THE GRACIOUS WORD, YEAR B

The Gracious Word
Year B

COMMENTARY ON
SUNDAY AND
HOLY DAY
READINGS

Wilfrid J. Harrington OP

Introductions to
the Liturgical Seasons

Philip Gleeson OP

DOMINICAN PUBLICATIONS

First published (1996) by
Dominican Publications
42 Parnell Square
Dublin 1

ISBN 1-871552-56-7

British Library Cataloguing in Publications Data.
A cataloguing record for this book is available from the British Library.

Cover design by
David Cooke

Printed in the Republic of Ireland by
Colour Books Ltd, Baldoyle, Co. Dublin.

Contents

Contributors

Wilfrid J. Harrington OP, author of more than twenty-five books on the Bible, lectures in scripture at the Dominican *studium*, Tallaght, at the Milltown Institute of Theology and Philosophy, and at Trinity College, Dublin. He is a regular contributor to summer schools at St Mary's College, Winooski, Vermont, and at Gonzaga University, Spokane, Washington, U.S.A.

Philip Gleeson OP lectures in dogmatics and liturgy at Tallaght and at the Milltown Institute. He also contributes to courses at the Irish Institute of Pastoral Liturgy.

Benedict Tutty OSB, whose drawing appears on page 34, was a monk of Glenstal. His works of art – in wood, metal, clay and enamel – appear in many churches in Ireland.

The line drawings by Michael Lydon (page 79) and Seán Adamson (page 105) first appeared in DOCTRINE & LIFE, in April 1964 and in March 1967, respectively.

Introduction

The three-volume *The Saving Word*[1] with scriptural commentary on the Sunday and feastday readings and accompanying relevant patristic texts and Church documents has served its purpose. It is now felt that a presentation of the Scripture commentaries alone would be welcome. What is on offer is by no means a mere reprint of the earlier commentaries. All the material has been thoroughly revised — in large measure rewritten.

Besides, there are significant new features. Among these are quite full introductions to the Gospels and shorter introductions to the major biblical writings. We offer a lengthy treatment of the infancy narratives of Matthew and Luke, obviously of special interest at Christmastide. And there is an analysis of the distinctive features of the passion narratives – of special relevance for preaching in Holy Week. And, something quite new, courtesy of my confrere Philip Gleeson, splendid introductions to the liturgical seasons. In short, this is, essentially, a new work.

Wilfrid J. Harrington OP

---

1. Wilfrid Harrington, Thomas Halton, Michael Krupa, Austin Flannery, three volumes (Wilmington, DE / Dublin: M. Glazier / Dominican Publications, 1980-1982).

Advent

Introduction to the Liturgical Season

The readings for Advent are a proclamation of hope, and a call to live Christian lives. They focus in a particularly moving way on the child of God whose birth will be celebrated at Christmas. They are full of the paradox of power and weakness which is one of the abiding themes of the liturgy of this time.

GOSPELS

The Gospels all point towards Jesus. He is the One who will come at the end of time, the One for whom John prepared the way and to whom he bore witness, the One whose coming was made known to Mary.

FIRST READINGS

The First Readings are prophetic passages, especially from Isaiah, about the Messiah and the messianic times. They help to give Advent its own particular flavour. They express the messianic hope of God's people, they give resonance to John the Baptist's call to conversion, they take up the theme of rejoicing (*Gaudete* Sunday), and they recall the promise made to the house of David.

SECOND READINGS

The Second Readings are in harmony with the Gospels and First Readings. They look forward to the coming of the Lord at the end of time, they contain expressions of hope and urge people to live Christian lives, they speak of Christian joy, and, on the fourth Sunday, they present Christ, the revelation of the mystery of God's saving plan.

Philip Gleeson OP

Advent

FIRST SUNDAY OF ADVENT

First Reading

Is 63:16-17; 64:1.3-8

This first reading is taken from the long poem Isaiah 63:7-64:11 a psalm of entreaty written by a returned exile not long after 538 B.C. Jerusalem lay in ruins; the task of re-building the temple had not yet been undertaken. The poem-prayer is typical of post-exilic prayers – the 'prayers of the chastened' – in that it recalls God's past goodness to his people and candidly acknowledges the people's ingratitude and sinfulness. The dominant note, however, is serene confidence in God's loving-kindness. The opening statement, 'I will recount the gracious deeds of the Lord' (v. 7), does not just introduce a chronicle of his mercies of the past; it is assurance that his steadfast love reaches into the present. There is, too, an urgency about the psalm as it strives to bring its hearers to a recognition of their plight from which God alone can deliver them. Not only recognition but acknowledgement: they are expected to make this prayer their fervent prayer.

'You are our Father' – the phrase occurs three times in our reading. God had become father of his people by redeeming them (Ex 4:22; Hos 11:1; Deut 32:5-6; Mal 1-6). Here the invocation of the Father is an expression of confidence: he can, and will, redeem this situation. There is a moving poignancy in this trustful 'Father' on the lips of self-confessed sinners (64:6-6). No attempt at whitewash here; there are no extenuating circumstances.

God is the Father who redeemed his people – and the Shepherd who led his people from Egypt. His people abandoned him, to its great loss. Jerusalem, the holy city of his dwelling, lay in ruins. Israel proclaims its sin: it has become an unclean polluted thing. It had cut itself off from its life-giving source and has become a heap of withered leaves scattered to the winds [Compare, 'Whoever does not abide in me is thrown away like a branch and withers' (Jn 15:6)]. The psalmist begs his God to rend the veil of his heavenly abode and appear in a theophany more majestic than that of Sinai; he beseeches him to bring about a new exodus of salvation. Deliverance is readily within the power of the divine Potter as he moulds, to his will, the clay of his people. Potter, yes, but Potter who is Father of steadfast love. That is the truth that makes all the difference.

At the opening of the Advent season this gracious psalm shows us Israel's confident expectation – even in the midst of the ruins of catastrophe – of a new exodus. This new age was to dawn half a millennium after the time of the optimistic poet.

And even though the Messiah has come we too, in the turmoil of our world, can look forward to the other coming of Christ when sin will be no more.

Second Reading   1 Cor 1:3-9

In the early Church, and it comes through in the earlier letters of Paul, there was lively expectation that the definitive coming of Christ, his Parousia, was imminent. This expectation was modified as the years went by but a looking to the day of our Lord Jesus Christ remained prominent in the New Testament. It was an attitude of joyful expectancy, a conviction that the Lord had not abandoned his people. He had gone to prepare for the day when he will finally gather his followers into the eternal Kingdom. This positive picture of the goal of Christian history was in time displaced by the more frightening image of the last day as a day of judgement and tribulation. For the faithful Christian, however, Christ will always come as redeemer, not as judge.

Of course, there is an aspect of truth in that other scene of judgement. It may be that our reading could make a nice balance. Here, as elsewhere, the clash of Corinthian enthusiasm and Pauline realism has served Christian theology. Paul insists that the 'grace' – God's gift of salvation bestowed on this community – must manifest itself. It will be seen in 'speech and knowledge of every kind' – in the various 'spiritual gifts' (vv. 4-7). Paul is going to deal at length with these charismatic gifts in chapters 12 to 14. At this point he merely acknowledges their presence in this community. He will be at pains to show that the presence of these gifts of the Spirit in no way means that Corinth is an exemplary Christian community – far from it!

The Corinthians may feel that they have already reached the goal - they are 'not lacking in any spiritual gift' (v. 7). Here lurks a warning, as the letter will show. The Lord will come, yes, but to reward fidelity and punish unfaithfulness (3:13; 4:3-4). The Corinthians must fight to retain what has been given (9:24-27). They can achieve this if they lean on the sustaining presence of the one who is to come! (v. 8). A faithful God is active in the activity of his Son who calls Christians into 'fellowship' (*koinonia*).

> Christian existence is a shared mode of being; if it is only through love that we really exist (13:2), others are as necessary to our being as we to theirs. Such reciprocity on the level of being creates the organic unity of the New Man (Gal 3:28; Col 3:10) who is Christ

(6:15; 12:12). The 'fellowship of the Son,' therefore, is quite different from the friendliness of a club (J. Murphy-O'Connor, *1 Corinthians*, New Testament Message 10).

Gospel   Mk 13:33-37

Chapter 13 of Mark, which rounds off the ministry of Jesus, is his farewell discourse. More immediately, it faces up to an acute Marcan concern. It is written, most likely, just after the Roman destruction of Jerusalem in 70 A.D. Some Christians, seemingly, had looked to that event as the moment of the End and were disillusioned when, afterwards, life went on as before. Mark is convinced that the End is near – but is distinct from the fall of Jerusalem. Following on a brief introduction (vv. 1-4) he treats of the signs of Parousia (5-23), the Parousia (24-27), and the nearness of the Parousia (28-37). Our reading is the conclusion of this third part and of the whole discourse.

The exhortation of v. 33 is Mark's introduction to the parable of the Doorkeeper (34-36). 'Beware' (vv. 5,9,23) is the keynote of the farewell discourse. 'Keep alert' means do not permit yourselves to fall asleep! 'Time' (see 1:15) is the appointed time fixed in an ordered divine plan. In its context the 'time' refers to the incalculable 'day or hour' of v. 32 (the End is near – but cannot be marked on a calendar). The call to watchfulness in v. 33 brings out the exhortation latent in v. 32.

The parable of the Doorkeeper, as Mark found it, had already gone through a process of reshaping. It certainly resembles the Watching Servants of Lk 12:35-38 – indeed both should be regarded as widely variant forms of the same parable. The main sentence of v. 35, 'Therefore, keep awake ... or else he may find you asleep when he comes suddenly,' is the application of the parable. Significantly, it is 'the master of the house' who will come, not the 'man' of v. 34: it is Christ himself. The parable is now understood in christological terms. Christ is the departing Lord and the parousia will mark his return. The doorkeeper represents the waiting disciples, the community of believers, and the divisions of the night are a symbol for the lapse of time before the coming. This meaning is borne out by Mark's care to bracket the first part of the parable with the warning, 'for you do not know when the time will come' (v. 33b), 'for you do not know when the master of the house will come' (v. 35b).

The opening 'Beware' (v. 5) and the final 'Keep awake' (v. 37) emphasize that Mark's real interest in this passage is centred in the exhortation, and his lesson is for all Christians without exception: 'I say to all.' The repeated call to watchfulness indicates how he wanted, not only this parable but the whole discourse, to be understood: not as a guide in calculating a deadline, but as an inspiration and a warning, to live one's life at each moment in preparedness for the meeting with Christ.

SECOND SUNDAY OF ADVENT

First Reading   Is 40:1-5, 9-11

In the light of the historical situation in which these words were first uttered, one cannot but be impressed by the confidence of the anonymous prophet who spoke them. Humanly speaking, there seemed no grounds for optimism. Hope cast on the dynasty of David, bolstered by the oracles of Isaiah, had sputtered out in the catastrophe of Babylonian conquest. The cream of the survivors of Judah were in exile in Babylon. And it was there that this man of vision – we name him Second Isaiah – gave us chapters 40-55 of Isaiah, a work fittingly known as 'The Book of Consolation.' God, this prophet assured his people, is about to come to lead his people once again out of slavery into their own land in a new exodus. Unlike the journey from Egypt to the promised land, this time there will be no straying, as Israel, led by Yahweh, will journey in solemn pilgrimage along a *Via Sacra*, a processional way, across the Syrian desert.

In his poetic vision the prophet hears the voice of God bid a crier run speedily to Jerusalem to carry the good news as the Lord leads his people to freedom. 'Good tidings': it is here the New Testament writers found their word 'gospel' – Good News. The herald is urged to proclaim the good news openly in the towns of Judah. His message is to be: 'Here is your God.' By new Testament times this was paraphrased in the synagogues of Palestine as: 'The Kingdom of your God is revealed.' The return from the exile, begun in 537 fell far short of the glowing picture painted here. Yet, all is not poetic imagery, for the restoration is a sign of salvation; it is in its measure, a redemption, a new creation. Later generations of Jews had patiently to await the fulfilment of God's word. And the message could sometimes be reinterpreted in moral terms: the highway to be made straight was one's way of life; the Kingdom was to be prepared for by repentance. It was still felt that the beginning of the messianic era would be associated with the desert. Thus did this biblical text and a later understanding of it prepare for the fulfilment that came in the person of Jesus and was ushered in by the Baptist.

Second Reading 2 Pet 3:8-14

One of the problems faced by the early Church was uncertainty as to the time-scale according to which God would conduct the history of salvation. We have already observed that, at first, Christians looked eagerly to an imminent return of Christ. Yet the End failed to materialize. On the whole, the Church quietly adjusted to the situation. The perspective of the author of our epistle is that, since the resurrection, humanity lives in the last phase of its history and awaits the 'Day of the Lord' which will mark the end of this present world. It is the confident view of a Christian of the early second century (2 Peter is generally dated about 120 A.D.). But there were some – as 2 Peter attests – who ridiculed the whole idea of the Lord's coming, thereby undermining the Christian view of history. It is to the consequent danger to faith that the author of 2 Peter addresses himself in today's reading.

The 'scoffers' had asked: 'Where is the promise of his coming? For ever since our ancestors [the apostles and first generation of Christians] died, all things continue as they were from the beginning of creation' (v. 4). They deny that history has any goal at all. Against their argument that the changeless nature of the universe forestalled the radical change demanded by the Christian hope, the author shows from the Old Testament that once before the world had been destroyed – by the Flood – and that God could just as easily destroy it again by fire (vv. 4-7).

Turning then to the 'beloved' faithful, he points out that the apparent delay of the Parousia may be explained in part by the fact that God's measure of time differs from ours (see Ps 90:4) and in part by his forbearance: 'not wanting any to perish, but all to come to repentance' (v. 9). But the Day of the Lord will surely come, if unexpectedly (see Mt 24:43). The just have nothing to fear. Expectation of the end will inspire them to live lives of holiness and godliness (3:11). Developing a Jewish idea that sin could delay the Coming (see Acts 3:19-20), the author suggests that righteousness can hasten the Parousia (vv. 11-12), thus providing an added incentive for virtuous living. And the fiery end of this world of ours is not really destruction: it will mark the emergence of 'new heavens and a new earth where righteousness is at home' (v. 13). See Is 65:17; 66:22; Rev 21:1,5).

Gospel   Mk 1:1-8

Mark states the theme of his gospel in his opening verse and then introduces the traditional prelude to the Good News: 'beginning from the baptism of John' (Acts 1:22). The title (v. 1) defines the whole work as 'the gospel of Jesus Christ': the gospel of the crucified and risen Lord – the gospel that is Jesus himself (8:35; 10:29). For Mark the gospel is somehow the presence of the saving power of Jesus. Two of Mark's significant christological titles are here at the start: Christ (Messiah) and Son of God. The beginning and abiding source of this gospel lies in the historical appearance of Jesus who, in the perspective of the Easter faith of the Church, was recognizable as the Son of God.

John the Baptizer solemnly proclaims the coming of the greater than he who will pour out the gift of the Spirit. Vv. 2-3 combine two scripture texts. John is the messenger (Mal 3:1) and the prophet (Is 40:3). The good news which concerns Jesus Christ begins with the wilderness prophet John, clothed like Elijah (2 Kgs 1:8) and subsisting on wilderness fare (v. 6). John is the sign that in the wilderness God is about to renew his covenant with Israel (Hos 2:14-23; Jer 2:1-3). This mission explains his clarion call to repentance or *metanoia*, a radical conversion, finding symbolic expression in baptism.

John who had uttered the call to repentance now proclaims the coming of the greater than he who will baptize the people with the Holy Spirit (vv. 7-8). His role of forerunner was already subtly intimated in v. 3 where the quotation from Isaiah 40:3 is changed to read 'his paths' (instead of 'the paths of our God'): 'the Lord' is now Jesus whose way John prepares. In contrast to the other synoptists who give a summary of the ethical preaching of the Baptist, Mark focuses on him as the pointer to the Coming One. Baptism 'with the Holy Spirit' is the promised outpouring of the Spirit for the time of salvation (see Joel 2:28-29; Is 44:3). In the parallel texts of Matthew 3:11 and Luke 3:16 this baptism is described as being 'with the Holy Spirit and with fire,' that is, a baptism of judgment. It is likely that the Baptist spoke only of baptism with fire. Here a threat of imminent judgment has been transformed into a prophecy of the outpouring of the Spirit, work of the risen Lord. In Mark, neither John nor Jesus preach judgment.

For an introduction to the Gospel of Mark see below, p 146.

THIRD SUNDAY OF ADVENT

First Reading   Is 61:1-2.10-11

In this reading we have the beginning and the close of a hymn (61:1-11) in which a post-exilic prophet declares that he has been sent by God to usher in the age of salvation for Jerusalem and all God's people. In the opening verses he speaks in his own name, while in the conclusion ('I will greatly rejoice ... ') he speaks in the person of the new Jerusalem. He is anointed with the Spirit of God to proclaim good tidings to the poor – the afflicted of every kind; to bring hope to the hopeless: to assure them of the care of their God. Luke tells us that Jesus found in this passage the programme of his own ministry. Coming, one sabbath, to the synagogue of his native Nazareth, he opened the scroll of Isaiah and read out:

The Spirit of the Lord is upon me,
because he has anointed me to bring good news to the poor.
He has sent me to proclaim release to the captives
and recovery of sight to the blind,
to let the oppressed go free,
to proclaim the year of the Lord's favour.

And, having read the passage, he declared to his hearers: 'Today this scripture has been fulfilled in your hearing' (Lk 4:16-21). In this way a passage, notable in its own right, has been given startling relevance. Who is the mysterious personage of the Isaian poem: the author? the Servant of Yahweh? a future bearer of good tidings? We cannot be sure. What matters for Christians is that Jesus made the prophecy his own. He was the Spirit-anointed one who preached good news to the poor. He manifested in his person the tender quality of the promised mercy. The saviour who was to come did show a gentle concern for people in their deepest need.

At the close of the reading Jerusalem is represented as exulting with joy in the good news brought to her. The Church, the new Jerusalem, should, so much more, be characterized by joyful hope. Hope is always the measure of faith. Joy and hope – *gaudium et spes* – fittingly describe the role of the Church and its message to our world. Any other message will not ring true.

Second Reading   1 Thess 5:16-24

In 1 Thessalonians 5:12-15 Paul had urged the Thessalonians to respect their leaders and live in peace with one another. He had exhorted them to admonish, encourage and help as the need arose – always in a spirit of patience. Then, in vv. 16-22, he passes to the positive demands of Christian love. Believers must 'always seek to do good' and that not only within the community but 'towards all.' In particular he exhorts to Christian joy, to prayer and thanksgiving. 'Rejoice always': this joy, of which Paul speaks more than once, is gift of the Holy Spirit (Gal 5:22). A characteristic of Christian joy is that it can exist together with trials and sufferings; these can in fact give rise to joy in that they take one closer to Christ (see Acts 5:41). 'Pray without ceasing' (see Lk 18:1) – constant prayer is a quality of Christian life. Prayer will take the form of thanksgiving: an eloquent way of praising God for his goodness.

It is clear from 1 Corinthians 12-14 that charismatic gifts, while being manifestations of the Spirit's presence in a community, could cause problems. The problem lay not in the gifts but in fact that some could not cope with them. Charismatics tended to give themselves airs. The answer was not in trying to stifle the gifts – that is the meaning of the admonition, 'do not quench the Spirit.' What was needed was discernment: to know whether there is gift of the Spirit. In Corinth Paul had to defend the gift of prophecy, that is to say, inspired, forthright preaching, against those who had exaggerated the importance of tongues. We may suspect a similar situation in Thessalonica; at any rate, there were some who 'despised' prophesying. In conclusion, Paul moves beyond the specific area of spiritual gifts and bids his readers hold fast to whatever is good and hold off from all that is evil.

We may see as the theme of the second reading that the salvation promised in Christ, the process of redemption already operative among us, is a source of present joy and peace. Even though the Christian is still preparing for the final coming of Christ, it is not an anxious worrying time, but a quiet confident waiting. Our prayer, to use the words of Paul (v. 23) is that the God of peace will keep us safe and blameless, spirit, soul and body, for the coming of our Lord Jesus Christ. After all, he who has called us to salvation is the faithful Father (v. 24).

Gospel   Jn 1:6-8.19-28

The subject of the gospel reading is the same as the previous Sunday – the witness of John the Baptist. But, today, we view the Baptist and his message in the distinctive colours of the fourth evangelist.

Verses 6-8 are an insertion (as is v. 15) into the hymn (1:1-18). More firmly even than Mark (1:7) John casts the Baptist in the role of witness: he came to testify, to witness. He is not the 'light,' the revealer; but he summons 'all' to faith in Jesus.

Before embarking on his gospel proper, John brings forward (1:19-51) a series of witnesses who bear testimony to the Messiah in a variety of messianic titles. The first part of the passage (which constitutes our reading) is the Baptist's vehement negative testimony: he is not the Messiah! Nor is he Elijah – traditionally, on the basis of Mal 3:1; 4:5, expected to precede the Messiah. And he is not the prophet-like-Moses who was to come (see Deut 18:15,18). He is a voice, only a heraldic voice – and yet the solemn voice of the wilderness prophet of Is 63. If he baptizes it is with water: a sign that one has repented. He is not more than a slave whose task it is to untie his master's sandal; and he feels unworthy even for that. There is polemic here. Not John himself, but disciples of the Baptist who still claimed John as the Messiah – are being put in their place (see Acts 19:1-4).

What matters to us is that the sense of joy, which is the keynote of today's liturgy, should be based on a growing conviction that, in the words of the Baptist, there stands among us, perhaps unknown to us, the one who will finally come in glory. Our hope is not all in the future. The work of our salvation has already begun.

FOURTH SUNDAY OF ADVENT

First Reading   2 Sam 7:1-5.8-11.16

David, his days of brigandage and forced exile ended, became king, first of Judah and then of the united kingdom of Judah and Israel. He had won for himself the city of Jerusalem and made it his capital (2 Sam 5). By installing the ark of Yahweh there he turned it into the religious centre of his domain (chapter. 6). Then, adverting to the incongruity that he had a palace while the ark of Yahweh was still housed in a tent, he planned to build a temple.

David consulted the prophet Nathan. In their first dialogue we have a fascinating example of the need for discernment of spirits (7:1-3). (Note second reading of previous Sunday). Nathan thought that David's proposal was great and enthusiastically gave the project his blessing: 'Go, do all you have in mind; for the Lord is with you' (v. 3). 'But that same night the word of the Lord came to Nathan ... '! (v. 4). The prophet had listened to his own heart; now he listens to the Lord. The Lord had pre-empted David's plan. The king had hoped to build a house (temple) for Yahweh; instead it is Yahweh who will build a house (dynasty) for David (7:4-17). It will be Solomon's task to build the temple. David receives the solemn promise that his dynasty would last forever: 'Your house and your kingdom shall be made sure forever before me; your throne shall be established forever' (v. 16). The temple liturgy kept this promise firmly before the people – notably Ps 89 which is read as the responsorial psalm today.

When Judah was overthrown and Jerusalem destroyed in 587 B.C., it seemed that this was one promise which had failed. Still, the Jewish people kept alive their hope that God would not renege on his promise and they continued to look forward to a Messiah who would be of the House of David. The expectation was fulfilled when Gabriel announced to Mary that she was to be the mother of the redeemer who, through Joseph, would be of the line of David. Gabriel's words echo the words of God's promise to David.

Second Reading
Rom 16:25-27

The doxology, which rounds off the letter to the Romans, may be a later addition by another than Paul. Authentic or not, it is certainly on all fours with the mind of Paul. It stresses what God has done, and is doing, for Christians, how he has done it, and what their response should be. God strengthens Christians in their faith (v. 25) and reaches out to others to bring them, too, into 'the obedience of faith' (v. 26). He achieves this through Paul's gospel – nothing other than Jesus Christ himself. This gospel is new but it has not sprung, unannounced, upon the world. God's 'mystery' – his saving plan for Jew and Gentile – had been announced by the prophets. But it was not understood until the 'now' of the era of salvation. Now, the good news can be proclaimed to all the world. The Christian response is a fervent 'thanks be to God!' – uttered, in Christian fashion, through Jesus Christ.

'According to the command of the eternal God' – or, as the Jerusalem Bible (JB) has it, 'the way the eternal God wants things to be done' (v. 26). It is not difficult for Christians, with hindsight, to see in the person and life of Jesus the fulfilment and more than the fulfilment, of the promises made in Old Testament times.

Yet the people to whom the promises had been first made could never have suspected that things would work out as they had. We too may have a very limited vision of what redemption is, and of how the coming of the Lord will be realized. Salvation history reassures us that God is faithful to his covenant – but in his way, for he is 'the only wise' (v. 27).

Our hope is secure, but we must be sensitive and open to God as he works out his plan of redemption in his own mysterious time and manner.

Gospel   Lk 1:26-38

Luke asserts the basic fact that Mary was called, and knew herself to be called, to be the mother of the Messiah. It was, for her, a profound spiritual experience, a matter between herself and her God, something that took place in the depth of her being. In giving expression to this personal, spiritual experience, Luke spontaneously turned to the Scriptures he knew so well. He brings before us the angelic messenger and his message: Gabriel, one of the 'Angels of the Face,' of Jewish tradition, who stand in the presence of God, and he provides the dialogue to bring out the significance of the call.

The angel describes the promised Son and his destiny (1:32-33) in terms borrowed from the Old Testament, especially from the oracle of Nathan (2 Sam 7:12-16) [first reading]. At this stage everything is still within the limits of the Old Law, but Luke will go on to explain that the intervention of the Holy Spirit will mean that Jesus must be named 'Son of God' in a new sense. Mary's question (v. 34) is a literary ploy, the evangelist's way of moving on to a new level. 'The Holy Spirit will come upon you' – in Genesis 1:2 the Spirit of God hovered over the waters, about to perform the great work of creation. Here, that divine power over-shadows Mary, about to perform a new and wonderful manner.

In Mary's consent (v. 38) we may see the true pattern of her humility. If she had been troubled and if she had asked a question (and we can trust the delicate perception of Luke) it is because she had been perplexed. Now that she knows the divine purpose she accepts that purpose unhesitatingly and with perfect simplicity. If heroics would be out of place at such a moment so, no less certainly, would be a protestation, even a suggestion, of unworthiness. Mary was too completely God's to think of herself at all.

This final reading for Advent brings together the great themes of this season. Luke sees Mary as summing up in her person the deepest and purest traditions of Old Testament piety. She was one of those whose trust was not in an external, political redemption. Over the centuries the expectation of deliverance had been purified and spiritualized, and there was a class who yearned for a deeper and more personal salvation. Mary was of this tradition.

The Infancy Narratives

Matthew 1-2; Luke 1-2

The Infancy Narratives of Matthew and Luke have had a notable influence on Christian tradition and have put a profound mark on Christian art. The long Christian appreciation of them has not been misplaced. We had sensed that there was something special here – that these texts said quite a lot more than they appeared to say. In our day we have, happily, come to realise that both infancy narratives – which are wholly independent of each other – are, first and foremost, christological statements. It is along this line, and only here, that we can grasp their true meaning. An overall look at these texts is appropriate as an introduction to the readings of Christmastide.

Matthew 1-2

Matthew and Luke shared a twofold tradition: Jesus' home was Nazareth; Jesus was descendant of David and, as such, appropriately born in Bethlehem. Reconciliation of these traditions has influenced the shape of their narratives. For Matthew, Jesus' birth in Bethlehem offered no problem; in his view, Bethlehem was home of Joseph and Mary. He has to move Jesus from Bethlehem to Nazareth. For Luke, on the other hand, the home of Joseph and Mary was Nazareth. he has to arrange to have Jesus born in Bethlehem. This contrived reconciliation, by each evangelist, of the dominant Nazareth tradition (throughout the gospels Jesus is counted a Nazarene) with the Bethlehem tradition would suggest that birth at Bethlehem is to be taken as a theologoumenon (a theological affirmation related as an historical event) – in this case an affirmation of the Davidic descent of Jesus.

In building his infancy narrative Matthew has made use of two main blocks of material: a cycle of angelic dream appearances and the Magi story. The material has been thoroughly edited by Matthew but the two blocks are still recognizably distinct. Angelic dream appearances: 1:20-25; 2:13-15; 2:19-23. It is evident that Joseph wears the cloak of the famous patriarch Joseph, especially in his being a man of dreams and in his going down into Egypt. The Magi story: 2:1-12. As it stands, this is a self-contained story, with no mention of Joseph. Matthew composed its sequel (2:16-18) when he combined it with the flight into Egypt episode.

A feature of Matthew's gospel is his use of formula citations which sit loosely in their context; they are particularly frequent in his infancy narrative: 1:22-23; 2:5-6; 2:15; 2:17-18; 2:23. Matthew has recognized the applicability of particular Old Testament texts to particular incidents in Jesus' career. He introduced them because they fit his theology of the oneness of God's plan and because they help to bring out, for his Christian readers, who and what Jesus is. Thus, the five infancy narrative citations tell us that the virginally-conceived Jesus is God-with-us, that as son of David he was, fittingly, born in Bethlehem, that, in being called out of Egypt, he re-enacted the Exodus of his people, that he suffered the Exile of his people, and that as the Nazorean he began his saving work.

THE GENEALOGY OF JESUS (1:1-17)

The Old Testament, especially Genesis and 1 Chronicles, makes skilful use of genealogies. In his turn, Matthew finds his genealogy to be an effective way of establishing the identity of Jesus. He traces Jesus' ancestry back to David and Abraham. In particular, he shows that the one whom Christians proclaim as 'Messiah' can be correctly claimed to be 'son of David'. The sequences of fourteen generations suggest that Jesus was born at the 'right' time.

Two features of the genealogy are of special interest: (1) The formula 'A was the father of B' (literally 'A begot B') is interrupted in v. 16. It is not said that 'Joseph was the father of Jesus,' rather: 'Joseph, the husband of Mary, of her was begotten Jesus, called the Messiah.' (2) The other feature, closely related to the first, is the unexpected presence of four women: Tamar, Rahab, Ruth, Bathsheba ('the wife of Uriah'). The point is that, in the Old Testament and especially in Jewish tradition, there was something irregular in the union of these women with their partners yet all four of them continued the lineage of the Messiah. Indeed they played such an important role that they were regarded as manifestly instruments of the Spirit. Clearly, then, they foreshadow the role of Mary. There was something 'irregular' about her relation with Joseph and she is 'with child of the Holy Spirit' (2:18). In that line of the Messiah Matthew had clearly seen the hand of God. We might add that it simply is not possible to reconcile this genealogy with that of Lk 3:23-38. But both of them tell us how to evaluate Jesus: theologically he is 'son of David,' 'son of Abraham,' (Matthew) and 'Son of God' (Luke).

THE BIRTH OF JESUS (1:18-25)

Joseph and Mary were betrothed. In Jewish society, bethrothal was something far more serious than our marriage engagement. Betrothal was really a marriage contract, except that the partners had not begun to live together. Joseph discovered that his betrothed was pregnant. 'Of the Holy Spirit' is Matthew's nod to the reader; Joseph was not aware of that factor and was in a quandary. He was a 'righteous'man, that is, Law-observant. He assumed that Mary had been unfaithful. The death penalty for adultery (Deut 22:23-27) was not then, if it ever had been, in force; divorce was the answer. This was the course Joseph decided on – except that he wanted to divorce her 'quietly.' It is not clear how he could have hoped to achieve this. And divorce would not have helped Mary at all. She would have been left on her own to bear her baby – in a thoroughly disapproving society. The 'righteous' man, Joseph, was a confused man. He desperately wanted to do the decent thing, but his 'solution' was no solution at all.

Happily for him – and for Mary – God took a hand. In a dream, all was made clear. Mary was not an unfaithful bride but a wholly privileged instrument of God. Her child, of divine parenthood, would be Saviour; he is the one who 'will save his people from their sins.' And here Matthew throws in his formula-citation. He looked to Is 7:14 (in the Greek) and found there a word of promise: 'the virgin would bear a son.' That son will be Emmanuel, God-with-us. Cleverly, Matthew has anticipated the close of his gospel: 'Remember, I am with you always' (Mt 28:20). In that unique child of Mary, a first-century Palestinian Jew, we meet our God. Paul has put it in his inimitable fashion: 'God was in Christ, reconciling the world to himself' (2 Cor 5:19).

THE MAGI STORY (2:1-12)

In this narrative, Matthew has cast back into the infancy the reactions that, historically, greeted the proclamation of the risen Lord: some believed and paid homage; others rejected the message and the preachers. In other words, christological revelation was followed by proclamation and by the twofold reaction of acceptance-homage and rejection-persecution. But this had been prepared for in the ministry of Jesus. The same pattern is presented in the infancy narrative.

There seems little point in looking for the homeland of the Magi – whom Matthew seemingly would regard as astrologers of some sort. Nor is there any point in looking to a comet, a supernova, or a planetary conjunction to account for 'his star' (1:2). A star which rises, goes before, and comes to rest over a place is no natural phenomenon but a miraculous (more precisely, a symbolic) star. More to he point is the fact that, for Matthew, the Magi represent the Gentiles, fittingly alerted not by an angel (as Luke's Jewish shepherds) but by a star. The liturgical tradition of the feast of Epiphany has caught Matthew's intent. The Magis' role as prefiguring the acceptance of Gentiles into the Christian community points toward the universal character of the gospel. Jesus is functioning as son of Abraham.

The Balaam narrative of Numbers 22-24, embroidered with Jewish tradition, would, skilfully used by Matthew, appear to have been the inspiration of the magi story. Balaam was summoned by Balak 'from the east' to curse Israel. Significantly, Philo calls him a *magos*. Similarly, Herod tried to use the magi for his own ends. In his oracle Balaam had declared: 'A star shall come out of Jacob, and a sceptre shall rise out of Israel' (Num 24:17). Here, credibly, is 'his star' (Mt 2:2).

FLIGHT AND RETURN (2:13-23)

The next two episodes are coloured by the story of Moses in Egypt – again as elaborated in Jewish tradition – and also echo the Exodus motif. The basic story line in 2:13-15 concerns the rescue of the child saviour from the machinations of the wicked king by flight into Egypt. Jewish tradition, as we find it, for example, in Josephus, had it that the Pharaoh of the Exodus had been forewarned by one of his 'sacred scribes' of the birth of a Hebrew who would constitute a threat to the Egyptian kingdom. Pharaoh and the whole of Egypt were filled with dread (see Mt 2:3). Pharaoh's plan was frustrated by a warning communicated in a dream to Moses' father. The parallels between this Roman legend and the pre-Matthean infancy narrative are manifest. Read against the background of Exodus 1-2 Jesus emerges as a Moses-figure. The Hosea quotation – 'Out of Egypt have I called my son' – refers to the exodus of Israel from Egypt. Matthew sees that Jesus relives the history of his people: not only the exodus but the previous going down into Egypt.

The story line in 2:16-18, involving the massacre of the male children in Bethlehem, echoes Pharaoh's decree against the male infants of the Hebrews. Matthew, with his formula citation of Jeremiah 31:15, works in another theme: that of the Babylonian Exile. Again, Jesus is associated with a tragic event of his people. The names in the three formula citations: Bethlehem (the city of David), Egypt (the land of the Exodus) and Ramah (the mourning place of the Exile) are theologically suggestive. The final episode (2:19-23), too, gives us three significant names: Israel, Galilee and Nazareth. The 'citation' here is really not such: Matthew is playing on the name Nazareth.

Quite likely, he is thinking both of the *neser*, 'branch,' of Is 11:1 and of *nazir* – one consecrated or made holy to God. At any rate he knows that this son of David, Son of God, is none other than Jesus the Nazorean.

As Matthew narrates the infancy narrative, it is the place where the Old Testament and the Gospel meet. If he brought forward some themes from the Old Testament with which to clothe the infant Jesus, he also brought back from the Gospel some evaluations of Jesus by the Christian community: son of David, son of Abraham, and messianic Son of God. He attaches the basic Gospel revelation, 'You are the Christ, the Son of the living God' (16:16) to the conception of Jesus. He has this revelation proclaimed to Gentiles and Jews, to be received by the former and rejected by the authorities among the latter. (Raymond E. Brown, *The Birth of the Messiah*. 231).

Luke 1-2

Luke, writing consciously in the style of the Greek Bible (the LXX), composed his narrative, broadly, in the shape of two diptychs: prophecies of the birth of John the Baptist and Jesus and narratives of the birth of both.

PROPHECY OF JOHN'S BIRTH (1:5-25)

The introduction (1:5-7) gives four items of information. The first three – time setting in the reign of Herod the Great, the names Zechariah and Elizabeth, their priestly descent – are items of tradition. The other, that they were aged and Elizabeth barren, reflects the stories of Abraham and Sarah, Elkanah and Hannah. Thus, the birth of John the Baptist is in continuity with the births of famous figures in the salvific history of Israel.

The pattern of annunciation (1:8-23) reflects that announcing Ishmael (Gen 16), Isaac (Gen 17) and Samson (Jdg 13) and carries echoes of Daniel 8:16-27; 9:21-23. The Lucan angel is named Gabriel (as in Daniel). The verses 15-17, which prophetically characterize the adult Baptist as an ascetic prophet calling upon Israel to repent, are culled from the ministry portrayal of him – 3:1-3; 7:24-35. The sign, required by the literary pattern, is dumbness, suggested by Dan 10:15. Since Elizabeth's pregnancy is going to be a sign for Mary (1:36) her seclusion (1:24-25) underlines its sign-value since no one could have known her pregnancy. For Zechariah and Elizabeth, Luke has looked to the Old Testament models of Abraham and Sarah; for the infant Baptist he drew on the description of John in the gospel story of the ministry. He has portrayed the Baptist in conscious parallel to Jesus – taking consistent care to keep the former on a lower level.

PROPHECY OF JESUS' BIRTH (1:26-38)

The structure again follows faithfully the pattern of angelic annunciations of birth. Hence, material not explained by the literary pattern is significant: the peculiar manner of conception (virginal), identity of the child (vv 32-33, 35), the portrait of Mary in vv 34 and 38. In 1:32-33 Jesus is described as the Davidic Messiah in terms taken from 2 Sam 7:9-16. The only thing specifically Christian here is that Jesus has been identified as that promised Messiah. Luke uses the technique of Mary's question and Gabriel's answer to point to the true identity of the Davidic Messiah: together they speak Luke's christological message. The Messiah is God's Son and his conception is not through marital intercourse (Mary) but through the Holy Spirit (Gabriel). It is Luke's dramatic version of an early christological formula, such as that in Romans 1:3-4.

The portrait of Mary in 1:38 is shaped from Luke's account of her in the ministry (8:19-21); as one who hears and does the will of God she is truly 'servant of the Lord.' Against the patriarchal background of Luke's biblical tradition, his focus on Mary is striking. It carries a typical Lucan message.

In contrast to Zechariah, we notice, Mary holds no official position among the people, she is not described as 'righteous' in terms of observing Torah, and her experience does not take place in a cultic setting. She is among the most powerless people in her society: she is young in a world that values age; female in a world ruled by men; poor in a stratified economy. Furthermore, she has neither husband nor child to validate her existence. That she should have found 'favour with God' and be 'highly gifted' shows Luke's understanding of God's activity as surprising and often paradoxical, almost always reversing human expectations. (Luke T. Johnson, *Luke*. 39).

MARY VISITS ELIZABETH (1:39-56)

In the structure of the Lucan infancy narrative this passage 'The Visitation', is a complementary episode, a pendant to the diptych of annunciations (1:5-38). Elizabeth is granted the perception not only that Mary is with child but that her child is the Messiah. Her canticle in praise of Mary (1:42-45) echoes Old Teastament motifs and anticipates motifs that will be found in the gospel (11:27-28). This narrative serves as a hinge between the two birth stories of John and of Jesus. And this meeting of women illustrates their respective situations. Elizabeth's pregnancy was not only a sign for Mary; it was also an invitation. The 'haste' of Mary was inspired by friendship and charity.

At Mary's greeting Elizabeth felt the infant stir within her – John, while still in the womb, is precursor (1:17) of the Lord. Enlightened by the prophetic Spirit she concluded that Mary is to be mother of 'the Lord.' That is why Mary is 'blessed among women' – the most blessed of women. Elizabeth went on to praise Mary's unhesitating acquiescence in God's plan for her – her great faith: 'And blessed is she who believed ... ' The song of Mary (1:46-55) moves from the reversal of Mary's condition from lowliness to exaltation (vv 47-49), to a general statement of God's mercy (50), on to a recital of his past and present reversals (51-53) and to a final statement on his mercy to Israel in fulfilment of his promise to Abraham (54-55). In some sort, throughout, Mary is representative of Israel.

THE BIRTH OF JOHN (1:57-80)

The birth of John marked the fulfilment of the angel's message to Zechariah. Circumcision was prescribed for the eighth day after birth. Elizabeth, to the consternation of relatives who had objected to her choice of name, was supported by her husband: the child's name was John. At that Zechariah found himself able to speak again. The infancy story of the Baptist closes (1:80) with a 'refrain of growth' indicating his physical and spiritual development. In typical Lucan style, reference to John's sojourn in the desert prepares the way for his next appearance (3:2). The canticle of Zechariah (1:68-79) begins with the fulfilment of God's promised visitation of his people and then focuses on John's role as 'prophet of the Most High.'

THE BIRTH OF JESUS (2:1-21)

The setting (2:1-7) is necessitated in part by Luke's assumption that Joseph and Mary lived in Nazareth before Jesus was born; for Matthew, their home was in Bethlehem. Luke has to get Mary to Bethlehem for the birth of Jesus there. His stratagem is the census of Quuirinius and he is certainly confused in his account of the census – an unhistorical event as he relates it. But, then, it may be that we have tended to take Luke too literally. His prime interest would seem to lie in the fact that the mighty Augustus was, unwittingly, an instrument of the Lord. Through his decree it came to pass that Jesus the Messiah was born in the town of David. When we look at it dispassionately we must admit that what we had taken to be the Lucan picture of many distant descendants of David crowding into the insignificant Bethlehem is not very likely – still less likely as following on a policy of the practical Romans. What Luke wants to show is that Jesus was born in the hometown of David as one who belonged there – not in lodgings like an alien. Manger and swaddling clothes (2:12) symbolize God's care and protection.

From the first, Mary is the caring mother, solicitously wrapping her baby and laying him in a manger-cradle. Luke is not suggesting anything miraculous about the birth – merely insisting that the 'servant of the Lord' is, in her loving care, reflecting God's care. In the annunciation to the shepherds (2:8-14) heaven and earth touch. The angels interpret the event and give it its true meaning: this child is Saviour, Messiah and Lord. The form of the proclamation (vv 10-11) and the canticle, the Gloria (v. 14), would seem, again, to glance at Augustus who, architect of the *pax Augusta*, was hailed as Saviour. Jesus, not he, Luke asserts, is Saviour and bringer of peace.

In the reaction (2:15-20) to birth and heavenly proclamation the shepherds are forerunners of future believers who will glorify God for what they had heard and will praise God for what they had seen. In this third part of the passage all the protagonists, Mary, Joseph, baby and the shepherds come together. Yet, only one figure constitutes a bridge from the infancy narrative to the ministry of Jesus, and that is Mary, his mother. She is that by being a believer and disciple (Lk 8:19-21; 11:27-28; Acts 1:12-14). This is what Luke intends by his declaration: Mary 'treasured all these words and pondered them in her heart' (2:19). One should look to the parallel assertion in 2:51 – 'his mother treasured all these things in her heart.' She, like the Twelve, will come to full understanding when Jesus will have risen from the dead. Until then, in the obscurity of faith, she pondered those puzzling events. It is a misunderstanding of Luke's purpose, and of his literary achievement, to claim, as some have argued, that these statements point to Mary as source of the evangelist's narrative. Luke had access to some traditions but the infancy narrative, as we have it, is his creation.

THE PRESENTATION (2:22-40)

We have seen that the Matthean magi story displayed the magi as reacting with acceptance and homage to the proclamation of the Messiah. Luke's shepherds play a similar role. But the magi story has two elements missing in the Lucan story up to now: the positive response of Gentiles and the rejection of the new-born Messiah. These are supplied in Simeon's double oracle (2:29-32, 34-35). In the setting of this episode (2:22-24) Luke has combined two different Israelite customs: (1) consecration or presentation of the child to the Lord (Ex 13:1, 11-16); (2) purification of the mother after the birth of a child (Lev 12:1-8). Luke's text gives evidence of his general knowledge of these customs and his inaccurate grasp of details. Simeon's Nunc Dimittis introduces the theme of salvation for the Gentiles (see Is 42:6; 52:10). In the second oracle (2:34-45) Simeon anticipates the rejection of Jesus by the Jewish authorities and the rejection of the Christian mission to Israel as described in Acts.

> As in the *Magnificat*, Mary is here portrayed as a personification of the people of Israel. Israel will be divided, and so will Mary's soul be run through by a sword … At the level of human drama, the revelatory significance of Jesus will not be obvious to all nor accepted by all. Jesus will be a 'sign of contradiction' (Luke T. Johnson, *Luke*, 57).

THE BOY JESUS IN THE TEMPLE (2:41-52)

This passage, concerning the twelve-year old Jesus, is hardly an infancy narrative and the repeated conclusion v. 52 (see v. 40) marks is as an addition. Originally, the story seemed to situate the 'christological moment' in Jesus' youth: here we have Jesus saying of himself what the heavenly voice will say at baptism. Obviously, for Luke, the punchline is v. 49: 'Did you not know that I must be in my Father's house?' Jesus, in his first spoken words in Luke's gospel, himself announces who he is: he is the one totally committed to God, his Father. By stressing Mary's lack of understanding (v. 50) Luke makes the historically accurate assertion that the christology of Jesus as God's Son was not perceived until after the resurrection.

> Luke is giving us a perceptive theological insight into history; there was a continuity from the infant Jesus to the boy Jesus to the Jesus of the ministry to the risen Jesus; and when Christian disciples like Mary believed in Jesus as God's Son after the resurrection, they were finding adequate expression for institutions that had begun long before (Brown, *The Birth of the Messiah*, 494).

The infancy narratives are independent of each other and are stylistically markedly distinct. They are concerned with quite different episodes. All the more striking, then, is their total theological agreement. For Matthew, as for Luke, Jesus, virginally conceived, is son of David and Son of God. He is Saviour of Jew and Gentile and destined to meet with acceptance and rejection. The whole is part of a divine plan long prepared in the salvific history of Israel. The Christian instinct has always reached beyond the surface of these narratives.

Christmastide

Introduction to the Liturgical Season

The readings for the Christmas season are full of joy at the light shining in the darkness, the revelation of God's love. They are an invitation to live in the light. At the heart of the whole season is the humanity of our God.

GOSPELS

The central Gospel for this season is the Prologue of John, which is read at Mass during the day on Christmas Day itself, and also on the second Sunday after Christmas.

But we also see the bright pictures painted by Matthew and Luke: the beginning of the Gospel according to Matthew, that is, the genealogy, the annunciation made to Joseph, the birth and naming of Jesus (Christmas vigil Mass); Luke's account of the birth of Jesus and the angels singing for joy (midnight Mass), and his account of the shepherds worshipping the child, and Mary turning things over in her heart (Mass at dawn).

On the feast of the Holy Family, the Gospel this year tells of the presentation in the temple.

On the solemnity of Mary, Mother of God (the Octave of the Nativity), the Gospel again puts us in the company of the shepherds, looking at Mary, Joseph, and the child, and it goes on to tell us that on the eighth day the child was circumcised and given the name, 'Jesus'.

On the Epiphany, the Gospel is that of the Magi, the traditional Roman reading for this day.

Then, on the feast of the Baptism of the Lord, the last day of the Christmas season, we move on to Mark's descriptions of the baptism of Jesus, the beloved Son, on whom the Spirit descended.

FIRST READINGS

Isaiah, so prominent during Advent, continues to be heard during the Christmas season. On Christmas Day, the Masses include readings from Isaiah which express delight at the wedding of God and God's people (vigil Mass) and proclaim a message of light and joy.

On the Epiphany, the First Reading is the traditional Roman one, the passage from Isaiah about kings and camels and gifts of gold and incense.

On the Baptism of the Lord, there is a passage from Isaiah about the beloved servant; this year Year B), the *ad libitum* reading offers the invitation to come to the water.

Besides these readings from Isaiah, the First Readings include Ecclesiasticus in praise of family virtue (Holy Family) and the *ad libitum* First Reading for the Holy Family puts before us the example of an Old Testament family, Abraham, Sarah, and Isaac. Numbers teaches us to invoke the name of God in blessing (Solemnity of Mary/ Octave of Christmas). Ecclesiasticus meditates on divine Wisdom rejoicing in God's presence and taking root in God's people (second Sunday after Christmas).

SECOND READINGS

The Second Readings harmonize with the Gospels and First Readings. On Christmas Day they include a passage from Acts, giving Paul's proclamation of Jesus as the fulfilment of the promise to the house of David (vigil Mass), two passages from Titus about the revelation of God's grace and God's kindness (midnight and dawn), and one from Hebrews about the revelation of the radiant light of God's glory (Mass during the day).

On the Feast of the Holy Family, Ephesians speaks about family virtues, and Hebrews commends the faith of Abraham, offering to sacrifice his only Son (Year B *ad libitum*).

On the Solemnity of Mary Mother of God, the Octave of Christmas, Galatians speaks of the child, born of a woman, and of the Spirit who enables us to call God, 'Abba'. On the second Sunday after Christmas, Ephesians addresses the theme of our adoption in Jesus. On the Epiphany, Ephesians announces the revelation of the mystery that pagans now share in the inheritance of God's people.

Finally, on the Baptism of the Lord, the Second Reading, from Acts, contains part of Peter's address to Cornelius and his household, about the beginning of the ministry of Jesus, anointed with the Spirit and with power. The *ad libitum* second reading is from First John about the water and the blood (Year B).

Philip Gleeson OP

Christmastide

First Reading   Is 9:1-7

This reading presents the child who is born to us as the complete ruler who will inaugurate a reign of unending peace (*shalom* – wholeness of life) and justice. Historically, the oracle was spoken on the occasion of the deportation of the people of Israel (the northern kingdom) in 732 B.C. It implies that salvation will be a reward of faithfulness as only those who have sown and waited patiently share in the harvest, and only those who have fought share the spoils of battle. The sufferings of the people are invoked in the opening lines: they have 'walked in darkness,' 'lived in a land of deep darkness,' 'been burdened by the yoke,' and felt the 'rod' of the taskmaster. These images of oppression are countered by the promise of light, joy and freedom that will come with the accession of a new Davidic king.

The composite throne-name of the royal child is prophetic: he possesses, to an eminent degree, the virtues of the heroes of his race – the wisdom of Solomon, the valour of David, the dedication of Moses and the prophets. Christian tradition and liturgy, in applying these titles to Jesus, acknowledge that he is the Emmanuel: God-with-us.

Second Reading   Tit 2:11-14

This passage from a letter written by a later admirer of Paul reminds us that we are moving on many levels when we speak about the coming of Christ. Even as on Christmas night we recall his first coming some two thousand years ago, we are still waiting for his final coming at the end of time (one way of expressing our conviction that God's saving plan moves towards a goal). There is the coming of Christ to each individual in the course of his or her life.

The purpose of God's freely-bestowed grace is not to take Christian men and women out of the world but to empower them effectively to renounce vice and to live virtuous lives 'in this world.' Beginning at Bethlehem and culminating on the cross, the process continues down the ages and will reach its perfection with the final 'manifestation of the glory of the great God and our Saviour Jesus Christ.' Our gracious God will have spoken his final word – word of salvation.

The angel said to the shepherds: 'Do not be afraid.
Listen, I bring you news of great joy ...'

(Lk 2:10)

Gospel
Lk 2:1-14

The setting is necessitated in part by Luke's assumption that Joseph and Mary lived in Nazareth before Jesus was born; for Matthew their home was Bethlehem. Luke has to get Mary to Bethlehem for the birth of Jesus there. His stratagem is the census of Quirinius and he is certainly confused in his account of the census – an unhistorical event as he relates it. But, then, it may be that we have tended to take Luke too literally. His prime interest would seem to lie in the fact that the mighty Augustus was, unwittingly, an instrument of the Lord. Through his decree it came to pass that Jesus the Messiah was born in the town of David. When we look at it dispassionately we must admit that what we had taken to be the Lucan picture of many distant descendants of David crowding into the insignificant Bethlehem is not very likely – still less likely as following on a policy of the practical Romans. What Luke wants to show is that Jesus was born in the city of David as one who belonged there – not in lodgings like an alien. Manger and swaddling clothes (2:12) symbolize God's care and protection.

From the first, Mary is the caring mother, solicitously wrapping her baby and laying him in a manger-cradle. Luke is not suggesting anything miraculous about the birth – merely insisting that the 'handmaid of the Lord' is, in her loving care, reflecting God's care.

In the annunciation to the shepherds (2: 8-14) heaven and earth touch. The angels interpret the event and give it its true meaning: this child is Saviour, Messiah and Lord. The form of the proclamation (vv. 10-11) and the canticle, the *Gloria* (2:14), would seem, again, to glance at Augustus who, architect of the *pax Augusta*, was hailed as Saviour. Jesus, not he, Luke asserts, is Saviour and bringer of peace (*shalom*).

Apart from symbolism, the simple circumstances of Jesus' birth are eloquent. He was born in poverty and the very first invited to share in the joy of Mary and Joseph were simple country folk, shepherds guarding their sheep. In our day Latin America has rediscovered this privilege of the poor.

CHRISTMAS DAY: MASS AT DAWN

First Reading
Is 62:11-12

The context is the joyful return of the exiles from Babylon and the restoration of Jerusalem, the 'daughter of Zion.' The city is no longer to be named 'forsaken' but is now 'sought out' – object of love. The people who live in Zion are God's 'holy people', 'the redeemed of the Lord.

All the titles used in this reading can be applied to the Church, the new people of God, a holy people redeemed by the Lord, a people no longer abandoned, the community of salvation. It requires prayerful insight to see the Church in such terms. It needs faith to see beneath the human and the sinful to the deeper reality of a holy people of God.

Second Reading   Tit 3:4-7

Quite undeservedly, God has lavished his goodness and loving kindness upon Christians – his loving kindness concretely manifested in Jesus. Before Christ came all were in the same state, ignorant, misled and enslaved by passions. But God freely, and without any merit on our part, sent his Son to cleanse and renew us. This author, a disciple of Paul, echoes a constant teaching of Paul: the call to salvation is a gratuitous act of God, independent of our deeds. Confronted with such generosity there is no place for self-righteousness; our response to God's Christmas gift must be one of humble thankfulness and acceptance.

The idea of the Spirit being poured out is a prophetic one (see Joel 3:1); it signifies the abundance of messianic blessings which were to appear in the eschatological era. This era has now arrived with the coming of Christ.

Gospel   Lk 2:15-20

This is a continuation of the passage read at midnight Mass. In their reaction to the heavenly proclamation of birth the shepherds are forerunners of future believers who will glorify God for what they had heard and will praise God for what they had seen.

Here all the protagonists – Mary, Joseph, baby and the shepherds – all come together. Yet, only one figure constitutes a bridge from the infancy narrative to the ministry of Jesus, and that is Mary, his mother. She is that by being a believer and disciple (Lk 8:19-21; 11:27-28; Acts 1:12-14). This is what Luke intends by his declaration: Mary 'treasured all these things and pondered them in her heart' (2:19). One should look to the parallel assertion in 2:51 – 'His mother treasured all these things in her heart.' She, like the Twelve, will come to full understanding when Jesus will have risen from the dead. Until then, in the obscurity of faith, she pondered those puzzling events. It is a misunderstanding of Luke's purpose, and of his literary achievement, to claim, as some have argued, that these statements point to Mary as source of the evangelist's narrative. Luke had access to some traditions but the infancy gospel, as we have it, is his creation.

The picture of Mary here is that of a loving and capable mother. Jesus was in very good hands. Furthermore, she is a deeply thoughtful woman. And she is a woman of faith who lived her life in faith.

CHRISTMAS DAY: MASS DURING THE DAY

First Reading   Is 52:7-10

The first lines of today's reading are familiar to us from Paul's use of them in Romans 10:15. A messenger ran along the mountain ridges to bring the good news of the return of the exiles from Babylon. His task is to proclaim salvation and peace. From now on, God is king and his reign will mean peace and prosperity. Watchmen on the ruined walls of Jerusalem take up the joyful message of the herald and announce it to the city: Jerusalem will be restored. The term for 'good news' in Greek is *euaggelion*, that is, 'gospel'. Here we see the true meaning of Gospel: it is the news of God's liberation. There is a note of universality; the event will not be of significance only for Israel. God's saving work will be so striking that 'all the ends of the earth shall see the salvation of our God.' We Christmas Christians must grasp the important truth that our salvation in Christ is in direct continuity with God's saving work in Israel.

Second Reading   Heb 1:1-6

Fittingly, in the second reading and in the gospel reading, two powerful texts, two prologues to writings of paramount christological importance, are brought together in this Mass of Christmas Day. 'Long ago God spoke to our ancestors in many and various ways': the Old Testament is the word of God; God spoke, but fragmentarily, through prophets. Now he 'has spoken' – once for all; and not any more by a prophet but through the Son. God has spoken his final word because this Son is the reflection of God's glory and bears the very stamp of his nature. High Priest of the new covenant, he has achieved purification of sin: in the Son and only in the Son was sin wholly expiated. We Christians do not listen for a whisper of angels. We hearken to the Word: 'the reflection of God's glory and the exact imprint of God's very being.'

Gospel   Jn 1:1-18
The sublime prologue of John's gospel takes up the theme of the
second reading and puts it in unmistakable Johannine terms. God has
spoken his final word – the Word-made-flesh who has pitched his tent
among us. The first part of the prologue (vv. 1-11) speaks about the
Son in metaphor, as a 'Word' who brings 'life' from God and as 'light'
in so far as he is revealer of God. The second part (vv. 12-18), in more
concrete language (Jesus Christ, the Father) describes the positive
response to Christ, and the life of Christians as children of God. (See
Second Sunday after Christmas.)

THE HOLY FAMILY
SUNDAY WITHIN THE OCTAVE OF CHRISTMAS

First Reading   Ecclesiasticus / Sirach 3:2-6.12-14
Ben Sirach (author of Sirach or Ecclesiasticus) has the down-to-earth
aim of teaching piety and morality and his book is an important witness
to the moral outlook of Judaism shortly before the Maccabean age, that
is to say, in the early second century B.C. The spirituality of the book
is grounded in faith in the God of the covenant, a faith which shows
itself in cult and in the practice of justice and mercy. Thus ben Sirach
exhorts to humility and kindness to the poor. He denounces pride, sins
of the tongue, adultery, covetousness and sloth. The book, in short,
abounds in practical religious counsels. Our passage is typical.

One of the more attractive characteristics of earlier, more traditional societies was the care and regard they showed for the elderly.
The text of this reading is a commentary on the command to honour
father and mother (Ex 20:12; Deut 5:16). Too often we think of the
fourth commandment merely in terms of obedience on the part of
younger children. Of much greater importance is the obligation of
grown children to ensure that their aged parents have a peaceful and
comfortable old age so that they can live their final years in dignity.
Although the father is the centre of attention here (as one might expect
in a patriarchal culture) the advice offered certainly does apply to both
parents.

First Reading *ad libitum*   Gen 15:1-6; 21:1-3
Abraham was chosen and called – the 'scandal' of divine election (Gen
12:1-3). He was called to *serve* the divine purpose and in this service
the scandal is resolved. 'I will make you a great nation' (12:2). All very

well – but Abram continued to be childless; his heir would be a slave born in his household (15:2-3). So much for the divine promise, he might well feel. Then, Abram does have divine assurance: his descendants will be countless as the stars. Abram 'believed the Lord; and the Lord reckoned it to him as righteousness' (v. 6). This will become a key text in Paul's defence of his Torah-free gospel, his doctrine of justification by faith (Gal 3:6-9; Rom 4:1-3). Twice more will Abraham hear the word of promise (Gen 17:8; 24:7); fulfilment will be through the child of promise: Isaac (17:16-19).

The second part of our reading (21:1-3) relates the birth of Isaac. The reference to 'laughter', found throughout chapters 17-21 wherever Isaac is mentioned, is a play on the name Isaac which, in Hebrew, sounds the same as the verb 'he laughed.'

Despite the perplexity and scepticism of the aged and childless Abraham and Sarah, God's purpose was achieved.

Second Reading   Col 3:12-21

This charming passage, with its image of dressing afresh (after the tattered rags of hate and division have been stripped off, 3:5-11) conveys the harmonious atmosphere of a truly Christian community – moving on to the peace of a Christian household. As 'chosen, holy, beloved', Christians are designated as the people of the new covenant. With special stress on mutual forgiveness the author faithfully echoes an exigent demand of Jesus (notably in the Lord's prayer, Mt 6:12-15; Lk 11:4; and in the parable of the unforgiving servant, Mt 18:32-35). Christians are recipients of unbounded divine forgiveness. But if we do not, generously, extend forgiveness to others, we have not really learned to know our loving Lord.

Above all, they must put on love. Almost every descriptive list of virtues in the New Testament culminates in *agape*, that special brand of brotherly and sisterly love which Jesus singled out as the very hallmark of discipleship (Jn 13:35). The verses, Colossians 3:15-17, show the positive face of morality in a most attracticve light. The 'peace' of Christ is inward security and contentment – the Lord's legacy to his Church. Verse 16 gives a glimpse of a Christian assembly at prayer. 'Do everything in the name of the Lord Jesus.' Doing things in his name reminds us of our belonging to him as members of his body, branches of his vine, empowered to act as his ambassadors in the world.

The Christian community spirit must not be only reflected in the home: it ought to begin there. Yet the demands here in vv. 18-21 leave us uncomfortable: wives are to 'be subject', husbands are 'not to be harsh,' children are 'to obey in everything,' fathers are 'not to provoke' their children – a far cry from the sublimity of vv. 12-17. These demands are time-conditioned, reflecting the outlook and presuppositions of another age and of another culture than ours. Significantly, v. 22 goes on to the master-slave relationship. Here is no fixed immutable ethic, binding for all time. The first part of the reading, rather than its close, truly depicts the atmosphere of the Christian family.

Second Reading *ad libitum*   Heb 11:8.11-12.17-19

In 11:1-40 the author of Hebrews deals with the faith of the Old Testament patriarchs (see the parallel in Wisdom 10) with the reminder that faith is necessary for those who move onward to draw near to God. Examples of enduring faith are marshalled from the traditions of the patriarchs. The faith of Abraham and Sarah is instanced in vv. 8-12. In Jewish tradition it was with Abraham that faith in the distant future was first given, along with hope founded in God's promise (see Genesis 12). 'And he went out, not knowing where he was to go' – a splendid comment on Genesis 12:1. Abraham is a type of our pilgrimage toward heaven: 'he looked forward to the city that has foundations, whose architect and builder is God' (Heb 11:10).

The supreme test of Abraham's faith is his readiness to sacrifice the child of promise: Isaac; see Genesis 22:1-19. A Palestinian-Jewish tradition represented Isaac as actually having been killed and then brought back to life. This is also the view of the author of Hebrews: 'he considered the fact that God is able even to raise someone from the dead' (11:19). The deed of Abraham has surely coloured the telling of a greater love: 'he did not spare his own Son' (Rom 8:32), 'he gave his only Son' (Jn 3:16). Abraham had put his faith in God, a seemingly capricious and callous God. For Abraham saw, what Paul and John and the author of Hebrews were to recognize, that his God is always a foolish God – a God who loves with divine abandon. He can make outrageous demands because he will always be faithful.

Gospel   Lk 2:22-40

In 2:22-334 Luke has combined two requirements of the Law: purification of the mother after childbirth and consecration of the first-born to the Lord. According to Lev 12:2-4, a mother was 'purified' forty days after the birth of a son. Mary made the offering of the poor: a pair of birds (instead of a lamb). The 'purification' regarded strictly ritual uncleanness and did not, of course, imply a moral fault in childbirth. If Luke has mentioned the purification of Mary it is because it happened to be associated with the presentation of Jesus in the Temple. The first-born son (he 'that opens the womb') belonged to the Lord (Ex 13:2.12) but was redeemed, bought back, by payment of a stipulated sum (Num 18:15-16). It is nowhere laid down in the Law that the first-born should be taken to the Temple and presented there. But Bethlehem is a mere five miles from Jerusalem. And, besides, Luke needs to get child and parents to Jerusalem and the encounter with Simeon and Anna.

It was fitting that Jesus, already acknowledged by shepherds (2:8-20), should, on coming to the temple, be greeted by one of the 'Poor Ones,' the *anawim*, who lived and manifested a distinctive feature of Jewish piety: they were those who did not trust in their own resources but relied in utter confidence upon God. Such a one was the righteous and devout Simeon who awaited, with faith and patience, the fulfilment of the hope of Israel, its consolation (see Is 40:1; 49:13; 51:12; 61:2). The Spirit had assured him that he would not die until he had seen the Messiah. Now the Spirit had moved him to visit the Temple and had revealed to him that the infant who was at this moment being presented there was indeed that longed-for Messiah.

The Matthean magi story (Mt 2:1-12) displayed the magi reacting with acceptance and homage to the proclamation of the Messiah. Luke's shepherds play a similar role. But the magi story has two elements lacking in the Lucan story up to now: the positive response of Gentiles and the Jewish rejection of the new-born Messiah. These are supplied in Simeon's double oracle. The *Nunc Dimittis* introduces the theme of salvation for the Gentiles (see Is 42:6; 52:10). Simeon realized that, in view of the fulfilment of the promise made to him (v. 26), death must be near; he can die in peace like Abraham (Gen 15:15) but more privileged than Abraham. His cup was filled to overflowing because he had gazed upon the 'salvation of God,' the Messiah whom God had sent to save his people. And not the chosen people only: the Gentiles were destined for salvation. In this passage, for the first time in Luke's infancy narrative, we look explicitly (see 2:1) beyond Jewish limits to a universalist horizon – salvation for all.

In the second oracle (2:34-35) Simeon anticipated the rejection of Jesus by the Jewish authorities and the rejection of the Christian mission to Israel as described in Acts. Though this infant had come as the Saviour of his people, he would be rejected by many of them, or he will stand as a sign of contradiction. He is the light that reveals the inmost thoughts; he is a sword of discrimination and a sword of testing (see Ezek 14:17). In face of him, 'inmost thoughts,' thoughts hostile to Jesus, will be mercilessly revealed. The parenthetical word to Mary – that the sword will pierce her heart – indicates that, as part of Israel, she, too, will be tested. But she will not fail.

After a prophet, a prophetess (2:36-38) – the delicate touch of Luke. Anna, now eighty-four, having lost her husband seven years after an early marriage, had chosen to remain a widow. She practically lived in the Temple, so uninterrupted was her prayer. A typical saint of Judaism, one of the *Anawim*, she is also an example to Christian widows (see 1 Tim 5:5, 9). Her prophetic instinct enabled her to recognize the infant Messiah and, gratefully, she spoke of him to whose who, like Simeon and herself, looked for the salvation of Jerusalem (Is 52:9), that is, of Israel, God's people.

We welcome Anna for another reason. The New Testament writings are male-centred (androcentric) texts and women are thin on the ground. Though we have come to learn that they are more present – present behind the inclusive term 'disciples' for instance – than we had suspected, it is still gratifying to find a woman singled out for special mention. All the more when it is one of the calibre of Anna. A 'little person' in her own estimation, she is great in the eyes of the Lord. She had been privileged to gaze upon the one who was the salvation of God: light to Gentiles and glory of Israel. And she, too, like the shepherds, was a preacher of the Good News. A lesson – a salutary lesson – of Luke's story is the declaration, exhilarating or disturbing according to one's thinking, that the first Christian preaching was done by unlettered and despised shepherds and by an elderly widow (2:20, 38).

SOLEMNITY OF MARY, MOTHER OF GOD
OCTAVE OF CHRISTMAS

First Reading   Num 6:22-27

This is a priestly blessing, one of the most solemn, and arguably the most beautiful, in the Old Testament. It is particularly apt on the first day of the year. Three times the Lord is invoked. Firstly that he might keep us continually in his protection. The second blessing is a prayer that God might always be well disposed towards us, that he would let his face shine on us. The climax is a prayer for peace, the highest gift of God and the pure sign of his benevolence, when he uncovers his face towards us. We pray God's blessing on our lives and on our work in the year ahead; we ask especially for inner peace and for peace among humankind.

Second Reading   Gal 4:4-7

God's saving plan has reached fruition: the sending forth of his Son marks the fulness of time. This Son of God, 'born of woman,' shares fully in our human condition. 'Born under the law', he like all his people of Israel wore the yoke of the law. But he was able to dispel the power of the law and free from its yoke all who, through him, would enter into God's family. Paul had (3:24-25) declared that the law was transitional; its role was that of *paidagógos*, 'custodian', 'disciplinarian', the slave who looked after the education of a minor until he came of age. Those under the tutelage of the law would come of age only – the whole letter makes clear – if they recognized and acknowledged the Son. As freely-chosen sons and daughters of God they are heirs of God's promise of salvation and blessedness.

Because their new status is well-nigh unbelievable, the Spirit of God, sent into their hearts, will assure them of their filial relationship; for, indeed, the vivifying Spirit of the risen Lord is the dynamic principle of adoptive sonship (Rom 1:3; 8:15-17). Speaking to the heart of the Christian, the Spirit gives one the assurance of being a child of God. Sons and daughters of God emboldened by this Spirit will joyfully address their loving Parent as *Abba* – in the intimate manner of the Son their Brother. How sad that formal religiosity so readily shatters this filial trust and casts the Father as a stern judge. Let us be guided by Paul – and by Jesus.

Gospel   Lk 2:16-21

This reading coincides with the Gospel of the Dawn Mass on Christmas Day. Verse 21, however, an addition here, refers to the circumcision and naming of Jesus which is commemorated today. The earlier verses recall Mary's motherhood and her faith as she pondered the meaning of events still veiled – a faith which had won for her a blessing (see 1:45).

The law of circumcising a male child on the eighth day after birth comes from Leviticus 12:3. The description here (v. 21) is parallel to 1:59-63, the circumcision of the Baptist, and here, too, the emphasis is on the bestowal of the name. Born under the law (Gal 4:4) Jesus submitted to the observances of the law – the law which he was destined to bring to an end. It was the father's right to name his child (see Lk 1:62) and in this case, too, the heavenly Father had bestowed the name, indicated beforehand by the angel (1:31). The name of Jesus ('Yahweh saves') was not unknown; it had been borne by Joshua (it is the same) and by Jesus ben Sirach, author of Ecclesiasticus. But here is something new, a name that fits perfectly the character and achievement of that Saviour announced to the shepherds, he who is Christ the Lord (2:11).

SECOND SUNDAY AFTER CHRISTMAS

First Reading   Ecclus 24:1-2, 8-12

The poem in praise of wisdom (24:1-31) is one of those rich and evocative Old Testament Wisdom texts which laid the groundwork for the Johannine theology of Jesus as the *Logos*, the Word. In Proverbs 8:22-31 and Job 28:12-27 Wisdom is personified: it existed before the visible world and was present with God at creation. Later texts like Ecclesiasticus 24 and Wisdom 7:22-8:1 attribute an active role to Wisdom in the creation of the world. The fact that Ecclesiasticus 24:23 explicitly identifies Wisdom with the *Torah*, God's 'instruction' to Israel helps us to understand today's reading which stresses the pre-existence of Wisdom ('from eternity, in the beginning, he created me') and its special presence in Israel ('make your dwelling in Jacob; I was established in Zion').

Because Wisdom (or the *Torah*) guided the lives of the people of Israel they were privileged above all peoples. God had clearly made his will known to them and had pointed out the way that would lead to salvation. In spite of the fact that the sages of Israel personified Wisdom and seem to refer to it as something outside God and operating independently of him, it would be quite wrong to think that they ever regarded Wisdom as a divine person distinct from Yahweh. Such an idea would be incompatible with their strict monotheism. If they personified Wisdom and spoke of its pre-existence they did so only to depict poetically and vividly God's plan for the whole created world. Such speculation did, however, prepare for the Christian doctrine of the pre-existence of Jesus (see Jn 1:1-18).

Second Reading   Eph 1:3-6.15-18

Our reading is formed of a blessing (1:3-14) and thanksgiving (1:15-16) leading into an intercession (1:17-2:22). The initial blessing is modelled on the Jewish *berakah*, a 'blessing' of God in response to his previous 'blessing.'

The blessing of Ephesians mentions the major themes of the letter and might be seen as a résumé of the letter. The God of Christians is the Father of our Lord Jesus Christ, the God who has revealed himself in Jesus. To acknowledge Jesus as Lord is to recognize God as Father (v. 3). God has chosen Christians for a purpose: to be holy and blameless before him – in simple words, to be like him (v. 4). We are predestined to be children of God, and we become God's children 'through Jesus Christ.' It is Jesus Christ who has revealed not only that God is Father but also how we are to realize our own divine sonship. If we Christians accept Jesus as 'Lord,' as the supreme influence in our lives, we must accept his view of God and acknowledge him as our Father.

In vv. 15-16 we have the writer's prayer of thanksgiving for his readers' faith and love, which runs, almost at once, into a prayer of intercession. He prays that his readers may really 'know' the 'hope' to which they have been called (vv. 17-18). He thus implies that, despite their faith and love, they still have to progress in their vocation. An understanding of the 'mystery' God's plan of salvation is possible only as gift of God. (See Fifteenth Sunday of the Year).

Gospel   Jn 1:1-18

Whatever may be said about the origins of the Prologue (most likely a pre-existing hymn) it now forms a fitting introduction to the Fourth Gospel since it tells us about the divine and eternal origins of him whose ministry is described in the following chapters. One cannot understand the unique significance of Jesus' message of salvation unless one is aware if his mysterious provenance.

The first words of John's gospel recall Genesis 1:1. In the Old Testament God's word manifested him: in creation, in deeds of power, in prophecy. John shows that Jesus Christ, the incarnate Word, is the ultimate revelation of God. The truth that all things were created through him is expressed first positively and then negatively. In vv. 6-8 John introduces the Baptist. He is the first in a file of witnesses who testify to the event of the incarnation. Witness is a fundamental idea in John. He designates as 'the world' those who refuse to accept Jesus and are hostile to him and to his disciples; they remain in darkness. Though his own people, on the whole, did reject him, those who had faith in the incarnate Word became children of God. To them he revealed his glory by his death, resurrection and ascension.

V. 14 is the climax of the hymn. By the incarnation God is present

visibly and personally to humankind and has become man in the fullest
sense. In the expression 'he pitched his tent among us' John recalls
how Yahweh dwelt among the Israelites in the Tent of Meeting (Ex
33:7-11). 'Glory' (*kabod*) is another expression of God's presence
(see Ex 40:34; 1 Kg 8:11). In such terms John is expressing emphatically that, in Jesus, God is present among humankind.

The prologue depicts Jesus primarily as the one who manifests the
Father to men and women. Since he alone was with God (v. 1) and
since he alone had seen God (v. 18), he alone could reveal the full truth
about God. Unlike the synoptists who presented Jesus as the Messiah
who inaugurates the Kingdom of God, John will continue in the rest
of the Gospel to present Jesus primarily as the Revealer of the Father
and of the Father's plan of salvation.

EPIPHANY

First Reading

Is 60-1-6

The background to this reading is the period of restoration after the
first modest return from exile in Babylon soon after 538 B.C. It is a
time of sadness and gloom as the returned exiles survey the ruins of
their city. The prophet's message is one of hope and confidence in
these difficult times; he sees in vision the new, restored Jerusalem
shining like a beacon with the glory of the Lord summoning all people
to come and worship the true God. Its relevance to the feast of the
Epiphany is in the approach of the pagan peoples from Midian, Ephah
and Sheba – descendants of Abraham (Gen 25:1-4) now coming into
their heritage – with their gifts of gold and incense and singing the
praises of the Lord. The opening verses of the reading sound the
keynote of joy and give the passage a universal bearing with the
recurring reference to peoples and nations. Jerusalem when restored
will be the centre of a a new and greater Israel – the Church.

The theme of light, so prominent here, will be taken up in the New
Testament, e.g. 'a light for revelation to the Gentiles' (Lk 2:31). The
contrast between light and darkness points forward to John's Prologue. In sum the message is: the light of deliverance has dawned for
Israel, and all nations will benefit by its radiance (a figure of redemption). The exiles – now a great host, unlike the first pathetic group – are
pictured as gathering for return to Jerusalem, bringing with them the
wealth of the nations (a reversal of the captivity). The nations themselves will come from afar to pay tribute and to worship the Lord who

has made his home in Jerusalem. Though addressed to Jerusalem or to Israel as God's chosen people now restored to their rightful place, the prophecy will be fulfilled in Christ ('the light of the world') and in the new Israel, the Church.

Second Reading   Eph 3:2-3.5-6

This reading effectively expresses the theological significance of the feast of Epiphany: the fact that God invites all, Jew and Gentile, to share on an equal footing in the new kingdom of his Son. This is the mystery: God's plan of salvation, hidden in the past, now revealed in Christ. It is difficult for us to share the sense of shocked bewilderment that Jews felt at the fact that pagans were to be accepted on equal terms with themselves; this is an aspect of the mystery that is particularly stressed in the passage. The emphasis is on the perfect equality of all men and women: in Christ all are part of the one body (the meaning of 'in Christ Jesus'). One can observe a definite shift with regard to Old Testament passages (like that of the First Reading) even when these, too, stress the universalilty of the new reign which would be established in Israel. The Magi of today's gospel are the first fruits of the Gentile world coming to receive their share in God's messianic blessings.

Gospel   Mt 2:1-12

In this narrative Matthew has cast back into the infancy of Jesus the reactions that, historically, greeted the proclamation of the risen Lord: some believed and paid homage; others rejected both the message and the preachers. In other words, christological revelation was followed by proclamation and by the twofold reaction of acceptance-homage and rejection-persecution. But this had been prepared for in the ministry of Jesus. The same pattern is presented in the infancy narrative. The negative reaction (of Herod and his advisers, the chief priests and scribes) turns the infancy narrative into a veritable gospel – for the gospel must have suffering and rejection as well as success.

There is little point in looking for the homeland of the Magi – whom Matthew seemingly would regard as astrologers of some sort. Nor is there any point in looking to a comet, a supernova, or a planetary conjunction to account for 'his star' (2:2). A star which rises, goes before, and comes to rest over a place is no natural phenomenon but a miraculous star – more precisely, a symbolic star. (The star may have been suggested by Balaam's oracle, especially in its Greek form: 'a star will arise from Jacob, and a man will stand forth from Israel', Num

24:17). More to the point is the fact that, for Matthew, the Magi represent the Gentiles, fittingly alerted not by an angel (as Luke's Jewish shepherds) but by a star.

The liturgical tradition of our feast of Epiphany has caught Matthew's intent. Note how all the details (the strange visitors from the east, the mysterious star, the gifts) lead up to the final gesture of homage and worship. The adoration of the child Jesus by the Magi fulfils Isaiah's prophecy (First Reading) of the homage to be paid by the nations to the true Israel in the person of the Messiah.

The adoration of the Magi has stirred the imagination of artists and poets down the centuries. There is a large element of mystery about these visitors from the east. Who were they? Where did they come from? They vanish from the gospel as swiftly as they appear. Later Christian tradition has filled in the details, giving them names, making them to be kings. The evangelist wants us to see the contrast between the faith of these pagan visitors and the unbelief of the Jewish leaders: the pagans have answered the call to faith in Christ while the chosen people have for the most part rejected it.

The Old Testament, and popular tradition based on it, form the basis of Matthew's magi story; its purpose is firmly christological. One may, however, find other interest in the characters of the story: in this respect the Magi. They are Gentiles, illustrating the universal breadth of the good news brought by the 'king of the Jews'. They are people of good will, open to God, ready to hear and follow the call of God. They are people prepared to follow a star, wherever it might lead. Open and starry-eyed, they are naive, guileless, easily taken-in by self-serving priests and a murderous king. They are romantic and lovable figures.

THE BAPTISM OF THE LORD
FIRST SUNDAY OF THE YEAR

First Reading   Is 42:1-4.6-7

This is the first of the four great Servant Songs of Second Isaiah. The anonymous prophet of the Exile paints a character portrait of a mysterious servant of God and describes the mission he is called by God to accomplish. The later Servant Songs (in chapters 45, 50 and 53) will fill in the picture with further details culminating in the great hymn of Isaiah 53 in which the redemptive death of the servant is described and his ultimate vindication and triumph. Jesus, in his person and mission, was to realise perfectly this prophetic role of the servant of the Lord, meek and humble of heart, totally dedicated to the will of the Father, accomplishing our salvation through his death and resurrection.

Point by point our passage speaks of: (1) the call or consecration of the servant to the task of bringing justice (that is, true religion, or knowledge of the true God); (2) the qualities of the servant: meekness, patience, mercy; (3) the mission of the servant: true justice or, equivalently, salvation; (4) the idea of 'covenant' suggesting the mediation of a new covenant between God and his people.

First Reading *ad libitum*   Is 55:1-11

The author of Isaiah 40-55, an anonymous prophet of the Exile, is, for convenience, named Second Isaiah. Our reading is the conclusion of his work. It is an invitation, addressed to the exiles in Babylon, to come to a banquet at which the food and drink are free (v. 1), at which fully-satisfying fare is offered (v. 2). The invitation is to a banquet with Yahweh himself, and mention of 'covenant' (v. 3) evokes the covenant meals of Genesis 15:7-20 and Exodus 24:9-11. He assures his people that the covenant with David (see 2 Samuel 7), despite the traumatic experience of the Exile, has not been set aside; it has been transferred to the people. This new Israel will not conquer or subdue nations. Rather, the nations will run to Israel because of its witness to Yahweh (vv. 4-5). The prophet insists that Israel (and consequently we) must 'seek the Lord,' which means here, as often in the Bible, turning to God with humility and a real sense of need of him (vv. 6-7).

A main theme of the passage is the ever-present possibility of forgiveness from God as it was revealed to Moses (Ex 34). It is perhaps in this sense that vv. 8-9 are meant, contrasting human hard-heartedness and grasping insistence on one's due with the Lord's generosity and loving-kindness.

The great 'Book of Consolation' of Second Isaiah had opened with stress on the permanence of Yahweh's word: 'the word of our God will stand forever' (40:8). It closes with emphasis on the effectiveness of God's word. It is not by chance that the prophet's word of consolation should begin and end with an insistence on the power of God's word. The author's message is one of comfort, inspired by the prospect of imminent return from exile (40:1-2). But it is, too, one of exhortation, designed to encourage the people to undertake the return. Just as, in prophetic preaching, exile represented alienation from Yahweh by sin, so the real return from exile, in the mind of Second Isaiah, is an authentic conversion, moral and spiritual, to Yahweh. This involves listening to his word. Return from exile is an effect of his word. Comparison with rain and snow is an assurance, in faith, that Yahweh is able to reinstate his people in their homeland. But, since this restoration is the work of his word, it will become effective for them only in so far as they respond to this word by returning to him from the 'exile' of sin (55:6-7). Far from dispensing them from the effort of a moral and spiritual return, Yahweh's power makes the return possible

Second Reading   Acts 10:34-38

A significant milestone in Acts is the conversion of Cornelius – so important in fact that, like the conversion of Paul, Luke has narrated it three times (10:1-48; 11:1-18; 15:6-18). In our passage Peter begins his discourse in the house of Cornelius. He proclaims the good news: God has no favourites. He would bring salvation to all people in Jesus Christ. The 'message' that 'spread throughout Judea' refers to the preaching of the good news of 'peace through Jesus Christ' by the apostles, sent first to 'the people of Israel.' Peter's vision (10:9-16) was what made him realize that Christianity was a religion for all people, not a preserve of Jews.

For today's feast the relevant passage in the reading is the description of the baptism: it is the 'anointing' of Jesus of Nazareth 'with the Holy Spirit and with power.' Luke, who all through the Third Gospel and Acts stresses the role of the Spirit in the life of Christ and of the early Christians, thus characteristically describes Jesus' baptism. In the resumé of Jesus' ministry which he places on Peter's lips in the present text he wants to express the idea that God was present in him, in his preaching and in his work, manifesting the divine power to the world and offering salvation to all. This discourse of Peter (10:34-43) is an example of the early Christian preaching (*kerygma*) to non-Jewish converts.

Second Reading *ad libitum*   1 Jn 5:1-9

A prominent theme of the First Letter of John is that the Christian is child of God – child of a Father who is Love. Our reading points out that the test of our loving lies in keeping the commandments. John really has one commandment in mind: that of love. The observation 'his commandments are not burdensome' reminds one of Matthew 11:30, 'For my yoke is easy, and my burden is light.' A prominent theme of Johannine preaching is the Christian's victory over sin and the evil one; here (vv. 4-5) 'world' is the same as the evil one. Victory is through the Son of God who has already overcome the evil one (Jn 12:31; 16:33). John, typically, insists on the reality of the incarnation; Jesus came 'by water and blood' – he is the Jesus of flesh and blood who was baptized in the Jordan and died on the cross (v. 6).

In John 19:34-35 the flow of blood and water from the side of the *dead* Jesus is a prophetic reference to the giving of the Spirit. The symbolic meaning is that the death of Jesus was life-giving. The author of 1 John seems to have in mind some who associated salvation and the coming of the Spirit with water (baptism) and not with blood (crucifixion). The significance of the threefold witness (Spirit, water, blood) is that Christians recognize the life-giving powers of the Spirit, of Baptism and of the Eucharist. All three are symbolized in the outpouring of Spirit, water and blood in John 19:30-35. The ultimate testimony, however, is that of God himself (1 Jn 5:9). Jesus is Son of God. To fail to acknowledge God's testimony to his Son is to make God a liar.

Gospel   Mk 1:7-11

The reading gives the Baptist's witness to Jesus (vv. 7-8) and the narrative of the baptism of Jesus (vv. 9-11). John, the Elijah-like figure who had proclaimed the call to repentance (1:2-6) now proclaims the greater than he who will baptize the people with the Holy Spirit. [See Second Sunday of Advent].

Jesus comes from Nazareth of Galilee to be baptized by John. The description of the baptism is matter-of-fact. There is no trace of the embarrassment shown in Matthew's text (Mt 3:14-15); Mark ignores the difficulty raised by the fact of Jesus submitting to John's baptism 'for the forgiveness of sins.' In Mark's eyes, Jesus is not only the true Israelite whose repentance is perfect; he is the Son of God receiving the sign of repentacne on behalf of the people of God. According to Mark, at the baptism Jesus alone saw and heard the heavenly happening (vv. 10-11). 'The Spirit' is the power of God coming upon Jesus, the Son, a consecration for his messianic mission: 'how God anointed Jesus of Nazareth with the Holy Spirit and with power' (Acts 10:38). The phrase 'like a dove'is found in all three synoptic gospels; its symbolism, likely, has reference to the mission of Jesus, although its precise meaning escapes us.

The title 'only Son' (for that is what 'beloved son' means) so solemnly attested (in terms echoing Psalm 2:7) transcends messiahship and points to a unique relationship to God; it expresses the faith of the early Church and marks a stage in christological thinking. The heavenly voice is for the Christian reader, telling one the truth about Jesus. The baptism story, as we find it in Mark, was meant to assert that Jesus was constituted and declared Son of God at the time of his baptism by John.

The heading of the gospel – 'The beginning of the good news of Jesus Christ, the Son of God' (1:1) – informs the reader of Mark's own point of view of Jesus' identity. In the baptismal scene the heavenly voice (the voice of God) declares of Jesus: 'You are my Son, the Beloved' (1:11). As Jesus is about to embark on his public ministry God solemnly affirms both his status and his call. Similarly, at the Transfiguration, God declares (this time for the benefit of the three disciples): 'This is my Son, the Beloved' (9:7).

Only at baptism and transfiguration does God appear as 'actor' in the story. And not alone does God, each time, declare that Jesus is 'Son': the baptism declaration confirms the truth of the heading and the transfiguration declaration confirms the truth of Peter's confession of Jesus as the 'Messiah' (8:29). Finally, at the climactic moment of the death of Jesus the title is *Son of God*: 'Truly this man was God's Son!' (15:39). This centurion is the first human being in Mark's story truly to penetrate the secret of Jesus' identity, because he was the one who had come to terms with the cross.

As for the *meaning* of 'Son of God,' the voice from heaven of 1:11 is a composite quotation from Psalm 2:7; Isaiah 42:1; Genesis 22:2. In Isaiah 42:1 the servant in whom God delights is one 'chosen' for ministry; in Genesis 22:2 Abraham's beloved son is his 'only' son. Most importantly, in Psalm 2, 'You are my son' is declared by Yahweh of the Davidic king. Consequently, God solemnly affirms that Jesus, the Anointed One from the line of David is the unique son whom he has chosen for eschatological ministry.

Lent

Introduction to the Liturgical Season

The readings for Lent are best understood in relation to conversion and baptism. They put before us the contrast between life and death, light and darkness, grace and sin. They ask us to choose life. They assure us that the God who created the human race will never abandon it. They promise newness of life in Christ.

GOSPELS

For the first and second Sundays, the Gospels are those of the temptation and the transfiguration.

For the third, fourth and fifth Sundays, in Year B the Gospels are all from John, and refer to the glorification of Christ through his cross and resurrection; they contain the images of the temple, the bronze serpent, and the grain of wheat.

FIRST READINGS

The First Readings are chosen, as always, to harmonize with the Gospels. They are also meant to take us through some of the great moments in the history of salvation, as part of the catechesis which characterizes Lent. In Year B we see the covenant with Noah after the Flood, the testing of Abraham and the promise made to him, God's Law given through Moses, the deportation to Babylon and the return to Jerusalem, and the promise, in Jeremiah, of the new covenant, the law written in people's hearts.

SECOND READINGS

The Second Readings harmonize with the First Readings and the Gospels, and try to provide a link between them. In Year B, they tell about the Flood as a type of baptism, God's not sparing his own Son, the wisdom of the cross, the life brought by Christ, and the obedience of the Son.

Philip Gleeson OP

Lent

First Reading   Gen 9:8-15

It is rather a pity that the whole passage (Gen 9:1-17) has not been set as this reading. The changed situation after the Flood raises a basic question: did the first blessing of creation, 'be fruitful and multiply' (1:28) still hold? The answer is that God has indeed renewed his blessing for the new generation. He has not abandoned humanity: he still wills procreation and increase (vv. 1,7). Human life is sacred because humankind was made in God's image (v. 5). The taking of human life (murder) is punished by death; God empowers humans to avenge murder (v. 6). This is an awesome responsibility. No more effectively could God express his abhorrence of murder. He grants to humans, in this circumstance, to enter into his own preserve of life. Respect for human life was to take a giant step even beyond this for, in the ethic of Jesus, there is no place at all for the taking of human life. The contrary practice of Christians down the centuries has not made void this word of the Lord.

'My covenant' (vv. 9-11) – the first in a series of patriarchal covenants that will serve as the preparation for the covenant at Sinai with the people of Israel. The term 'covenant,' which in its technical theological sense concerns the relations of humankind with God, was borrowed from human social experience, from the fact of treaties and alliances between individuals and peoples. In practice, the religious use of the term regards a special type of covenant, that in which one partner takes the initiative and imposes the conditions. Therefore, God lays down the terms, demanding of his people that it would keep the covenant (17:9; 19:5). See Sirach 44:18 'Everlasting covenants were made with him [Noah] that all flesh should never again be blotted out by a flood.' The most striking comment is that of Second Isaiah in his moving hymn to the New Jerusalem: 'This is like the days of Noah to me: just as I swore that the waters of Noah would never again go over the earth, so I have sworn that I will not be angry with you and will not rebuke you. For the mountains may depart and the hills be removed, but my steadfast love shall not depart from you, and my covenant of peace shall not be removed, says the Lord, who has compassion on you' (Is 54:9-10).

God's covenants illustrate the way God deals with humankind – his justice, his mercy, and his readiness always to give another chance.

God knows and understands human weakness; he asks only that we not turn away irrevocably. And that is the real significance of the new covenant made in Christ. It is God's complete and final answer to all those tentative beginnings and subsequent fresh starts made by humankind over the centuries. Christ is for those who need him – he is the saviour of men and women. That knowledge is, like the rainbow for Noah, our hope. And in it too we become more than ever aware that once 'brought to life in Christ' our Christianity must issue forth in good works here and now. Therein lies the challenge.

Second Reading   1 Pet 3:18-22

Peter is exhorting Gentile Christians to persevere in their faith in face of persecution. He points to Christ as the basis for their hope. Jesus may have been put to death 'in the flesh,' that is, as far as his earthly life was concerned. But that was beginning rather than end. In his resurrection he was 'made alive in the spirit' and proclaimed to all his definitive victory over evil.

Christ's victory is communicated to men and women in baptism. Through it we share in his resurrection and are therefore assured of eternal salvation and ultimate triumph over all that is evil. Like Noah, the Christian is saved by passage through water. The baptized person has a firm ground of hope in time of trouble. Christ has already won the victory over the force of evil. The Christian who pledges oneself to God with 'a good conscience' thereby professes faith in God's power and goodness and so can look, without fear or disappointment, to the living Lord for the grace and strength to keep the pledge one has given.

> This whole passage has taken us over a trajectory of salvation; from the death and resurrection of Jesus (v. 18) to his descent into Sheol (v. 19) to his triumphant exaltation at God's right hand (v. 22). Although this 'journey' imagery (specifically the descent into Sheol) is unique in the New Testament, it is a theme picked up in the writings of the early Fathers and used in the creed. For 1 Peter, too, this saving journey was part of the 'creed' on which the energetic witness of the community must be based (Donald Senior, *1 & 2 Peter*. New Testament Message 20, 3).

Gospel   Mk 1:12-15

With the emergence of the beloved Son (1:9-11) a new era has begun, the era of eschatological hope. An essential feature of this hope is the overthrow of evil. And thus it is that, confirmed in his divine Sonship and anointed with the Spirit for his task (vv. 10-11), Jesus faces a trial of strength. The Spirit 'drove' – a strong word – Jesus into the wilderness. In the setting of the temptation, a struggle with evil, the wilderness is the traditional haunt of evil spirits (symbolized by 'wild beasts'); and there Jesus encounters Satan, the prince of evil, the enemy of God.

Jesus was tempted; the Greek word carries all the nuances of temptation, trial, tribulation, test. For Jesus, temptation did not end here (see 14:32-42), and the implied victory over Satan, reflected in his subsequent exorcisms, will have to be won all over again on the cross. Here we are doubtless to understand that the ministering angels supplied Jesus with food; Mark has no reference at all to a fast of Jesus. At this first struggle Jesus is not God-forsaken as he will be at his last (15:34).

Now that Jesus has been acknowledged as God's Son and has thrown himself into a totally committed struggle against evil, he can begin to preach the Good News (vv. 14-15). Mark's first words are ominous: 'after John was arrested (lit. delivered up).' The fate of the Baptist was to be delivered up to his enemies in accordance with the divine will (6:17-29). The alert reader, conscious that Jesus suffered a like fate, will perceive in John a type of the suffering Messiah. Jesus came preaching 'the gospel of God,' the good news from God. It is the christian message of salvation (see 1 Thes 3:2,8-9; 2 Cor 11:7; Rom 1:1; 15:6). And the summary of that preaching uses early christian theological language. Like the Forerunner, Jesus calls for a thorough-going conversion: but, more urgently, he calls on people to embrace the Good News. While the sentence, 'The reign of God has come near; repent and believe the Good News' is an admirable summary of the preaching of Jesus, Mark himself undoubtedly understood the words 'believe the gospel' in the christian sense of faith in the good news of salvation through Jesus Christ. And this is how his reader must take it.

SECOND SUNDAY OF LENT

First Reading   Gen 22:1-2.9-13.15-18

It is clear that what took place in this episode was a test of Abraham's faith. But, for Abraham himself, it represents his agonizing effort to do what he thought God really wanted of him. Human sacrifice was known to the Canaanites, and the patriarch lived among them. It is not inconceivable that in his steady effort to find and do God's will he might have thought that God – the Author of life – asked this deed of him. Rarely, if ever, was a man summoned to give greater proof of his faith and of his obedience. Ironically, it is Isaac, hitherto the reward of that faith, who becomes the focus of its supreme test. For Isaac, sole son of parents 'past the age' and 'as good as dead' (Heb 11:11-12), was the only possible way in which God's promises to Abraham could be fulfilled. Now God asks him to sacrifice his 'only son'!

A poignant story indeed. 'Take your son, your only son Isaac whom you love ... and offer him as a burnt offering ... So Abraham rose early in the morning.' The man who had, without hesitation, at the Lord's bidding set out from his homeland (12:1), now, without question, sets out to do this awful deed. He obeyed with a heavy heart, a heart pierced to the quick by Isaac's unsuspecting question: 'Father ... the fire and the wood are here, but where is the lamb for a burnt offering?' The tragic dignity of Abraham and his sad readiness to give his son stirred a Christian sentiment. The deed of Abraham has surely coloured the telling of a greater love: 'He who did not withold his own Son, but gave him up for all of us' (Rom 8:32); 'God so loved the world that he gave his only Son' (Jn 3:16. Abraham had put his faith in God, a seemingly capricious and callous God. For, Abraham saw, what Paul and John were to recognise, that this God is always a foolish God – a God who loves with divine abandon. He can make outrageous demands because he will always be faithful.

Second Reading   Rom 8:31-34

The celebrant/reader should not be satisfied with this snippet but ought read on to v. 39 or, preferably, read the whole passage 8:28-39. We learn at once who God is: he is God *for us*. It is as good a definition of God as we might hope for. He is the loving God who created us and called us to be his daughters and his sons. The question: 'Will he not with him also give us everything else?' can have one answer only. The giving of his Son shows, beyond doubt, that God is in deadly earnest. Father and Son are prepared to go to any length to save humankind from themselves. God gave his Son without condition; he took the risk. The death of his Son was, at the deepest level, a sacrifice made by God.

In 8:33-34 we have two questions with ironical answers. Who can bring a charge? God – who justifies! It is really another way of putting the question: 'If God is for us, who is against us?' Can we imagine that the God who, in our helplessness, has, at such a cost, taken his saving initiative, is now going to be our Judge? And who will condemn us?

Christ Jesus, who died for us, who intercedes for us! Again it is another way of putting a question, this time the question, 'Who will separate us from the love of Christ?' Christ's love of us is dramatically manifest in his sacrificial death and in his efficacious intercession. Tribulation and distress cannot separate us from the love of Christ. No trials of our human lot can come between the Christian and that unyielding love.

Gospel   Mk 9:2-10

While it is no longer possible to say what it was that transpired upon the mountain – was it vision? was it deep religious experience? – we must seek to understand what the episode means for Mark. Perhaps his pointer, immediately before (9:1), to an imminent parousia, and the presence of Elijah and Moses, may help us to understand his purpose. In ch. 13 Mark has to contend with some who, having pinned their parousia-hope on the destruction of Jerusalem and its temple in 70 A.D., were disillusioned because that hope had been dashed. Was Jesus after all no greater than Elijah and Moses who, too, had been rapt to heaven? He was not really the Messiah, then, and that is why their expectation had been disappointed.

In Mark the aspect of revelation made to Jesus (see Lk 9:28-32) yields wholly to the theme of revelation granted to the disciples. And now the entire first part of the narrative prepares for this. Jesus leads the three disciples 'up a high mountain' where he was transfigured 'before them' (v. 2). Moses and Elijah appear 'to them' and it was for the disciples' benefit that a heavenly voice was heard, speaking of Jesus in the third person (v. 7). The 'three dwellings,' one each for Jesus, Elijah and Moses, would have put all three on an equal footing. Peter really 'did not know what to say;' he has, yet again, wholly misunderstood. The voice from heaven will set the matter straight. The cloud which now overshadows them is the cloud of God's *Shekinah* (the 'presence' or 'dwelling' of God) and the medium of his manifestation. 'This is my Son, the beloved' – in contrast to 1:11 the words are here addressed to the disciples: they hear the divine approbation of Jesus as the messianic Son. Elijah and Moses have disappeared and he stands alone. 'Listen to him' – the Beloved Son is also the prophet-like-Moses whose teaching must be heeded (see Dt 18:15-19).

The faith of the disciples in Jesus the Messiah had been confirmed. But this was only the beginning. Their problem remained – Jesus must die before he would be glorified. His mission was not that of a conquering hero; he was to be the Suffering Servant of Yahweh whose victory lay in apparent defeat on the cross. The disciples would have to work that one out for themselves and would find the solution only in the light of the resurrection. So it is with us. God's ways never seem to be ours. Unlike Peter we must resist the temptation to pick and choose – to build a tent – at any particular juncture. Rather we should strive to 'listen to Jesus' in the whole of his teaching and make it effective in the whole of our lives.

THIRD SUNDAY OF LENT

First Reading   Ex 20:1-17

This reading is one of the two versions of the Decalogue – the other being (Dt 5:6-21). The Ten Commandments should be viewed in their original Sinai setting. There they are clearly part of the covenant God made with his people; they are an expression of the profound and abiding nature of the covenant. They are not so much a set of laws to which God expected and exacted obedience as declarations of willing loyalty offered to God by his people.

It may be that commandments four to ten are the original seven commandments. They deal with interpersonal relationships and are found in other codes of law since they are the core of 'natural law.' Crime in other ancient codes is against humans. In the Bible it is seen as a affront to God himself. The distinctive commandments, one to three, make that point, dramatically. Morally and religiously, the decalogue is superior to other ancient codes. Yet we Christians must be aware that we do not live by the ten commandments: we live by the 'law' of Jesus (Mt 7:24).

Second Reading   1 Cor 1:22-25

For Paul, Christianity was the message of the cross of Christ and he let nobody forget it. He proclaimed, without apology, a crucified saviour, knowing full well that this would shock Jews and scandalize the Greek world of his time. For Jews awaiting the advent of a Messiah who would inaugurate the sovereignty of Israel over the Gentiles, it was incredible that one who had been crucified as a criminal could be the Messiah. Did not their own law state clearly: 'anyone hung on a tree is under God's curse' (Dt 21:23)! See Gal 3:13. The fact of crucifixion automatically disqualified Jesus from being the Messiah. The Greek mind, consistently seeking for a philosophical system that would satisfactorily explain humankind and the world, found the idea of God becoming human repugnant. The incarnation, quite apart from crucifixion, was 'madness.'

It seems to be characteristic of God to confound human wisdom. He accomplishes by 'foolishness' what the greatest human wisdom cannot achieve. And his wisdom and saving action are, paradoxically, revealed in Jesus Christ, crucified and risen. Those 'who are the called,' that is, those who hear and heed the divine invitation, see in Christ 'the power of God and the wisdom of God.' For in him is salvation and new life.

The cross of Christ is hard to accept until we reflect on the fact that it is but the practical expression of 'God so loved the world.' Israelites knew that God loved one – there was ample evidence of it. What they did not guess at was how much God loved them. Only the cross of Jesus would speak that. It was also a strangely fitting way of making the point.

Gospel   Jn 2:13-25

The cleansing of the temple which John has at an early stage of Jesus' ministry is, more credibly, put by the synoptists at the close of the ministry (Mk 11:15-18 and parr). What matters is not when it happened but what it means. Jesus passes judgment on the Jewish sacrificial system. By word and deed, in the fashion of the Old Testament prophets, (Jer 7:11; Mal 3:1), he protests against the profanation of God's house and signals that its messianic purification was at hand. 'The Jews' – the hostile religious authorities – recognize that Jesus' action was deed of one who was a prophet and claimed to be Messiah.

John spells out the significance of the deed. He recalls the words of Psalm 69:10 'Zeal for your house will consume me.' The symbolic action had been predicted for the messianic age by Zech 14:21 'there shall no longer be traders in the house of the Lord of hosts on that day.' After the resurrection (vv. 17,22) the full meaning of what Jesus did and said became clear to his followers. Jesus, the risen Messiah, had taken the place of the temple and all it stood for. The centre of God's presence among his people is no longer a place; it is henceforth a person. The new sanctuary is the risen body of Jesus. In this new temple dwells the fullness of the Spirit. And that Spirit comes to those who believe and dwells with them so that they too in their turn become temples of God.

FOURTH SUNDAY OF LENT

First Reading   2 Chr 36:14-16, 19-23

The Chronicler's work (1,2 Chronicles, Ezra, Nehemiah) is a third century B.C theology of history. The author brings to life again before the eyes of his contemporaries an (idealized) Davidic theocracy. This recalling of the glories of David is designed to make his readers ponder on their vocation as God's people. The story of the restoration (Ezra, Nehemiah), coming after the failure of the monarchy, would show how God had remained faithful to his people. As a new beginning it would turn their hope towards the full establishment of God's kingdom.

Our reading, the conclusion of 2 Chronicles, catalogues the sins of Zedekiah and his people and tells of the end of Jerusalem and its temple, and of the Babylonian exile. The candid confession of sin and the acknowledgment that the chastisement was richly deserved are typical of post-exilic writings. No less typical is the optimism: the book closes on the note of restoration (vv. 22-23). Jerusalem is not destined for oblivion; God's promises are not nullified by his people's sins; his mercy overcomes his wrath. Despite setbacks, the life of God's people will continue. Significantly, it is with this passage that the Hebrew canon of the Old Testament ends, pointing forward in hope towards an unforeseen future.

Second Reading   Eph 2:4-10

From the start the author of Ephesians writes with enthusiasm of God's gifts to humankind through Jesus the mediator. He elaborates on the gifts: 'Blessed be the God and Father of our Lord Jesus Christ who has blessed us in Christ with every spiritual blessing in the heavenly places … He destined us for adoption as his children through Jesus Christ, according to the good pleasure of his will … a plan for the fullness of time, to gather up all things in him, things in heaven and things in earth' (1:3,5,10). The power of God which was at work in Christ's resurrection and ascension has already been at work in us, in so far as we have been 'raised' from the death of our former Gentile (and indeed Jewish) existence. To this extent we already share in Christ's dominion over the rest of creation (2:1-6). The description of our previous existence as a 'death' and of our new life as a participation in Christ's resurrection and ascension reinforces the author's insistence that we have been saved by grace alone (vv. 7-9). God's saving grace is so radical, in fact, that even our good actions have been 'prepared' by God (v. 10). Our part in the process of redemption is to be grateful, to trust in Christ, to accept the gift with all humility and begin to act in accordance with our new status – for we are 'created in Christ Jesus, for good works that we should walk in them.'

Gospel   Jn 3:14-21

The dialogue with Nicodemus (Jn 3:1-21) treats of new birth. The phrase rendered 'born anew' (vv. 3,7) can equally well mean 'born from above' and, typically, John intends both meanings. True to the procedure of the gospel Nicodemus understands the statement of Jesus at its surface level (v. 4); Jesus then explains that he means spiritual rebirth from above; his baptism, which brings about this rebirth, is not in water only – as was the baptism of John – but of 'water and Spirit' (v. 5). Then, in our reading, comes an enigmatic reference to the death of Jesus (vv. 14-15) and a clear statement of the marvellous love of God (vv. 16-18).

In v. 14, John gives a double significance to the verb 'to be lifted up.' First, it is the physical fact of being elevated upon the cross, just as the bronze figure of a serpent was raised by Moses over the stricken Israelites (Num 21:4-9); but it also evokes the spiritual elevation of Jesus by the Father – that glorification which was granted him through his death. Like the bronze serpent of old, the raised-up Son of Man will be an effective sign of salvation for all who look on him with trust.

Verses 16-21 develop what has gone before. The hope of salvation offered through the descent and exaltation of the Son of Man is now traced back to its ultimate source: God's marvellous love. It was God who set the process in motion, wishing that the world be saved from sin. V. 16 ('God so loved the world ... ') is the very foundation of the gospel; together with 1:14 ('the Word was made flesh') and 12:32 ('I when I am lifted up from the earth, will draw all people to myself'), it constitutes the 'good news' proclaimed by John.

Yet, not everyone will benefit from the loving initiative of God; some, by hardening their hearts against belief in Jesus, will seal their own condemnation. Jesus brings judgment with him, necessarily; he is like a light that shines into the heart of each person, and the way we react to this light determines our destiny. If, loving darkness and deceit and selfish ways, we turn away wilfully from God's light, we cannot come to God; we renounce the right to be called his children. For John, salvation or damnation begins already, here on earth, according to one's acceptance or rejection of Jesus, the only Son of God. The essential judgment is not passed by Jesus (or by the Father) but is contained in the choice we make when we are confronted by him.

In the verses 13-15 concerning the ascent to God the emphasis is on difficulty. Ascending to God is not something that one can do alone – it requires the prior initiative of the one who descended – and it involves the spectre of death.

> Just at the point that the ascent to God may seem overwhelmingly difficult, the gospel offers both strong encouragement and a grim warning. The strong encouragement is the classic, 'For God so loved ... ' To a weary world or faltering pilgrims it is a way of saying that God is coming to meet them, coming to them with unfathomable love. And if the ascent to God demands a form of death, the One who is being approached is not simply a bemused spectator. On God's part too there is a form of death – the giving of an only child so that the world may be saved. Thus what is demanded of the one who would approach God, however difficult it may be, is made possible when seen in the context of God's self-giving. (T. Brodie, *John*, 199).

FIFTH SUNDAY OF LENT

First Reading   Jer 31:31-34

Jeremiah's grim mission was 'to pluck up and to pull down, to destroy and to overthrow' (1:10). It was his hopeless task to try to bring his people so see that without a radical change of heart, a genuine conversion, they were living in a fool's paradise. Never could God permit his city to fall and his temple to be destroyed, they were convinced. In truth, the Babylonians were God's judgment on a grossly unfaithful people. Because there was not the slightest hint that the people were going to change their ways, Jeremiah has to insist that the nation is doomed. But, when Nebuchadnezzar had captured and destroyed Jerusalem did the prophet crow over it and call out: 'I told you so!'? Far from it. The time for threats is over. Disaster has struck and here is a shattered people. His prophetic service had been to try and bring his people to their senses. His service now is to comfort them in their bewilderment.

Jeremiah saw that the old covenant would be replaced by a new one (31:31-34) when God would act directly on the human heart, when he would write his law on that heart, and when all men and women would know Yahweh. The Sinai covenant was conditional on the people's willingness to obey the law – and the people had failed to obey.

Jeremiah now foresees a whole new basis for covenant. What is new is that there is a change in the manner in which the divine will is to be conveyed to the people. Yahweh is to by-pass the process of speaking and listening and project a new vision of himself: a God of compassion and mercy and overwhelming love. Jeremiah's own experience is reflected here. He had preached to a hopelessly obdurate people; he is convinced that God must take a hand and change the human heart (see 32:37-41). He glimpses the era of the Spirit as Paul will paradoxically characterise it – the 'law of the Spirit of life' (Rom 8:2).

The greatest tribute to Jeremiah was paid by the one whose way he had prepared. On that night before the Lord went to his death, he brought the most solemn promise of the prophet to fulfilment: 'this cup that is poured out for you is the new covenant in my blood' (Lk 22:20). God had set his seal on the life and message of his servant.

Second Reading   Heb 5:1-9

The priesthood of Christ is a central theme of the letter to the Hebrews and our reading is a key passage in the unfolding of the theme. It is well to look to the context (4:12-16) where it is urged that the demands of God's word spoken through Christ are stringent and there is no escaping them. We will be judged on how we have responded. This might seem to impose an impossible responsibility, but there is no need for discouragement. We have confidence in knowing that Jesus is our merciful high priest who will give us all the help we need to be faithful. He has entered heaven but he is united to us still in his perfect understanding of our trials and difficulties. The distance between us, abolished by the incarnation, has not been broadened again by the ascension. He is always ready and able to help us because he is always our compassionate High Priest.

The passage 5:1-10 falls naturally into two parts: (1) the qualities requisite for the priestly office (1-4): (2) Jesus possesses these qualities (5-10). A high priest is a human being officially instituted as a mediator between God and humankind, who pleads the cause of men and women before God, who offers the gifts of mortals to God, especially sacrifice for sin. A true high priest must be compassionate, showing benevolence and indulgence to sinners and must be chosen and called by God (1-4). In proving that Jesus was these qualities, the author proceeds in reverse order, dealing first with his vocation and then with his fellowship in human suffering. Christ did not take the dignity of high priesthood upon himself: God who, in Ps 2:7, hails the Messiah as his Son (see Heb 1:5), declares him in Ps 110:4 to be a high priest forever after the order of Melchizedek. If he possesses the premier condition of priesthood, divine vocation, he also possesses the fundamental quality of the priest, compassion towards sinners (7-10). These verses present the Son in an attitude of suppliance before the Father. At once priest and victim, he learned the difficulty of obedience; and, being perfected in suffering, he brought salvation to those who obey him. Vv 7-8 (surely referring to the Gethsemane prayer; see Mk 14:32-42) indicate the means (suffering) by which the saving mission of Christ is effected. Vv. 9-10 indicate the result for himself and for those who trust in him. Through his obedience Jesus gained an enriching experience, a practical comprehension of and appreciation of suffering which would enable him fully to sympathize with his brothers and sisters. 'For we do not have a high priest who is unable to sympathize with our weaknesses, but we have one who in every respect has been tested as we are, yet without sin' (4:15). [See Thirtieth Sunday of the Year]

Gospel   Jn 12:20-33

In the Fourth Gospel Jesus often speaks of his 'hour,' his supreme moment, when all that he has come to do on earth will be accomplished. (In 2:4; 7:30; 8:20 the 'hour' has not yet arrived; in 13:1; 17:1 he knows that it has come at last). Twice, in today's gospel reading, he speaks of this fateful 'hour' (vv. 23,27). The time for his passion has come and he fears it and yet longs for it. His soul is troubled. Should he ask the Father to save him from the cross? No! he sets his mind to fulfil his task: 'It is for this reason that I have come to this hour.' Further, he is sure that in this hour of crisis and suffering he will be glorified. Here, in the attitude of Jesus to his coming passion, we find a parallel with Heb 5:7-9. The high priest experiences the pain of obedience, yet accepts it totally, and through it is glorified.

Our passage is concerned with the relationship between death and life – between sacrificial death and fuller life. In vv. 20-22 we hear that some Greeks wish to speak with Jesus. Surprisingly, instead of acceding to their request, he states a fundamental theme to guide all his followers: 'unless a grain of wheat falls into the earth and dies, it remains just a single grain, but if it dies, it bears much fruit' (v. 24). Following Christ involves despising one's earthly life and possessions and being ready to yield up everything for his service. Jesus explains more fully in vv. 32-33 the relation between his sacrificial death and the life of humankind. In his own person he exemplifies the general principle: life, through death – 'I, when I am lifted up from the earth, will draw all people to myself' (v. 32). This *'lifting-up'* means, in the language of the Fourth Gospel, two things. It is both the physical posture of the crucifixion (see 3:14 'as Moses lifted up the serpent in the wilderness ... ') and the divine act by which Jesus was glorified, on account of his obedient death. Just as he is lifted up in torment by sinful men, even so he is raised in immortal triumph, by the Father, to be the saviour of all. And through his death and glory, he will draw all humankind to himself, to give them faith and life and forgiveness.

> Jesus speaks of an implied invitation: if lifted up from the earth he will draw all people to himself. The lifting up refers both to dying (on the cross, cf v. 33) and to ascending to God. Thus the seed which fell to the earth and died will be lifted up from the earth and will indeed bear much fruit. As in the bread of life discourse (6:44), 'drawing' refers to a profound inner action upon the human heart. And 'all people' has a sweeping universalism.
>
> Thus to people everywhere who may be cowed by fear and death Jesus offers a strengthening vision: one need not be immobilised by the forces of darkness; rather one may be drawn, along with others, towards one who is above the earth. (T. Brodie, *John*, 417).

Passion Sunday and Sacred Triduum

Introduction to the Liturgical Season

Passion Sunday and the Sacred Triduum are the centre of the Church's liturgical year. They proclaim the suffering, death and resurrection of Jesus. They evoke the whole history of salvation. They recall the two great sacraments of Baptism and Eucharist. They call for conversion, and encourage us to bear witness to the risen Lord.

GOSPELS

The gospel readings take us through the Passion (Passion Sunday and Good Friday) and proclaim the Resurrection (Easter Vigil and Easter Sunday). If Mass is celebrated during the evening of Easter Sunday, the account of the road to Emmaus may be read. We also hear the account of the entry into Jerusalem (the procession on Passion Sunday). And, on Holy Thursday, there is the great symbol of Jesus' washing the feet of the disciples, a gesture which helps to show the meaning of the whole paschal mystery.

READINGS FROM THE OLD TESTAMENT

Again we read from the book of Isaiah, the third and fourth songs of the suffering servant (Passion Sunday and Good Friday). We are reminded of the institution of the Passover meal (Holy Thursday). The Easter Vigil is provided with seven readings from the Old Testament: the creation; the sacrifice of Abraham; the crossing of the Red Sea (never to be omitted); the passage from Isaiah about the everlasting love and faithfulness of the Lord, the creator and husband of his people; the invitation in Isaiah to come to the water; the passage in Baruch calling the people back to faithfulness; the passage in Ezekiel about the Lord pouring clean water over his people, and giving them a new heart.

READINGS FROM THE NEW TESTAMENT

Readings from the New Testament take up the theme of the passion, 'He was humbler yet ... ' (Philippians, Passion Sunday); 'He learnt to obey through suffering ... ' (Hebrews, Good Friday). They give us the tradition about the two great sacraments, the Eucharist (1 Corinthians, Holy Thursday) and Baptism (Romans, Easter Vigil). The Second Reading on Easter Sunday is a choice between Colossians on dying and rising with Christ, or 1 Corinthians, on Christ our Passover. And, on Easter Sunday, the first reading is from Acts, Peter's witness to the resurrection addressed to Cornelius and his household.

Philip Gleeson OP

Passion Sunday and Paschal Triduum

PASSION (PALM) SUNDAY

Processional Gospel   Mk 11:1-10
Bethphage and Bethany are the villages nearest Jerusalem on the road
from Jericho. it is idle to speculate whether the precise directions of
Jesus (vv. 2-3) indicate a previous arrangement with the owner of the
colt. Mark clearly presents Jesus as displaying supernatural knowledge in making these arrangements. One 'that has never been ridden'
is a common requirement in a beast used for a religious purpose. The
garments (v. 7) provide an improvised saddle; the spreading of
garments on the road (v. 8) was a form of royal homage (see 2 Kgs
9:13). 'Leafy branches' recall the procession on the feast of Tabernacles (or Dedication). Despite the 'many' of v. 8, Mark does not give the
impression that the accompanying crowd is large; yet they walk
behind and before Jesus, forming a procession. 'Hosanna' is a trans-
literation of a Hebrew phrase meaning 'Save now'; it became an
acclamation (like Hallelujah).

The entry as depicted here meant the coming of a Messiah who was
poor, an advent in humility, not glory. What is at stake, for Jesus, is the
nature and manner of his messiahship. At this moment, coming to the
city that will so soon see the passion and death, he can manifest
himself. But he does not come as a temporal ruler or with worldy
pomp. He comes as a religious figure, a prince of peace, 'humble and
riding on a donkey' (Zech 9:9).

Alternative Processional Gospel   Jn 12:12-16
This visit of Jesus to Jerusalem is unlike his former visits – 2:12-22;
5:1; 7:10. Here Jesus' approach is described as a *coming* – not as a
'going up.' He received an enthusiastic reception. A 'great crowd' met
him with cries of 'Hosanna!' and carrying branches of palm. The
quotation in v. 13 is directly from Psalm 118:25-26. The reference is
messianic, as in v. 15 (see Zechariah 9:9). The phrase 'he who comes
in the name of the Lord' applies perfectly to Jesus, who comes in the
name and with the power of God.

If there were overtones of nationalistic enthusiasm in the festive
welcome, Jesus quickly moved to defuse it. 'Jesus found a young
(little) donkey and sat upon it' (v. 14). Jesus did not come as a temporal
ruler or with worldly pomp. Significantly, where the text of Zechariah

9:9 begins 'Rejoice greatly ' the Johannine text substitutes 'Do not fear'.The manner of the entry of this humble King anticipates Jesus' declaration to Pilate: 'My kingdom is not from this world' (Jn 18:36).

> In the kingdom of Caesar there is fear but not in the realm of the one who sits on a little donkey. The nature of this other realm is not easy to grasp, and so, as the text notes (v. 16), it is only after Jesus was glorified that the disciples, in remembering, understood the scripture and the corresponding events (cf 2:22). The implication, therefore, is that the realm has to do with Jesus' glory, and that, if the disciples could only have grasped it, it was in some sense already present in the picture of Jesus seated on the donkey. (T. Brodie, *John*, 410)

First Reading   Is 50:4-7

In this extract from the third Servant Song (Is 50:4-9) the enigmatic figure is presented firmly as a teacher who has to learn before he can communicate his message to others (50:4-50. This message evidently meets with opposition and prompts the persecution of the Servant by the very people to whom he brings comfort (v. 6). But this is all part of the Servant's training. It is by suffering that his true mettle is proved and he is shown to be a faithful Servant. Through his confidence in Yahweh's unfailing support (v. 7) he testifies to Yahweh's power to draw victory out of apparent failure and to the ultimate triumph of his message. The problem of who precisely the Servant is does not obscure the central point that he is one in tune with God who hears God's message.

This is the challenge presented to us by the Servant whom we Christians, through the experience of salvation, know Jesus to be. We can see how perfectly well he was attuned to the will of the Father, knowing his word and bringing it to people.

Second Reading   Phil 2:6-11

It is widely accepted that this hymn is pre-Pauline. Paul has adopted it with some characteristic additions ('even death on a cross', 'in heaven and on earth and under the earth', 'to the glory of God the Father'). Christ Jesus, the subject of the poem, is in 'the form of God': the word 'form' designates the divine sphere in which God dwells. But Jesus did not snatch at and jealously guard the glorious condition that was his by right. Instead he 'emptied' himself; the nature of this *kenósis* ('emptying') is explained by the clauses that follow: he rendered himself powerless as a slave is powerless. Jesus, truly human, wished to share to the full the weakness of the human condition, except for sin (Gal 4:4; Rom 8:3; Heb 2:17). Like the slave he had chosen to become, he was obedient unto death; and the utter abasement of Jesus is emphasized by reference to the manner of his death, that of a common criminal. But from the depths plumbed by his self-renunciation, God has exalted his Servant to unparalleled heights by resurrection and ascension. And he has granted him the title of 'Lord.' The hymn reflects the words of Jesus himself: 'Was it not necessary that the Messiah should suffer...?' (Lk 24:26).

But Paul cites the hymn not primarily for its christological depth but because it is a reminder to his readers of the 'mind' of Jesus, which should also be theirs (Phil 2:5). Jesus' career is not to be contemplated from afar, it is to be imitated. Christology is not just to be studied, it is to be lived. All Christians are to realize Jesus' career in their lives by 'emptying' themselves in the service of their fellows in humility and by finding God's will in the seemingly most hopeless circumstances. For nothing is more apparently hopeless than death. The whole purpose of Jesus' career is not that he should live, suffer, die and rise instead of us, but that we should be able to model our own lives on his. If Jesus is Saviour, his Church is Servant and will be properly successful only at the price of service and humiliation to the point of death.

The Passion   Mk 14:1-15:47

Mark's gospel is a theology of the cross – *theologia crucis*. Understandably, this concern comes to a head in his Passion Narrative. It is evident in the Gethsemane episode (14:32-44) – 'he began to be distressed and agitated' (v. 33): Jesus is shattered. He died with an anguished shout: 'My God, my God, why have you forsaken me?' (15:34). Mark has Jesus die in total isolation, without any relieving feature at all.

It is only after death that Jesus is clearly recognized and acknowledged by any human in the awed confession of the centurion: 'Truly, this man was God's Son!' (15:39). Mark is making a theological point: salvation is never of oneself, not even for Jesus. That awful and awesome journey to the cross is comfort for all who have seen in Jesus of Nazareth the image of the invisible God. It is the consolation of all who have found in him the ultimate asssurance that God is on our side. It is, above all, comfort to all who find it hard to bear the cross. It was not easy for the Master.

PROPHECY OF FAILURE   MK 14:26-31

On the way to the Mount of Olives Jesus spoke forebodingly of the fate of his disciples. He quoted Zechariah 13:7 to the effect that since Jesus the caring shepherd will be struck down his defenceless sheep will be scattered. He then promised, in a reversal of the scattering, that after his resurrection he will be again their shepherd in Galilee. Peter, who had earlier challenged Jesus (8:27-34) now again challenges him (14:29). Mark, like the other evangelists, has Jesus predicting Peter's threefold denial. Peter vehemently rebutted the warning and the others echoed his avowal of readiness to die with Jesus. The reader knows that the Twelve will fail, abysmally; but Jesus will not abandon them. Mark is holding out hope to Christians who may fail.

GETHSEMANE   14:26-31

At Gethsemane Jesus asked his 'disciples' to pray – they will not act as disciples. Jesus himself went apart to pray; he realised that he was on his own. Mark's Gethsemane-scene shows that Jesus did not fully understand God's way, shows that he did not want to die. While we can plausibly assert that Abba was Jesus' preferred address to his God, the word *abba* occurs only once in the gospels – here in Mk 14:36. There is a fittingness to its appearance here: the familiar title seems to be wrested from Jesus at this awful moment. He prayed, explicitly, that the cup be taken from him. He did not contemplate suffering and a horrible death with stoical calm. He was appalled at the prospect. He knew fear. He was brave as he rose above his dread to embrace what his God asked. But he must know if the path which opened before him was indeed the way that God would have him walk. He found assurance in prayer: the utterance of his trustful Abba already included 'thy will be done.' His decision was to trust God despite the darkness of his situation. His prayer did not go unanswered – though the answer was paradoxical. As the Letter to the Hebrews puts it: 'he was heard because of his reverent submission' (5:7). The obedient Son cried out to the Father and put himself wholly in the hands of the Father.

If Jesus said of the disciples, 'the spirit indeed is willing, but the flesh is weak,' that statement is not irrelevant to his own situation. Jesus himself had experienced human vulnerability: distress, agitation, and grief even to the point of death, to the point of asking the Father that the hour might pass him by and the cup be taken away. 'The Son of man is given over to the hands of sinners' (14:41). In the Old Testament God gives over the wicked to punishment; here, in contrast, a just man is 'given over' by God. At the end Jesus invited his disciples:

'Get up, let us be going.' Jesus still includes his disciples, even though they had failed him.

It is important that Mark has so closely woven the theme of discipleship misunderstanding with that of Jesus' testing. It is his most dramatic answer to any objection to a suffering Messiah. Jesus himself had been brought to the brink of rejecting it. The evangelist leaves no doubt that suffering messiahship is not easily accepted; he knows, as fully as Paul, that the cross is foolishness and scandal. The three disciples did not understand. The reader is duly warned. One must watch and pray. Good intentions are not enough. Discipleship is a way of life. And the course of that way has been plotted by Jesus: 'Get up, let us be going ... '

THE ARREST 14:43-52

Jesus was ready and the drama opened without delay. The Son of Man went to his fate in obedience to a divine purpose (see 14:21). His lot was indeed bitter: 'One of the twelve' was hastening to betray him. Judas was accompanied by an armed rabble, one dispatched by the religious authorities; their plot was bearing fruit (14:1-2). There is no mention of temple police (Lk 22:52) or Roman troops (Jn 18:3,12). The 'betrayer' is, literally, 'the one who deliverd him up' – Judas is serving a divine purpose. Judas greeted Jesus in the manner in which a disciple would salute his rabbi; yet betrayal with a kiss is singularly distasteful and Luke underlines the fact (Lk 22:48). In the Marcan narrative Jesus does not speak to Judas. The person who wounded the high priest's slave is not named in contrast to Jn 18:10 where the wielder of the sword is Peter and the slave is named Malchus; while Luke notes that Jesus healed the wound. Mark gives the impression of a clumsy attempt to defend Jesus by someone other than a disciple. Jesus protested at the manner of the arrest: it characterized him as a man of violence. But he was a man of peace, a teacher who did not need to disguise his teaching. The phrase 'day by day in the temple' implies a longer Jerusalem ministry than the few days allowed by Mark. Reference to the fulfilment of the scriptures does not point to specific texts but asserts that here God's will is being done: the Son of Man is being delivered up. The 'all' who fled are the disciples. They forsook him. Even one who still 'followed' Jesus after the disciples had deserted quickly lost heart. Jesus was left all alone. Traditionally, the 'young man' of vv. 51-52 has been taken to be the evangelist. Rather, it would seem that, for Mark, this was a would-be disciple. His shameful flight dramatised disciple failure and carried its message for later disciples who may have failed. Ultimately it is a message of hope because of the promise of restoration (14:28; 16:7).

BEFORE THE JEWISH AUTHORITIES 14:53 -15:1

The opening verse (14:53) makes two affirmations: the leading away of Jesus and the assembling of priests, elders and scribes. Mark has built on the tradition that Jesus was brought before the Jewish high priest (see Lk 22:54; Jn 18:13). Peter is introduced – he had followed Jesus 'at a distance.' It will soon emerge how very far behind he is on the way of discipleship. Jesus' testimony is framed by Peter's denial. He was faithful unto death, while Peter proved unfaithful. At Caesarea Philippi Peter showed that he could not accept the notion of suffering messiahship (8:31-33). Now he would disassociate himself from the suffering Messiah. But first the trial of Jesus gets underway.

The opening remark (v. 55) harks back to 3:6; 11:18; 12:12 and 14:1 – Jesus had long been tried and condemned. All that remains is how to make away with him. His enemies needed evidence. And the witnesses were there. Jesus is the suffering Just One surrounded by false witnesses. The influence of the psalms is manifest: 'for false witnesses have risen against me, and they are breathing out violence' (Ps 27:12); 'Malicious witnesses rise up' (Ps 35:11). Mark stresses their lack of agreement. The repetition of the lack of agreement (v. 56b 'and their testimony did not agree,' v. 59 'But even on this point their testimony did not agree') is the frame for a Marcan insertion: the temple saying, v. 58. He thus signals the special importance of the saying.

Mark emphasises the falsity of the testimony. Yet, there is wide attestation that Jesus had spoken against the Temple (see Mt 26:61; Jn 2:19; Acts 6:14). Besides, the cursing of the fig tree episode does present Jesus as 'destroying the temple:' 'the fig tree that you cursed has withered' (Mk 1:21). He did claim to have brought the temple to an end: that is the point of the mocking repetition of the charge as he hung on the cross (15:29). Ironically, the taunt was true, symbolically demonstrated by the rending of the temple veil (15:38). The temple had lost its meaning for Christians. And this was because Jesus had built another temple 'not made with hands' – the community. This was his purpose in calling and forming disciples. John offers a different explanation: Jesus spoke of the temple of his body (Jn 2:21).

It suits Mark's purpose that the testimony of these witnesses cannot be the decisive factor in Jesus' trial. That must be the formal messianic claim of Jesus himself (v. 62). When pressed by the high priest to respond to the charges, Jesus maintained a rigid silence (vv. 60-61a).

The silence of Jesus, carefully emphasized ('but he was silent and did not answer, v. 61) is dramatic preparation for the solemn confession of v. 62. The high priest was forced to take direct action; his question and Jesus' answer form the heart of this passage. Thoroughly Marcan, these verses are the culmination of his christology. The titles 'Christ' and 'Son of God' stand in the heading of the gospel (1:1). The high priest now ironically bestowed them on Jesus (Son of the Blessed is the equivalent of Son of God). When Jesus was acknowledged as Christ at Caesarea Philippi he enjoined silence (8:30). But now Jesus himself, positively and publicly, acknowledged that he is the Messiah, and that he is indeed Son of God. But he did so on his own terms, in terms of 'Son of Man.' With his firm 'I am' he made, for the first and only time, an explicit messianic claim. He could do so because now there was no risk of triumphalist misinterpretation : he was manifestly a suffering Messiah (see 8:31). The use of 'the Blessed One' and 'the Power', though not really precise Jewish terminology, do, for Mark, provide a 'Jewish' colouring. His 'you will see' refers to the Christian perception of Jesus 'at the right hand of God' by resurrection and 'coming with the clouds of heaven' at the *parousia*.

Jesus' confession provoked the death-sentence and that is how it had to be because he cannot be known for who he is until he has died and risen from the dead (see 9:9). In terms of the trial-narrative, his claim was self-incriminating. The Sanhedrin can now achieve its stated purpose (v. 55). The rending of garments had become, in the case of the high priest, a carefully regulated formal judicial gesture. Only Mark (followed by Matthew) specifies a charge of blasphemy. It reflects the situation of the early church: Jewish authorities had begun to regard the Christian claims for Jesus as blasphemous. And Christians would have suffered for their confession of him (see 13:9-11).

The mocking episode (v. 65) appears to be a separate element of tradition introduced by Mark at this point. The 'some' implies members of the Sanhedrin. That Mark intends the implication is evident when we note that he has made them explicitly mock Jesus on the cross (15:31). Historically unlikely, it is fitting in Mark's narrative. The leaders had sought his death from 3:6 and now triumph has its hour. The irony of this scene is that Jesus is being mocked as a prophet just as his prediction of Peter's denial is being fulfilled.

PETER'S DENIALS   14:66-72

With v. 66 we return to Peter. In the setting and form of the denials,

Mark is on traditional ground. His title for Jesus, however, is 'Nazarene' (see 1:24; 10:47; 14:57; 16:1), indicative of his interest in Galilee. At the initial stage Peter was evasive, pretending not to understand what the maid was saying (v. 68). On the basis of this first (traditional) denial Mark has built the other two, so producing his familiar triadic pattern. Peter had to come out and deny that he was 'one of them', a disciple of Jesus (v. 70).

Finally, he was forced to disassociate himself from Jesus, calling down the wrath of God upon himself if what he says is not true (v. 71). The progression is patent: evasion, denial of discipleship, denial under oath that he had ever known Jesus at all. The cockcrow – Mark alone mentions that the cock crowed a second time – caused Peter to remember Jesus' prediction of his denials and his own vehement protestation (14:30-31). 'He broke down' – an approximate translation of an enigmatic verb, but the general idea is clear enough: Peter was utterly shattered.

The denial-story brings the disciple-misunderstanding theme (prominent throughout the gospel) to a head. Peter had publicly disassociated himself from Jesus. The sheep had been effectively scattered and the stricken shepherd was wholly on his own (see 14:27). As they see themseles in disciples who could betray and deny and forsake, Mark's readers are not likely to feel complacent. Mark insists on the loneliness of Jesus during his passion: up to the moment of death he is alone, more and more alone. His intention is not only to awaken us to the poignancy of this painful solitude. He wants us to perceive in that starkness the truth that Christ alone saves.

In the story of Peter's denials Mark may well have had christian experience in view. Persecution could be, and was, sharp and painful. Not all could bear up with what must have been heroic courage. What then?

> Was all hope lost for those who failed and denied Christ? A Peter who had once denied and later borne witness could constitute an encouragement that repentance and a second chance were possible. For that reason it may have been important to underline the seriousness of what Peter had done. Before his arrest Jesus had warned his disciples, 'Keep on praying lest you enter into trial/ testing/temptation [*peirasmos*], precisely because they were not yet sufficiently strong. But with bravado, Peter by attempting to follow had entered into peirasmos and failed. (R.E.Brown, *The Death of the Messiah*, 625).

BEFORE PILATE 15:1-15.

Mark picks up the thread of the story which had been interrupted by the account of Peter's denial. This second meeting of the Sanhedrin served to introduce the trial scene which followed. Jesus was 'delivered over' to Pilate: the recurrence of this expression throughout the passion narrative is a reminder that all of this is happening 'according to the definite plan and foreknowledge of God' (Acts 2:23). It is enough to name Pilate – all Christians know who he is. By the high priest Jesus had been asked, in Jewish terms, if he were the Messiah, the Son of the Blessed. The Roman uses a title that has meaning for him: King of the Jews. In his eyes the title was political and, if Jesus really claimed it, was equivalent to high treason: political authority was Rome's prerogative. Pilate's question falls into a pattern wherein a title is bestowed which is true of Jesus but not in the sense understood by those who bestow it (3:11; 8:29; 14:61; 15:2).

Mark has firmly presented the passion of Jesus as proclamation of his kingship and the crucifixion as an enthronement. The theme appears at once in Pilate's question: 'Are you the King of the Jews?' (15:2). Jesus did not reject the title but he did imply ('You say so') that he understood it differently. Pilate repeatedly calls him King of the Jews (15:9, 12); indeed, in v. 12 he is 'the man whom you (the chief priests) call the King of the Jews.' The soldiers payed homage to 'the King of the Jews' (15:16-19) and the official charge against Jesus read: 'The King of the Jews' (15:26). Priests and scribes mocked him as 'the Messiah, the King of Israel' (15:32). If, for Mark, this is a narrative of the enthronement of Christ as king, it is such in light of Jesus' profession of 14:62 – which sealed his fate (14:63-64). Jesus' royal status is wholly paradoxical. Jesus' royal authority could never resemble the authority of earthly kings (see 10:42-45).

The priests hastened to press charges against him; Jesus preserved the silence that is a feature of the suffering Just One (see Is 53:7). Pilate's 'wonder' is more than surprise, it conveys a sense of religious awe (see 5:20; Jn 19:8-11). Outside of the gospels we find no trace of the Passover amnesty described here (v. 6); it would seem to be an inference drawn from this isolated Barabbas incident. Interestingly, Luke makes no mention of the custom. Barabbas was in prison with other rebels who had killed during a political affray. The crowd came to plead for this man, and Pilate presented them with an alternative: they might have instead 'the King of the Jews.' He had seen through the charges made against Jesus. Mark puts the responsibility where he believed it belonged, at the door of the priests. As in all the gospels,

Pilate was convinced of Jesus' innocence, but yielded to pressure. It is he who is really on trial; John has developed this feature in masterly fashion. Pilate's strange appeal to the crowd as to what to do with this King of the Jews is very effective. The nation rejected its king and called for his death on the cross. Pilate helplessly protested Jesus' innocence – 'Why, what evil has he done?' – but they clamoured for blood. Pilate yielded, 'wishing to satisfy the crowd.' He released a murderer and condemned an innocent man. Jesus was scourged: a severe flogging was the normal prelude to crucifixion. Pilate 'delivered him' (v. 15): he had played his role in a drama directed by God.

HAIL, KING OF THE JEWS!   15:16-20a

Into the narrative of the sentencing and execution of Jesus (15:6-15 + 21-32) Mark has inserted the incident of mocking by soldiers (15:16-20), thereby highlighting the title 'King of the Jews.' This brutal mockery is, ironically, Jesus' investiture. The soldiers led him inside the palace, the Roman procurator's headquarters in Jerusalem. The 'whole cohort' means, most likely, those who were around at the time. But the statement does add to the mock solemnity of the situation: this 'King' had his palace guards. The 'purple cloak' was, very likely, one of the red-coloured military cloaks; the 'crown' (diadem) was a rude replica hastily woven of thorns. A 'purple' cloak and a 'crown' of thorns furnished a mock ritual of kingly dignity. Striking and spitting seem out of place and probably come from the other mocking scene in 14:65. Here the emphasis is on royal 'homage.'

The irony of the situation is patent, and it admirably serves Mark's christology. Jesus is King, but only in humility (11:7-10) and suffering. Now they can lead him out to his throne: the cross.

Death by crucifixion was, and was intended to be, degrading. Even choice of the place of Jesus' execution was a calcaluted insult. Archaeological research has shown that Golgotha, a disused quarry, was, at that time, a refuse-dump. There was nothing of majesty about the death of Jesus, no trace of glory.

CRUCIFIXION   15:20b-32

The Marcan drama reached its climax in the crucifixion scene. The evangelist had prepared for Jesus' death in 3:6; from that point on, explicitly or by allusion, he continued to harp on it. In painting this scene he has drawn upon Old Testament passages portraying the figure of the suffering Just One, who suffers but is finally vindicated. Various motifs which build up the image of the Just One, taken mainly from the

ARTIST: MICHAEL LYDON

psalms, surface in this passage. Mark's concern is to establish that everything took place according to the scriptures, that is, according to the will of God.

It was customary for the condemned man to carry his cross beam. Mark tells us that a certain Simon of Cyrene (a town in North Africa, but perhaps Simon now lived in Palestine) was 'impressed' by the soldiers to carry the beam. Alexander and Rufus were evidently known to Mark's community. Golgatha, an Aramaic name, means 'a skull.' The name may have been suggested by a skull-shaped hill; though the text speaks only of 'place' and does not specify hill. It was presumably outside the city wall and close to a road (v. 29). It was Jewish custom, based on Prov 31:6-7, to provide condemned criminals with drugged wine as a means of lessening their torment. Jesus, in Gethsemane, had accepted the Father's will, and accepted it whole-heartedly; he will not take the wine. And they crucified him. 'So, in the simplest possible terms, the dread act is recorded' (Vincent Taylor). By custom, the clothes of the condemned fell to the executioners. Mark, with Ps 22:18 in mind, saw in this, too, a divine purpose.

The evangelist marks the time off in three-hourly intervals (15:25,33,34). For that matter, precise statements of time are a feature of the trial and passion narrative: 14:72; 15:1, 25, 33, 42; 16:1. This is to indicate that the passage of time was in accord with the will of God. Nothing at all has happened by chance or unexpectedly. The third hour is 9 a.m. It is impossible to reconcile this time reference with Jn 19:14 where Jesus was sentenced at 12 noon of 14 Nisan. John's purpose is to have Jesus die at the hour when the Passover lambs were slaugh-tered. Both evangelists are making theological statements.

The superscription (15:26) is in accordance with Roman practice; for Mark it indicates that the King is now enthroned. All the gospels agree that Jesus was crucified between two criminals. Many manu-scripts of Mark carry as v. 28: 'And the scripture was fulfilled which says, He was reckoned with the transgressors.' It is a borrowing from Luke 22:37, but it does make explicit the intent of Mark who would have seen in this disturbing fact a fulfilment of Isaiah 13:12. Two sets of taunts were now levelled at Jesus. The fact that there were passersby suggests crucifixion near a roadway. Their taunt was influenced by Lamentations 2:15 and Psalm 22:7-8 – 'They wag their heads'; 'He committed his cause to the Lord; let him deliver him, let him rescue him.' And they 'derided', literally 'blasphemed' him. They were, of course, really blaspheming God, so doing the very thing that justified Jesus' condemnation to death (14:64). Their words harked back to the temple charge in 14:58. The irony is that precisely by not saving his life (8:35), by not coming down from the cross, Jesus was bringing the temple to an end (15:38) and building the new temple.

The mocking invitation for Jesus to come down from the cross was echoed by the leaders of official Judaism. The presence of the chief priests and scribes at the crucifixion and their cruel railing cannot be historical. But, in Mark's storyline it is fitting that they should be the principal scoffers. They, the implacable opponents of Jesus, had to be fitted in at this climactic moment. 'He saved others' – a reference to Jesus' ministry of healing, regularly described as *sózein*, 'to heal' or 'to save' (e.g. 5:23,28,34). It is in his death that Jesus accomplished salvation and was perceived to be the Son of God. This becomes clear in the episode of 15:27-39. Here, Jesus was three times challenged – by the passersby (vv. 29-30), by the religious leaders (vv. 31-32a) and by those crucified with him (15:32b) – to come down from the cross and thereby save himself. Jesus would not rise to the challenge. As one who had warned the disciples, 'Those who want to save their life will lose it' (8:25), and as the Son who wills what the Father wills (14:36), Jesus made no attempt to save his life. Mark is making a theological point: salvation is never of oneself, not even for Jesus. Nor is there any hope of salvation from an Elijah-figure (15:35-36).

Up to now Jesus had been 'King of the Jews,' now he is 'the Messiah, the King of Israel.' Since Maccabean times 'Jews' had become the Gentile name for the people of Israel, so King of the Jews is normal in dealing with Pilate; the priests, naturally, used 'Israel' as a self-designation. Jewish tradition had anticipated that in the days of Messiah the true Israel would be established. Now Jesus was being ironically addressed as the King of this eschatological Israel. They were still looking for 'signs' (see 8:11-12): if Jesus does come down from the cross they will 'see' and believe. But there can be no 'seeing' until Jesus has died and risen. Temple saying and christological titles, prominent in 14:58 and 14:61-62, are brought together here (15:29,32); the significance of both is being worked out on the cross. The denouement comes in 15:38-39. Meanwhile, Jesus' isolation is total: even his companions in suffering deride him (v. 32b).

Mark has firmly presented the crucifixion of Jesus as an enthrone-ment. The title appears at once in Pilate's opening question: 'Are you the King of the Jews?' (15:2). Jesus accepted the designation but with the implication that he understood it differently. Pilate consistently calls him King of the Jews (vv. 9, 12). The soldiers paid homage to the 'King of the Jews' (15:16-19) and the official superscription, 'The

King of the Jews' was fixed on Jesus' cross. The priests and scribes mocked him as 'Christ, the King of Israel' (v. 32). For Mark this is a narrative of the enthronement of Christ as King; and it can be such in light of the christological profession of 14:62. Jesus' royal status is wholly paradoxical.

DEATH AND REVELATION 15:33-39

The grim drama was being played out. Crucified at the third hour (9 a.m.), Jesus had spent three hours in agony. Now, at the sixth hour (noon), broke the hour of darkness, of momentary demonic triumph – 'your hour, and the power of darkness' (Lk 2:53). Jesus had begun his mission in an encounter with Satan (Mk 1:12-13) and carried on the war in his exorcisms. Now, helpless on the cross, he seemed to be crushed by these very powers. The close of that time of darkness, the ninth hour (3 p.m.) marked the hour of fulfilment.

Paradoxically, it seemed to sound the nadir of Jesus' defeat. This is brought out by the twofold reference to a 'loud cry.' The expression *phóne megalé* occurs only four times in Mark. In 1:26 and 5:7 it is the loud cry of a demoniac, one oppressed by an evil spirit. Jesus himself now (15:34,37) reacted with a loud cry to the intolerable pressure of evil. He suffered the absence of God: his cry of dereliction was one of total desolation: 'My God, my God, why have you forsaken me?' His words are the opening of Psalm 22 – a lament. Lament is the cry of a suffering righteous person addressed to the One who can bring an end to suffering. Mark has Jesus die in total desolation, without any relieving feature at all. It would have seemed that, up to this point, Jesus' isolation could go no further: deserted by his disciples, taunted by his enemies, derided by those who hung with him, suffocating in the darkness of evil. But the worst was now: abandoned by God. His suffering was radically lonely. But his God was 'my God' (v. 34). Even in this, as at Gethsemane, it was 'not what I want, but what you want.' Here, even more than then, the sheer humanness of Jesus was manifest.

> In the tragic drama of the Mark/Matthew Passion Narrative Jesus has been abandoned by his disciples and mocked by all who have come to the cross. Darkness has covered the earth; there is nothing that shows God acting on Jesus' side. How appropriate that Jesus feel forsaken! His 'Why?' is that of someone who has plumbed the depths of the abyss, and feels enveloped by the power of darkness. Jesus is not questioning the existence of God or the power of God to do something about what is happening; he is questioning the silence of the one whom he calls 'My God.'

If we pay attention to the overall structure of the Mark/Matthew Passion Narrative, that form of addressing the deity is itself significant, for nowhere previously has Jesus ever prayed to God as 'God.' Mark/Matthew began the Passion Narrative with a prayer in which the deity was addressed by Jesus as 'Father,' the common form of addresss used by Jesus and one that captured his familial confidence that God would not make the Son go through the 'hour' or drink the cup (Mk 14:35-36; Mt 26:39). Yet that filial prayer, reiterated three times, was not visibly or audibly answered; and now having endured the seemingly endless agony of the 'hour' and having drunk the dregs of the cup, Jesus screams out a final prayer that is an inclusion with the first prayer. Feeling forsaken as if he were not being heard, he no longer presumes to speak intimately to the All-Powerful as 'Father' but employs the address common to all human beings, 'My God.' (The fact that Jesus is using psalm language – a fact to which Mark does not call our attention – does not make less noticeable the unusualness of such terminology on Jesus' lips.)

Mark calls our attention to this contrast between the two prayers and makes it more poignant by reporting the address in each prayer in Jesus' own tongue: '*Abba*' and '*Eloi*,' thus giving the impression of words coming genuinely from Jesus' heart, as distinct from the rest of his words that have been preserved in a foreign language (Greek). As he faces the agony of death, the Marcan Jesus is portrayed as resorting to his mother tongue. (R.E. Brown, *The Death of the Messiah*, 1046).

The bystanders thought that Jesus called on Elijah, who was popularly believed to come to the aid of the just in tribulation. Misunderstanding hounded Jesus to the end. 'Vinegar' is the Roman soldiers' *posca*, a mixture of water, sour wine and egg. The gesture was kindly meant (v. 36), but Mark, likely with Psalm 69:21 in mind, thinks of it as an addition to Jesus' misery. Again the 'loud cry' is significant: it depicts Jesus' awareness of his struggle with evil. All the more so because Mark describes a sudden, violent death – 'breathed his last' is not strong enough to convey his meaning (v. 37). Jesus died abandoned, seemingly crushed by the forces of evil. This is perfectly in keeping with Mark's *theologia crucis*. Forthwith he can point to the victory of Jesus.

At the end of the passage 15:27-39, Mark focuses on the theme of Jesus as 'the Son of God.' In contrast to the mocking challenges hurled at the dying Jesus (15:29-32) there is an emphatically positive response to Jesus' death. The centurion in charge of the execution stood facing a helpless victim on a cross and watched him as he died. He declared, in awe: 'Truly, this man was God's son!' (15:39). His declaration is to be viewed in the context of the rending of the temple curtain from top to bottom (15:38). The temple had lost its significance (see 11:12-25; 13:2; 14:58). It was the end of the cult through which God had hitherto mediated forgiveness of sin and salvation. Mark's theological point is that salvation is now mediated uniquely through the shedding of his blood by the wholly faithful Son of God. Jesus had already proclaimed as much. He had done so in his words to the disciples: 'For the Son of Man came not to be served but to serve, and to give his life a ransom for many'(10:45). And in his words at the last supper: 'This is my blood of the covenant which is poured out for many' (14:24). The temple is gone. God's Son is henceforth the 'place' of salvation.

> Before the Sanhedrin Jesus answered affirmatively the high priest's question about his being the son of the Blessed (God) in terms of seeing the Son of Man (14:61-62); now the Roman centurion has seen 'this man' and identified him as the Son of God ... [One may express] the totality of the picture in Mark 15:39: 'Mark makes the Roman centurion a faithful representative of Gentile Christianity which saw the significance of Jesus as the son of God revealed par excellence in the drama of the cross.' He is the first of that believing community which in the language of 14:58 constitutes another sanctuary not made by hand, replacing the Jerusalem sanctuary made by hand, the veil of which has just been rent into two from top to bottom. (R. E. Brown, *The Death of the Messiah*, 1152).

THE FAITHFUL WOMEN   15:40-41

The Twelve had fled. Yet, Jesus had not been wholly deserted – a little group of women disciples remained. Mark says of them: 'They used to follow him and provided for him while he was in Galilee; and there were many other women who had come up with him to Jerusalem' (15:41).

The women had 'followed him' – *akolouthein* is a technical term for discipleship. Although this is the only place in the gospel where the discipleship of women is mentioned in *explicit* terms, we should not overlook the reference to 'many other women.' We must recognize that throughout the gospel 'disciple' is an inclusive term. It is becasue they had continued to follow him, if only 'at a distance' (v. 40) – as women they could not be at the very place of execution – that the final message is entrusted to these women (16:1-8). They alone, of all disciples, had followed to the cross. Luke is the evangelist who gets the credit for alerting us to Jesus' solicitude for womankind. But Mark had, beforehand, made his telling contribution. The chosen male disciples had abandoned Jesus (14:50). These women disciples have stood steadfast and have not been ashamed of Jesus. They are those of whom the Son of Man will not be ashamed (8:38).

THE BURIAL 15:42-47

The story of Jesus' burial was important because it established that Jesus had really died and because it assured that the women who found the empty tomb had seen that the body had previously been laid in it. Mark sticks to his three-hour scheme even though the 'evening' (6 p.m.) would mean that the sabbath had begun. The 'day of preparation' (v. 42) – here is where we learn that Jesus died on a Friday. The Twelve had fled at the arrest of Jesus (14:50). It was left to another to bury him. Joseph of Arimathea, a Sanhedrin member, was concerned to fulfil the law – here, that the body of one hanged should not be left overnight on the tree (Deut 21:23). Joseph was duly granted the corpse of Jesus (Mk 15:42-46). It would be hasty, dishonourable burial of one executed on a charge of blasphemy. The body was not anointed. It was simply wrapped in a linen shroud and placed in a niche of that disused quarry. A far cry, indeed, from the royal burial of the Fourth Gospel (Jn 19:38-42). We need to be sensitive to the theological concerns of the evangelists. The only witnesses of the burial are women, a preparation for the final passage of the gospel (16:1-8).

HOLY THURSDAY
MASS OF THE LORD'S SUPPER

Despite the well-known divergence between the Synoptic gospels and John on the precise date of the last Supper, its Passover setting remains clear. The first three gospels present the meal as a Passover meal. So, Lk 22:15 – 'I have eagerly desired to eat this Passover with you before I suffer.' John presents Jesus as the true Passover lamb: he died at the hour when the Passover lamb was slaughtered and, in his case, the prescription regarding the Passover lamb ('You shall not break any of its bones', Ex 12:46) was observed (Jn 19:36). The relationship between Eucharist and Passover is firmly embedded in the tradition.

First Reading   Ex 12:1-8, 11-14

This reading gives the account of the institution of the Passover as an established feast in Israel and indicates the prescribed ritual. The Passover was originally a simple feast of nomadic shepherds. The use of unleavened bread went back to a spring agricultural festival marking the early harvest and the offering of the first fruits. Our text represents a stage when both festivals were combined and firmly linked to the exodus event. The feast of Passover came to be regarded as a memorial, recalling God's fidelity to his covenant, and as an assurance that God would be faithful to his promises. At each Passover Israel looked backward to the first Passover and forward to the final deliverance which God had promised. In the Church the Eucharist is the memorial of the death and resurrection (of the Passover, see Jn 13:1) of Christ; at each Eucharist we look back to his death and forward to his coming again.

Second Reading   1 Cor 11:23-26

Paul begins by setting down the words used by Jesus to institute the Eucharist. These are introduced by the technical terms 'to receive' and 'to deliver' which place him as an intermediary in a chain of tradition. Paul's version of the words of institution is most closely related to that of Luke (22:15-20), and it has been plausibly suggested that it records the usage of the Church of Antioch. A distinctive feature of Paul's version is the twice repeated 'Do this in remembrance of me.' For Paul, authentic remembrance is concerned with the past only insofar as it is constitutive of the present and a summons to the future. What he desires to evoke is the active remembrance of total commitment to Christ which makes the past real in the present, thus releasing a power capable of shaping the future. The 'proclamation' takes place in and through the eating of the bread and the drinking of the cup.

The attitude of the participants is crucial. If their imitation of Christ (11:1) is non-existent or seriously defective, then, no matter how carefully the ritual gestures are performed 'it is not really the Lord's supper that you eat' (v. 20). Only if the participants have truly put on Christ (Gal 3:27), which is equivalent to putting on love (Col 3:14), is there effective 'proclamation' of the death of Christ in the Eucharist.

Gospel   Jn 13:1-15

Jesus knows that he is about to give the supreme manifestation (see 15:13) of his abiding love for his disciples. He himself brings out clearly the meaning of what he does, the act of humble service he now renders. The opening words (13:1) are a caption for all that is to come in chapters 13-19, the demonstration of Jesus' love for his own – a love to the end *(eis telos)* – without measure. He *lays aside* his garments (13:4,12) as he spoke of laying down his life (10:18). The disciples are to 'have share' with him (v. 8): the washing of the feet expresses symbolically that they are brought into communion of life with Jesus through his death, a supreme act of self-giving and humble service. It is necessary to be washed by Christ, giver of life, if one is to have part with him in eternal life – one must share in his death and resurrection.

'I have set you an example.' The disciples are not to look only to his ultimate gesture of love: humble service should characterise all the living of his followers. Here is a moving lesson in *diakonia*. Jesus is indeed Lord and Teacher; he has authority. But his style and exercise of authority is marked by *service*. And, bringing together the second reading and gospel, it follows that true union with Christ in the Eucharist, and consequently true communion among Christians, is possible only in this atmosphere of loving service.

The Mass is the celebration of the Christian Passover. The whole of Jesus' life, culminating in his death and resurrection, was a passage from 'this world' to the Father, from death to life, from sin to grace, *for us*. By faith we appropriate the Passover, we share in Christ's life, death and resurrection. The Eucharist, the meal at which we receive Christ as bread and wine, is the special sign, symbol, the 'sacrament' of this faith, But signs, symbols or 'sacraments' are effective only *as such*, that is, only if, and in so far as, they are received as expressions of the deeper reality which they convey. The reality which Christ gives to us in the Eucharist is himself as the 'man for others.' If we really receive him as such we must ourselves become 'people for others', servants of our fellows. Our Passover, of which the Jewish Passover is the model and Christ's Passover is the cause, is our continual 'passage' from selfishness to service.

GOOD FRIDAY

First Reading   Is 52:13-53:12

The fourth and finest of the songs of the suffering servant of Yahweh, Israel's deepest insight into the meaning of suffering, contemplates the fate of the man upon whom rests the hopes of Israel. Whatever may be said about the identification of the servant of this song, he surely stands forth sharply as an individual. Christians could not fail to discern in him the lineaments of their Lord.

The servant is innocent yet has suffered – in this respect he resembles Job. But there is something more: 'he was wounded for *our* transgressions, crushed for *our* iniquities.' The servant is innocent, gentle, humble. He is the one God has chosen to establish righteousness on earth. He achieves his goal through suffering as he bears the chastisement *we* had earned. His burden is the sin of others; his attitude in face of reproach and insult is silence; his sacrificial death, a gesture of love, counters human wickedness. The servant is truly the man for others, dying that others might live. His ultimate triumph and exaltation are glimpsed beyond present persecution, beyond rejection by his own people, beyond ignominious death.

The present passage has been called 'the fifth gospel' because it appears to anticipate so vividly Jesus' suffering, death and eventual triumph. The close correspondence between this Song and the Passion narratives is best explained by the recourse which the evangelists (along with other New Testament theologians) had to this passage. It provided a context in which to interpret what must have been one of the most severe challenges to faith in the person of Jesus. How could the all-powerful God permit his chosen servant to be subjected to the ignominy of death by crucifixion? The flow of the poem suggests that it was an offering of expiation leading to the ultimate vindication of the victim and opening up the possibility of life for his descendants. The Johannine Jesus could, in the spirit of the Servant, declare, 'I, when I am lifted up from the earth, will draw all people to myself' (Jn 12:32).

Second Reading   Heb 4:14-16; 5:7-9

A major theme of the letter to the Hebrews is the priesthood of Christ. The coming of the Son into our world is presented in cultic terms. It is almost as if he had come precisely to be our high priest who offers sacrifice for us (2:17; 8:1-6; 9:11-14; 10:1-18) and who intercedes for us. The fact that Jesus the high priest has entered the heavenly sanctuary (6:20; 7:26; 8:1; 9:11) is a motive for holding fast to the faith we confess (4:14-16).

Verse 15 is a reply to a latent objection: may not this surpassing greatness of the high priest imply an aloofness towards human misery. 'Sympathize' here means to enter into and share the suffering of others. We need have no fear. Our high priest can sympathize with us in our temptations; he can help us because he has experienced our trials and sufferings. Having such a high priest – now passed into the presence of God – Christians can advance with full confidence to present themselves before God. The 'throne of grace' is the throne of God's mercy. It is because it is now accessible to sinners that it is the throne of grace; the way of access is Christ the Priest, the link between God and humankind. Christians who approach the throne encounter the loving mercy of God who bestows on them his favours.

The passage 5:1-10 shows that Jesus has perfectly met the requirements of priesthood: he is a human person, officially constituted a mediator between God and humankind, who pleads the cause of men and women before God and who offers their gifts to God, especially sacrifice for sin. A true priest will be compassionate, greatly understanding of sinners; Jesus is eminently endowed with this quality.

Verses 7-10 show Jesus in prayer – Gethsemane is manifestly in mind. We are shown the means (suffering) by which the saving work of Jesus is effected (vv. 7-8), as well as the result for himself and those who trust in him (vv. 9-10). Through his obedience he gained an enriching experience, a practical understanding and appreciation of suffering which would enable him to sympathize fully with his brothers and sisters. He has entered heaven but he is joined to us still in his perfect understanding of our trials and difficulties. The distance between us, abolished by the incarnation, has not been broadened again by the ascension. He is always ready and able to help us because he is always our compassionate high priest.

The exhortation of the author of Hebrews brings encouragement to Christians in their experience of suffering. It underlines the humanity of Jesus; he shared in our human condition and he can identify with our sufferings since he suffered deeply himself. He gives us hope in suffering, for in and through his suffering he responded in loving obedience to his Father. In death as in life he bore witness to a loving God's limitless love of humankind.

The Passion   Jn 18:1-19:42

While one acknowledges that the portrait of Jesus in the Synoptic gospels is already, and inevitably, coloured by Easter faith, the Jesus of John is startingly different. Contrast is sharpest between Mark and John.

One need but compare the two Passion Narratives (Mk 14:32-15:47; Jn 18-20), beginning with the arrest of Jesus (Mk 14:43-50; Jn 18:1-11), to see that the stories are, in several respects, historically incompatible. A look at the brief account of arrests will suffice to make the point.

THE ARREST OF JESUS Jn 18:1-11. See Mk 14:43-50.

Mark 14:43-50. The story-line: Jesus is 'still speaking' his closing words of the Gethsemane episode (14:32-42). Judas plays an essential role, leading the arresting crowd (sent by the Jewish authorities) to where Jesus was to be found and then, at night-time and in a group, identifying the right man. Jesus, quite passive, was at once arrested. The unnamed slave of the high priest was wounded by one of the bystanders; Mark gives the impression of a clumsy attempt to defend Jesus by someone other than a disciple. Jesus, now a prisoner, does protest at the manner and timing of his arrest: he is not a man of violence and there was no call for this show of strength. All the frightened disciples deserted him.

John 18:1-11. The story-line: Here reference to the 'words' of Jesus points not to Gethsemane (an episode absent from the Fourth Gospel) but to the solemn prayer of John 17. Judas guides not a 'crowd' but a Roman military detachment as well as Temple police. Jesus, fully aware of all that was to happen, takes the initiative and strides forward to accost the band of soldiers and police; there is no need for Judas to identify him, as is expressly noted. They are seeking 'Jesus of Nazareth.' At the God-presence in him, manifest in his declaration 'I am' (*egó eimi*) they are rendered powerless – stricken to the ground. Jesus, completely in charge of the situation, lays down his terms: they may arrest him, on condition that they do not detain the disciples. These do not desert him, as in Mark; he protects them. It is 'Simon Peter' who strikes out and cuts off the right ear of 'Malchus' – the story has grown from its Marcan form. Jesus rebukes Peter (instead of protesting at the manner of his own arrest, as in Mark). Only now is Jesus arrested, and only because he permitted it to happen.

It is evidently the same incident, but how different the telling. The fact is: each version is completely at home in its proper setting; it just would not do to switch the accounts. This alerts one to the manner of proper understanding. There is little doubt that Mark's version is closer to what really happened. It would, however, be a mistake to think that Mark is primarily concerned with 'facts' and that, consequently, he does not propose a christology; or that, at best, he puts forward a low christology. It is one of the unfortunate results of such concentration on the Johannine picture that the christology of the other evangelists has been underrated. Indeed, the Marcan christology is not 'inferior' to the Johannine. It is notably different.

Fleeting reference above to Gethsemane suggests a further point of comparison. In Mark 14:32-36 we encounter a shattered Jesus, crushed to the point of death at the prospect of a gruesome death. He prayed, explicitly, that 'the hour might pass from him.' He needed to be assured that the path which opened before him was indeed the way that God would have him walk. John, on the other hand, though clearly aware of the Gethsemane tradition, studiously avoids the Gethsemane episode. He has Jesus declare: 'Now my soul is troubled. And what should I say – "Father, save me from this hour?"' (Jn 12:27). So far, reminiscent of Mark. Then comes a distinctively Johannine twist: 'No, it is for this reason that I have come to this hour.' The Johannine Jesus explicitly refuses to pray the Gethsemane prayer. It is inconceivable that he could speak the words of Mark 14:36 because the Johannine Jesus 'knows all that was to happen to him' (Jn 18:4). There is a clash of christologies. For us, it is not a matter of choosing between them. It is, rather, a question of understanding both of them.

We could, usefully, examine the saying in John 18:5-6 – 'I am' (*egó eimi*). There are four absolute 'I am' sayings in the Gospel (8:24,28,58; 13:19) e.g. 'When you have lifted up the Son of man, then you will realise that I AM' (8:28). Each time there is an echo of the divine name of Exodus 3:14 or, more immediately, of Isaiah 43:10-11. Jesus declares: I am the bearer of God's name and power. The meaning in 18:5-6 is close to this: the name has the power to paralyse Jesus' enemies.

John presents the Passion as the triumph of the Son of God. The *dramatis personae* are sharply characterized. Despite appearances, *Jesus* is always in control. He is the Judge who judges his judge (Pilate) and his accusers ('the Jews'). He is the King who reigns, with the cross for a throne 'I, when I am lifted up from the earth, will draw all to myself.' *The Jews* are not the whole Jewish people but its leaders who see Jesus as a danger to them, the Establishment, and who are determined to destroy him.

Such are 'the Jews' in the story-line. For John and his contemporaries 'the Jews' are the leaders of a later Judaism vigorously opposed to the now distinctive Christian movement. *Pilate* recognizes, and three times acknowledges, the innocence of Jesus. He desperately tries to compromise but ends by yielding to political blackmail. He is a man who will not make a decision for or against Jesus – and finds himself trapped.

JESUS BEFORE THE JEWISH AUTHORITIES 18:12-24

Jesus was brought before Annas, a former high priest who had been deposed by the Romans but who still had considerable influence. This was not a formal trial but an interrogation. The episode throws light on the confrontation of the evangelist and his community with contemporary Judaism. Jesus becomes a defender of his followers against attacks of Judaism. Jesus was then sent to Caiaphas the actual high priest. In view of his cynical political decision (and unwitting prophecy), 'it is better for you to have one man die for the people' (11:50), Jesus cannot expect justice. As in the Synoptics John, too, has Peter's denials of Jesus (18:15-18, 25-27).

JESUS BEFORE PILATE 18:28-19:16a

The synoptic accounts of the trial before Pilate tell us little whereas John's dramatic reconstruction does bring out the significance of it. Only John makes clear why Jesus was brought to Pilate in the first place and why Pilate gave in to having him crucified. Only John shows the interplay of subtle (and not so subtle) political forces on Pilate and indicates how Pilate's original questioning of Jesus concerned a political charge against him. Yet Mark, we now realize, has given the key to the trial in the title 'King of the Jews' (15:2); thereafter he stresses that it is as king of the Jews (Messiah) that Jesus is rejected by the crowd and crucified.

There is a theological reason for John's stress on the Roman trial. We are to see Pilate in the light of the rest of the Fourth Gospel. He provides an example of an attitude to Jesus which purports to be neither faith nor rejection: the typical attitude of those who try to maintain a middle position in an all or nothing situation. Pilate's refusal to make a decision for or against the Light leads to disaster. Because Pilate will not face the challenge of deciding for the Truth in Jesus and against the Jews, he thinks he can persuade the Jews to accept a solution that will make it unnecessary for him to declare for Jesus. This is the Johannine view of the episodes of Barabbas, the scourging, and the delivery of Jesus to the Jews as 'your King.' For John this trial is our own tragic history of temporizing and indecision. Pilate, the would-be neutral man is frustrated by the pressure of others. He failed to listen to the truth and decide in its favour. He, and all who would follow him, inevitably end up enslaved to this world.

The Johannine presentation of the Roman trial is highly dramatic. It is structured, chiastically (a.b.c.d c'b'a'), in seven episodes or scenes. There are two settings or stages: the outside court of the praetorium where 'the Jews' are gathered; the inside room where Jesus is held prisoner. Pilate goes back and forth from one stage to the other. The atmosphere is notably different in either setting. Inside Jesus and

Pilate engage in calm dialogue; outside is clamour as Pilate is pressurized to find Jesus guilty. Pilate's passing from one setting to the other is expressive of an internal struggle: while becoming increasingly convinced of Jesus' innocence he finds himself being forced to condemn him.

Scene 1. OUTSIDE. Jews Demand Death (18:28b-32).

The Jews who had brought Jesus to Pilate would not enter the Gentile praetorium. To do so would involve ritual defilement and prevent them from celebrating Passover. Pilate went out to them; they insisted that Jesus was a criminal deserving death. The execution would be according to Roman law: death by crucifixion. Jesus had already referred to his death as a 'lifting up' – on a cross! 'And I, when I am lifted up from the earth, will draw all people to myself' (12:32).

Scene 2. INSIDE. Pilate and Jesus on Kingship (18:33-38a).

Pilate questioned Jesus: 'Are you the King of the Jews?' Jesus wanted to know how he understood the title: in a political or in a religious sense? He himself proclaimed the otherworldly realm of truth; he separated his kingship from anything that could threaten Pilate. His purpose was to bear witness to 'the way things really are' – the way God is, the way God is related to the world.

Pilate's response, 'What is truth?' is not to be understood as a profound philosophical question... Ironically it is a self-condemnation: his failure to recognize truth and hear Jesus' voice shows that he does not belong to God (Brown, *The Death of the Messiah*, 752f).

Scene 3 OUTSIDE. Pilate Finds Jesus Not Guilty (18:38b-40).

Pilate had shown that he was not on the side of truth. He had turned from the light. *He* was the one on trial. He went outside and declared that, having interrogated Jesus, he could find no case against him. V. 38a is the first of Pilate's three 'not guilty' statements (see 19: 4,6). He tried the ploy of the Passover amnesty: 'Do you want me to release for you the King of the Jews?' They shouted back: 'We want Barabbas' – a known bandit.

Scene 4. INSIDE. Soldiers Scourge Jesus (19:1-3).

Pilate, in failing to give Jesus justice, is forced to a travesty of justice. He ordered Jesus to be scourged. Scourged though he had already pronounced him innocent! His scourging of an innocent man proves that man's innocence! Pilate is getting more deeply embroiled. The soldiers twisted some thorn branches into a mock crown (diadem) and decked Jesus in a cast-off soldier's cloak. The saluted him: 'Hail, King of the Jews!' The kingship theme, already introduced in the dialogue with Pilate, would persist. Ironically, this mockery serves as a declaration of who Jesus is.

Scene 5. OUTSIDE. 'Behold the Man!' (19:4-8).
Pilate had Jesus presented to the crowd – all bloody as he was from the scourging and decked in the mock crown and robes: 'Here is the man!' He was showing them a pathetic human being who was no threat to either Rome or 'the Jews.' They howled for his death: 'Crucify him!' In exasperation Pilate retorted: 'Crucify him yourselves; I have no case against the man.' They shot back: 'According to our Law he ought to be put to death: he has claimed to be Son of God.'

> By the end of the enquiry the divinity of Jesus as a threat to the unicity of God was emerging as the great issue between Jews and Christians, and John describes it as the factor beneath the surface in the Roman trial (Brown, *The Death of the Messiah* 829f).

Scene 6. INSIDE. Pilate and Jesus on Power (19:9-11).
Pilate was now quite alarmed: the unbelieving politician is superstitious. He came inside and asked Jesus: 'Where are you from?' Jesus was silent. When Pilate invoked his authority he was told, bluntly: 'You would have no authority over me if it had not been decreed so from above; but those who have handed me over to you are more guilty than you.' Pilate was now desperately anxious to release Jesus. He had been challenged by Truth – and had sought to compromise. He was hopelessly trapped. His next attempt to have the case dismissed was met with naked blackmail: 'If you set this man free you are not Caesar's friend; anyone who makes himself king is a challenge to Caesar.' Pilate was aware that his standing in Rome was, just then, not very secure; he could not risk a suggestion of disloyalty to the emperor. Time had run out on him. He could no longer evade a decision.

Scene 7. OUTSIDE. Jews Obtain Death (19:12-16a).
Pilate yielded to the Jewish demand for Jesus' crucifixion. John's account of the passing of the sentence of death is detailed, dramatic and theological; the only points of parallel with the synoptics are in the repeated call for crucifixion and the outcome of Jesus' being 'handed over.' The Old Testament background to this verb (*paradidómai*), used by all the evangelists, implies that Jesus was 'delivered up' to his enemies 'according to the definite plan and foreknowledge of God' (Acts 2:23); there was a mysterious divine purpose. The real trial was

over when the Jews uttered the fateful words: 'We have no king but Caesar.' This is akin to the statement in Matthew's account: 'His blood be on us and on our children!' (Mt 27:25). Both evangelists are reflecting not history but apologetic theology. The tragedy of Jesus' death was viewed through the hostility between Church and synagogue in the late first century A.D. The audience at the trial is made to voice a Christian interpretation of the Jewish rejection of Jesus.

John also tells us that this was the hour when the Passover lambs were being sacrificed in the Temple. It is supreme Johannine irony: the Jews renounce the covenant at the very moment when the priests begin to prepare for the feast which annually recalled God's deliverance of his covenanted people. By the blood of a lamb in Egypt Yahweh had marked them off to be spared as his own. Now, they know no king but the emperor and they slay another Lamb. At that moment, just before the Passover, as Jesus set out for Golgotha to shed his saving blood, the trial of Jesus ends with the fulfilment of that proclamation at the beginning of the gospel: 'Here is the lamb of God who takes away the sin of the world!' (1:29).

THE CRUCIFIXION OF JESUS 19:16b-30

Jesus was led out, laden with the cross-beam and without human assistance, to Golgotha, the Place of the Skull. 'Carrying the cross by himself' – there is no Simon of Cyrene: John's christology has no room for Jesus' needing or accepting help. Jesus was crucified between two others. Pilate had ordered an inscription which was affixed to the cross: 'Jesus of Nazareth, the King of the Jews;' he had the notice written in Hebrew, Latin and Greek. The annoyed Jews protested: 'It should read, "this man *claims* to be king of the Jews."' Pilate retorted: 'What I have written, I have written.' As representative of imperial Rome Pilate had made a heraldic proclamation, couched in the sacred and secular languages of the day – a worldwide proclamation of Jesus' Kingship. Supreme irony!

In 19:26-27 John has by the cross the mother of Jesus and the beloved disciple. The scene is surely symbolic as a new relationship is set up between the mother and the disciple. The disciple 'took her to his own.'

> What is peculiar to the beloved disciple, what is 'his own', is neither his house nor his spiritual space but the fact that he is the disciple *par excellence*. 'His own' is the special discipleship that Jesus loves. The fact that the mother of Jesus is now the disciple's mother and that he has taken her to his own is a symbolic way of describing

how one related to Jesus by the flesh (his mother who is part of his natural family) becomes related to him by the Spirit (a member of the ideal discipleship). (Brown, *The Death of the Messiah* 1024).

JESUS' LAST WORDS 19:28-30

Jesus was conscious that his hour had drawn to its close; all had now been accomplished. In response to his call 'I am thirsty' John specifies that a sponge full of sour wine was raised to his lips 'on a bunch of hyssop' – a small plant that could not sustain a sponge. Significantly, in Exodus 12:22 it is specified that hyssop be used to sprinkle the blood of the paschal lamb on the doorposts of the Israelite homes. Plausibly, John introduced the unlikely hyssop here to suggest that Jesus is fulfilling the role of the paschal lamb. The last word of Jesus, 'It is finished!' is a cry of victory: now Jesus will draw all people to himself.

> In *John* Jesus, who has come from God, has completed the commission that the Father has given him, so that his death becomes a deliberate decision that all is now finished, taken by one who is in control... Accordingly his 'It is finished' refers both to the work the Father has given him to do and to the fulfilment of Scripture. As 'Lamb of God' he has taken away the world's sin, thus fulfilling and completing the role of the paschal lamb in OT theology. (Brown, *The Death of the Messiah* 1078).

'Then he bowed his head and gave up his spirit' (v. 30b). In 7:37-39 Jesus promised that when he was glorified those who believed in him would receive the Spirit. His last breath was the outpouring of the life-giving Spirit – *his* Spirit.

REACTIONS AT THE CRUCIFIXION 19:31-37

The final episode, the *not* breaking of Jesus' legs and the flow of blood and water is the only part of John's crucifixion narrative which has no parallel in the synoptics. True Passover Lamb, not one bone of Jesus was broken (see Ex 12:46). The flow of blood and water is another proleptic reference to the giving of the Spirit – following on Jn 19:30. The risen Lord will give the Spirit on Easter day (20:22). Spirit-giving is multifaceted; but always the Spirit comes from Jesus because it is Spirit of Jesus. The beloved disciple (surely the 'he' of v. 35) bears witness to the christological and salvific dimension of the death of Jesus. Note that blood and water flow from the *dead* Jesus. The drama of the cross does not end in death but in the flow of life that comes from death. The death of Jesus on the cross is the beginning of Christian life.

THE BURIAL OF JESUS 19:38-42

Joseph of Arimathea – a secret disciple of Jesus – got permission from Pilate to remove the body of Jesus. He and that other secret disciple, Nicodemus, gave Jesus a royal burial. They bound his body in linen cloths, sprinkling a lavish quantity of perfumed spices between the folds. Then they laid him in a new unused tomb in a nearby garden.

Previously in John's Gospel believers who adhered to Jesus and were identified as his disciples have been contrasted with those who believed but were afraid to have it known that they were disciples. At this 'hour' of the death and burial of Jesus the beloved disciple in 19:31-37 is the example par excellence of the first group of believers. Hitherto Joseph and Nicodemus in 19:38-42 have belonged to the second group; but now they are presented as transformed through Jesus' victory on the cross. (Brown, *The Death of the Messiah* 1267).

THE EASTER VIGIL

For the Easter Vigil there are seven Old Testament readings before the two New Testament readings of the Mass. These Old Testament readings may be reduced to three and, in special circumstances, even to two, with the proviso that the third, the narrative of the crossing of the Red Sea (Ex 14:15-15:10) must be read. Where a selection needs to be made it is preferable to choose those readings which have a more direct bearing on the paschal theme and carry a message for Christians today. If three readings are to be selected, one would suggest the first, third and seventh.

A. Old Testament Readings

First Reading   Gen 1:1-2:2

Few passages of Scripture are more at home in a liturgical setting because this, in its present form, is assuredly already a liturgical text. At its close one has the over-powering impression that indeed God *is* the Creator of all that exists – that all he has made is *very good* And one should have grasped the deeper and more comforting truth that *humankind* is the pride of God's creation: his image, his representative.

'Let us make humankind in our image, after our likeness' (1:26). This is the high moment of the story of Genesis 1-11. The earth had been shaped, and the sky with its lights; the waters had been gathered into their place. Grasses and cereal plants and fruit trees flourished. Birds and fishes teemed; cattle, wild beasts and creeping things roamed the earth. The world was riotously alive. All was good. God looked, complacently, on the works of his word. The world pulsed with life. Yet, there was an emptiness, a silence. There was wanting the crowning glory, the masterpiece. There remained the desire of God, his need of a counterpart. 'Let us make human beings in our image.' God will not remain alone. He set to creating a creature that would correspond, one with whom he can speak and who would listen. In God's creation human beings are unique in that they are God's counterpart; their *raison d'être* is their relationship to God. With humans alone, in all creation, can God have dialogue. Because he is a loving God, that dialogue will be free. His counterpart will respond to him in freedom – or not at all. Humankind is God's image: his representative to administer the earth in his name.

'Have dominion': the commission reflects the relationship of God to creation. Humankind is ever God's representative, with a dominion that carries heavy responsibility. The earth has been entrusted to humankind, but it remains God's property: 'The earth is the Lord's and all it contains' (Ps 24:1). Humans have been granted no licence to exploit – in a destructive sense – nature, to despoil the earth. Humankind's special obligation, as image of God, is a call to respect for the natural world. God has concern for *all* of his creation, not only for humankind. Human dominion over the earth is meant to be a wise and benevolent rule so that it may be, in its measure, the sign of God's lordship over his creation.

In Genesis 1, a refrain runs through the litany of creation: 'God saw that it was good' – leading to the climactic declaration: 'God saw everything that he had made, and indeed, it was very good' (1:31). The Creator alone can say this of his creation because the Creator alone can see the whole of it. *We* cannot look upon our world and declare, with truth: 'It is very good.' We cannot blind ourselves to so much that is, to our eyes, far from good. Job understood this. When he sketched the facile authority of the Creator over chaos and the heavens and the great waters (Job 26:5-13), he exclaimed, in awe: 'These are indeed but the outskirts of his ways; and how small a whisper do we hear of him!' (26:14).

Second Reading   Gen 22:1-18

The restoration of creation as God had willed it began with God's call
to Abraham. The new relationship with God is based on total faith in
him, symbolized here by Abraham's readiness to give up his only son
Isaac. A poignant story indeed. The man who had, without hesitation,
at the Lord's bidding, set out from his homeland (Gen 12:1), now,
without question, sets out to do this awful deed. He obeyed with a
heavy heart, a heart pierced to the quick by Isaac's unsuspecting
question: 'Father, the fire and the wood are here, but where is the lamb
for a burnt offering?' The tragic dignity of Abraham and his sad
readiness to give his son stirred a Christian sentiment. The deed of
Abraham has surely coloured the telling of a greater love: 'He did not
withhold his own Son, but gave him up for all of us' (Rom 8:32); 'God
so loved the world that he gave his only Son' (Jn 3:16). Abraham had
put his faith in God, a seemingly capricious and callous God. For,
Abraham saw, what Paul and John were to recognize, that his God is
always a foolish God – a God who loves with divine abandon. He can
make outrageous demands because he will always be faithful.

Third Reading   Ex 14:15-15:1

The reading describes the final act in the drama of the Hebrews'
liberation from Egyptian slavery. It marked the decisive confrontation
between God's protection of his people and the obduracy of Pharaoh.
The crossing of the Sea of Reeds and the defeat of the Egyptians
became the great symbol of God's saving actions in history. Here in
Exodus (and in the Vigil liturgy) it flows into the song of victory of Ex
15. Later, the author of Revelation will have the conquerors of the
Beast sing, beside the heavenly sea, 'the song of Moses, the servant of
God, and the song of the Lamb' (Rev 15:2-4). When Israel saw what
God had achieved 'they believed in the Lord and in his servant Moses'
(Ex 14:31). We, too, contemplating the mighty work of God in our
Exodus, believe in God and his holy Servant Jesus (see Acts 4:30).

Fourth Reading   Is 54:5-14

Already in the eighth century B.C. the prophet Hosea had introduced
the daring figure of Yahweh as the husband of his people (Hos 1-3).
Two centuries later, the unknown prophet of the Exile takes up that
image to comfort a shattered people. God seemed far away and Israel
a wife forsaken. Israel receives the promise that the Lord, the Holy
One, will take her back into his love and that their renewed relationship

would abide – 'with everlasting love I will have compassion on you.'
The Church, the Bride of Christ, is heir of this promise.

Fifth Reading   Is 55:1-11

The previous reading sang of Yahweh's enduring love; this reading,
virtually its continuation, sings of his eternal covenant. It is an appeal
to the exiles to turn from the ineffective things of this world to the word
of God which alone achieves its purpose and can satisfy human
longing. We Christians can be encouraged by the assurance of 'an
everlasting covenant, my steadfast, sure love for David' – an assurance
in the improbable setting of the ruins of the house of David! Why?
Because the thoughts and ways of the Lord are not subject to human
limitations (vv. 8-9) and the word of the Lord *will* accomplish its
purpose (vv. 10-11). We, disciples of the Word, have no grounds for
pessimism nor any excuse for discouragement.

Sixth Reading   Bar 3:9-15; 32-4:4

Part of the great wisdom poem of Baruch (3:9-4:4). It is a call to return
to God, source of true wisdom. Israel is privileged to be recipient of
this wisdom; if Israel lives by it, it will have life and peace. Wisdom
is to be sought and found in Torah, the law of Moses. From a Christian
perspective this wisdom is embodied in Christ. An exhortation to seek
wisdom is all the more poignant on the Easter night when Christ
crucified, the wisdom and power of God (1 Cor 1:24), triumphs over
death.

Seventh Reading   Ezek 36:16-28

The capture and destruction of Jerusalem and exile of the people had
not only convinced the nations of the powerlessness of Yahweh but
had led Israel to doubt his might and his protection. Ezekiel reminds
the exiles that the disasters had not come because of God's impotence
but were caused by their sins. He assures them that their God will act
– because he owes it to himself to vindicate his honour. He will gather
his people, cleanse them from their sins and put a new spirit within
them. Thus he would show himself to be their God and they would
once again be truly his people. The hauntingly beautiful passage
36:24-28 is very like Jer 31:31-34. God will cleanse his people of their
sin, giving them the new heart and spirit which will render them
capable of fidelity to the Lord. For the Christian, this cleansing is to be
understood in the new life celebrated in baptism.

B. New Testament Readings

First Reading
Rom 6:3-11

This reading takes us to the very heart of Christianity. The death and resurrection of Jesus are his 'Passover' to the Father. They are likewise the Passover of Christians, the new exodus to salvation. On Calvary Jesus died to this order of things, to the 'flesh' in its weakness and mortal nature; at his resurrection he entered into a new order of being, into a life glorious and immortal.

Baptism incorporates one into this Passover of Christ and into all that his Passover symbolizes and achieves. The Christian, in baptism, has shared in the death of Christ. Therefore, as far as sin is concerned, the baptized one is dead to its power. Sin no longer has absolute rule over us (v. 6) Having been buried with Christ in baptism (vv. 4a,5a,8a) we are now to regard ourselves as in fact dead, as far as the power of sin is concerned (v. 11a). This is, of course, only half the story. By dying Christ conquered sin (he 'died to sin', that is, he died rather than sin); and by rising he conquered death. If by baptism we shared in that death, do we not also share in that overcoming of death? We do but not yet! While our participation in Christ's death is described in the past tense, our participation in the resurrection is described exclusively in the future tense. It is an instance of Paul's constant insistence on the fact that our share in the glorified life of the Lord belongs to the future. Jesus is Lord not because he transports us out of this world but because he enables us to serve him in the confines of this world.

But, if we do not yet share the glory of Christ's resurrection, this share in his glory is enough for now: For the first time, we can choose not to sin. For the first time, it is possible that exhortations to good can be followed. By it Christians are crucified, die, with Christ to a purely earthly order of things. They die to weak human nature which is prey to sin and death. They die to it in the sense that now another power is present in them, the power of the risen Christ which gives them the means of triumphing over sin and eternal death. In baptism, too, they rise with Christ to the new life which he now enjoys because, through his resurrection, Christ is the life-giving Spirit. All this is the paschal mystery which is operative in Christian life: death to sin and life to grace. This conviction of Christians is hope and challenge: we should live by the Christ-life we have received.

Gospel
Mk 16:1-8

Mark relates that the three women named in 15:40, intending to anoint the body of Jesus, came to the tomb when the sabbath had ended. There a 'young man' (an angel) informed them that the crucified Jesus of Nazareth whom they sought was 'not here': he had been raised. The women were given a message for the Twelve: Jesus is going before them into Galilee (v. 7). But what kind of messengers did they turn out to be? For, disconcertingly, the closing statement runs: 'So they went out and fled from the tomb, for terror and amazement had seized them; and they said nothing to anyone, for they were afraid' (16:8).

The abrupt ending of Mark has long been seen as a problem. Even early Christians had been puzzled by this startling closure of the gospel. Attempts were made to round off Mark's work. The manuscript tradition has preserved three different endings – notably the familir Longer Ending (16:9-20). Narrative critics rightly view 16:8 not only as Mark's intended ending but as a classic example of the literary feature of unresolved conflict. Its purpose is to involve the readers. They are made to wonder how they would have acted had they found themselves in the situation of these women. The open-ended Marcan conclusion challenges and demands response. The Marcan story is not rounded off precisely because the readers are asked to write its ending.

It remains to be seen whether we, confident of the victory of the Lord of life, will quietly and passionately minister in his name in our Galilee – the boardroom, factories, homes, relationships, voting booths, pulpits – to which Christ sends us. Yet one thing is sure: He has gone there ahead of us, and there we can see him, just as he promised' (R. A. Olsen, 'Mark 16:1-8', *Interpretation* (1993), 409.

Easter Season

Introduction to the Liturgical Season

The readings for the Easter season evoke the presence of the risen Lord in the Church, and they speak about the life and worship and witness of the Christian community, animated by the Holy Spirit.

GOSPELS

The Gospel of the second Sunday of the Easter season is from John, the appearances of Jesus to the apostles on the first day and on the eighth day.

In Year B, the Gospel of the third Sunday is Luke's account of the appearance to the Eleven and their companions in Jerusalem. The Gospels for the fourth Sunday show Jesus as the Good Shepherd. Those for the fifth, sixth and seventh Sundays are taken from John, the discourse and prayer of Jesus at the Last Supper, about life and love and Spirit and unity.

FIRST READINGS

The First Readings are from the Acts of the Apostles, arranged in 'a three-year cycle of parallel and progressive selections'. They give a picture of the early Church's way of life, its witness to the resurrection, and its growth. They include material about prayer, breaking bread, baptism, laying on of hands, and Church order, which remind us that this is a time of reflection on the life of the Church, including its liturgy.

SECOND READINGS

For Year B the second readings are from First John, and are chosen to express 'the spirit of joyous faith and sure hope proper to this season'.

ASCENSION DAY

The Easter season includes Ascension Day, on which the Gospel is from one or other of the synoptics, and the First Reading is Acts' account of the ascension. The Second Reading is from Ephesians, about God raising Christ from the dead and making him sit at his right hand. An *ad libitum* Second Reading is given for Year B, a passage from Ephesians reflecting on Christ's ascension on high.

PENTECOST

The Easter season ends with Pentecost Sunday. The Gospels are passages from John about fountains of living water, symbolizing the Spirit (vigil Mass), and about Jesus breathing on the disciples and saying 'Receive the Holy Spirit' (Pentecost Sunday). An *ad libitum* Gospel for Year B is a passage from John about the promise of the Spirit.

An interesting choice of First Readings is given for the vigil Mass of Pentecost: the Tower of Babel, the theophany on Mount Sinai, Ezekiel on the dry bones being brought to life, or Joel on the pouring out of the spirit on all humankind.

The Second Readings are Romans on the Spirit who pleads for us (vigil Mass); First Corinthians on the variety of gifts and the one Spirit (Pentecost Sunday); Galatians on the fruits of the Spirit (Year B *ad libitum*).

The First Reading for Mass during the day is Acts' description of Pentecost, with all its implications for the life of the Church.

Philip Gleeson OP

ARTIST: SEÁN ADAMSON

Eastertide

First Reading
Acts 10:34.37-43

From now until Pentecost Sunday inclusive, first readings are drawn from Acts of the Apostles. Since Acts is the second volume of one work (the third gospel being the first) it should be understood for what it is; more correctly a sequel to Luke's gospel than a history of the early Church. Given this close relationship, we are not surprised to find that the structure of gospel and Acts runs along parallel lines. The narrative of the ministry of Jesus is formed of two more or less equal parts: the first, covering the preaching in Galilee, centres in the Twelve and ends with the mission confided to the Twelve; the other part, the journey to Jerusalem, begins with the mission charge to the Seventy, and has material not found in Mark and Matthew. Similarly, Acts has two parts: one in which Peter has a leading role and which looks to Jerusalem (1:1-15:35); the second, centered in Paul, breaks out of this geographical framework and turns towards Rome (15:36-28:31).

In Acts Luke is concerned with showing the progress of the Good News throughout the whole world (1:8). He is especially interested in the passing of the preaching from Jews to Gentiles and in the progress of the Gentile mission. Behind the continuous spread of the Gospel throughout the provinces of the Empire he sees the power of the Holy Spirit. Luke was aware that the Gentile mission had been set on foot before Paul had begun to play his part and he knew that Paul was not the only architect of the Gentile Church. But since his purpose was to portray the spread of the Church, he could not have chosen a more dramatic and effective way of doing so. For it is true that Paul the missionary and Paul the theologian has set his stamp on Christianity.

Our reading is part of Peter's speech in the home of the Roman centurion, Cornelius. The discourse gives an outline of the ministry of Jesus, ending with the narrative of his resurrection. Noteworthy is the emphasis on the fact that Peter and his companions were eyewitnesses of the resurrection – more precisely, that they had encountered the risen Lord. They are witnesses so that they can be sent to preach redemption, the forgiveness of sin.

The risen Saviour continued to be with his Church after the resurrection. And it was because Jesus had risen again from the dead that the apostles could preach the reality of redemption, of the forgiveness of sin. Because God was with him, Jesus during his ministry went about doing good. God is present in a special way with his people in the person of the risen Christ. In him the fulness of God dwells, an overflowing plenitude of divine power and goodness, bringing new divine life to all who believe in Christ. This is the power of Christ's resurrection of which Paul speaks in Philippians (Phil 3:10).

Each successive generation of Christians can proclaim, and must proclaim, the reality and the significance of the resurrection as confidently as Peter did. The Church does so unceasingly, but does so in a special manner at Easter. And down the ages the opening words of the Easter Mass have brought us Christ's reassuring message: 'I have risen and am with you still, alleluia.' The passage of years has made no difference. The risen Lord is the same yesterday, today and forever.

Second Reading   Col 3:1-4

According to the author, baptism is a participation in Christ's death and resurrection, symbolized by the ritual of being 'plunged' into water (2:12). This real sharing in Christ's death and resurrection has profound and far-reaching repercussions in the Christian's present moral life. It entails the rejection of all that is 'earthly' (3:2-5), that is, all that is opposed to God. It calls for the pursuit of the 'good life' – not by the world's standards but as the good life has been lived by Jesus. Here we have the reality of *Christian* freedom. Though by one's sacramental death in baptism the Christian is liberated from past constraints, one is, nevertheless, bound to lead a new life in conformity with the gospel.

Alternative Second Reading   1 Cor 5:6-8

Paul is concerned in 5:1-13 with a case of incest in the Corinthian community. He argues that this 'immoral' person, like yeast within a lump of dough, affects the whole community. The historical context does not exhaust the meaning of the image. We today cannot expect to share fully in the newness of Christ's sacrifice if we cling to the evil and wickedness of our life without Christ.

Gospel   Jn 20:1-9

John has preserved two versions of the women's visit to the tomb – 20:1-3 and 11-13. Underlying the first of them (vv 1-2) would seem to be the earliest form of an empty tomb narrative in any gospel. John has introduced the Beloved Disciple and has, for his own dramatic purpose, reduced the original group of women to Mary Magdalene – preparing the way for the later christophany to her (vv 14-18). It is this christophany, and not an angelic spokesman, which explains the meaning of the empty tomb (vv 12-13). But the tradition which was thus rewritten is early indeed.

Thoroughly Johannine is 20:1-10. At Mary Magdalene's disturbing news (v. 2) Peter and 'the other disciple' hurry to the tomb. In the tradition, Peter's companion was unnamed. John has introduced him as the Beloved Disciple so that his coming to faith might interpret the significance of the empty tomb. The burial cloths and, more unexpectedly, their arrangement, are a sign that Mary's interpretation of the empty tomb ('they have taken the Lord out of the tomb', 20:2) is not the correct one. Jesus has not been 'taken' anywhere. Rather, he has left mortality behind him. Only the Beloved Disciple (vv. 2,8) seeing the sign, believes – 'he saw and believed' (v. 8). Manifestly, he believed, even *before* any appearance of the risen Lord, in the risen Christ himself. The fact of the matter is that while the 'beloved disciple' is a real person and the source of John's tradition, he also represents the christian disciple who is sensitive, in faith and love, to the presence of the risen Jesus. With this one exception – theological exception – of the Beloved Disciple who saw with eyes of faith, the 'empty tomb' is never regarded as a reason for faith. The conviction that Jesus can no longer be found in the tomb because he is risen Lord (and not for any other reason) follows on encounter with the risen Lord.

What is the *significance* of the resurrection of Jesus? The confession: 'God raised Jesus from the dead' implies more, much more, than the deed of raising from the dead. It implies that the kingdom of God – the rule of God – is indeed come in Jesus. The resurrection should not be regarded as an isolated fact. In declaring 'Christ is risen' one is acknowledging that God's saving promises have been accomplished in Jesus. Jesus had seen his whole life and his whole mission in relation to the fulfilment of such promises: 'We had hoped that he was the one to redeem Israel' (Lk 24:21). It was because of their former hope in him that the disciples were able to interpret the resurrection as God's confirmation of all that Jesus stood for. Because he was raised from the dead, Jesus holds decisive significance for us. Because of the fact of his resurrection we know that meaningless death – and meaningless life – now have meaning. Jesus had died with the cry on his lips: 'My God, my God, why have you forsaken me?' (Mk 15:34). The sequel was to show that God had never abandoned Jesus. We have the assurance thnat he will not abandon us.

If the life of Jesus showed the meaning of his death, the life-and-death of Jesus showed the meaning of his resurrection. As Jesus' lifestyle, his praxis of the kingdom of God, had prepared for his death, his resurrection was the vindication of all he stood for. This involves more than the authentication of his message. Resurrection, for one thing, underlies the reality of Jesus' Abba-consciousness, his communion with God, which death could not interrupt. The resurrection of Jesus demonstrates that God is indeed the God of humankind who holds out, to all of us, the promise of life beyond death. In other words, the resurrection of Jesus is not only something that happened to him; it reaches to us. And not only as it concerns our future resurrection. Already, as risen Lord, Jesus himself is present to us and with us in our striving to give substance to the Kingdom. He is Emmanuel – God-with-us.

SECOND SUNDAY OF EASTER

First Reading   Acts 4:32-35

A picture of a Christian community ideally faithful to the gospel message. As in 2:42 'they devoted themselves to the apostles' teaching and fellowship, to the breaking of bread and the prayers.' It is a community of shared faith and shared possessions: a faith in the resurrection and power of the Lord, and a distribution of goods now seen as common property. The motivation for the generous distribution is spelled out in 4:34 – 'there was not a needy person among them.' There is no romantic glorification of poverty. Concern is for the poor a preoccupation of Luke. He has sketched a picture of the ideal Christian community as a challenge to, and model for, his own community

Second Reading   1 Jn 5:1-6

Through the Sundays of Easter (two to seven) the second reading is from the first letter of John. It is helpful to give, in summary, the message of the letter. The author's primary purpose is not to exhort his readers to practise virtue or to fly sin, but to make them understand the sublimity of their conditions as Christians. Christian existence is defined as a vital relationship to God. It is a matter of birth to the life of God, of fellowship with Father and Son: the faithful are born of God, they abide in God, they know God. In short, they have 'eternal life'; and for John, eternal life is the very life of God. This life, possessed by the Christian, is a reality, but it is mysterious: what the faithful are now, and as they will be hereafter, is attested only by faith. Therefore, the author multiplies the criteria by which the believer gauges the genuineness of one's Christian life; hence the frequency of 'by this' and the verb 'to know' (2:3,5; 3:10,14,19,24; 4:2,6,13,18,20). Since it is a participation in the divine life, Christian life must reflect the qualities of God. If we are children of God, in fellowship with him, it is impossible that we should not be conformed to him.

God is Light (1:5) and Love (4:8): *Light* because he is the absolute good and because our moral conduct should be modelled on his justice and holiness (2:20; 3:7); *Love* because he is the source of all the tenderness and generosity that the verb 'to love' suggests. The Christian is called to walk in the Light (1:6-7) and to abide in Love (4:16) by observing the commandments (2:3-7; 3:22-24; 5:2-3), summed up in the two precepts of faith in the name of Jesus and of brotherly/sisterly charity (3:23). To believe in the divine Love which is incarnate in Jesus and, in turn, to love their brothers and sisters – such is the message addressed by John to Christians.

But John does also intend to recall – by implication at least – the fundamental norms of the Christian life. In the realm of faith his readers must readily accept the apostolic witness (1:5; 3:21-24), as well as the testimony of God (4:6,9,13) and the intimate word of the Spirit (2:20,27). Their relationship with their brothers and sisters is coloured by their care to observe the commandments, centred in the precept of charity (2:3-11; 3:11-24, 4:7 - 5:4). They must take their stand against the unbelieving world and face up resolutely to its allurements (2:12-17; 3:13; 4:1) bolstered by confidence in the person of the Saviour (2:1-2; 3:5,8; 5:6-7). The Christian life makes demands and its sublimity is matched by a practicality that calmly accepts the realities of human existence.

A prominent theme of the letter is that the Christian is child of God – child of a Father who is Love. Our reading points out that the test of our loving lies in keeping the commandments. John really has one commandment in mind: that of love. The observation 'his commandments are not burdensome' reminds us of Mt 11:30, 'For my yoke is easy, and my burden is light.' A prominent theme of Johannine preaching is the Christian's victory over sin or the evil one; here (vv. 4-5) 'world' is the same as the evil one. Victory is through faith in the Son of God who has already overcome the evil one (Jn 12:31; 16:33).

John, typically, insists on the reality of the incarnation; Jesus came 'by water and blood' – he is the Jesus of flesh and blood who was baptized and died on the cross (v. 6).

The spiritual message of this letter is basically the same as that of Paul, but it is more theocentric than Paul and goes to the Father. Here the ideal is not to live 'in Christ' but to 'abide in God,' in the 'Father and Son.' But this does not prevent John from emphasizing, just as strongly as Paul, the indispensable mediation of the incarnate Son of God: it is through the Son that the believer receives the very life of God. All the while, be it said again, a writing of such elevated spirituality, cast in the realm of Father and Son, keeps a close and constant grip on the world of humankind and testifies to a simple and demanding moral realism: fellowship with God, participation in the divine life, is impossible without absolute fidelity to the Commandment. This short writing has an abiding message for those far advanced in the Christian Way – and for all Christians.

Gospel   Jn 20:19-31

The risen Christ appears to his disciples only to entrust them with a mission. The mission is nothing more or less than the one he has received from the Father and, indeed, accomplished by his death and resurrection: the reconciliation of men and women with their Father (the forgiveness of sins). He greeted his disciples with the common Jewish salutation 'peace be with you.' Jesus considered peace a gift that comes from God, which established a relation of harmony and friendship not only between the Israelite and neighbour but also between the Israelite and God. Jesus had declared during his lifetime that the world cannot give true peace and that he had come to bestow it (Jn 14:27). Now as glorified Lord he communicates his peace to his disciples and thus binds them to himself and to one another in a union of love and harmony.

To carry out their mission they are enlivened and inspired by the Holy Spirit – which is Christ's Spirit, making them one with him. They are to be Christ's body to the world. One of the effects of the gift of the Spirit was that they could forgive sins. John did not tell us who could exercise this power or how it should be exercised. It would be blatantly anachronistic to read back into this text the later sacrament of reconciliation. What one can confidently say is that the Church's use of the sacrament of reconciliation is one valid and legitimate way of exercising the power over sin given by the risen Jesus to his disciples.

The episode of Thomas (vv. 24-29) is of great importance for the fourth evangelist and is, indeed, climactic in his gospel. (Chapter 20 is the close of the gospel proper, chapter 21 being an appendix). The disciple, Thomas, passes from unbelief to belief. The last word of a disciple in the gospel is a full-blooded christological profession of faith.

Thomas refuses to accept the word of the other disciples and insists on having concrete proof of the reality of the resurrection of Jesus (vv. 24-25). In the event, he comes to belief without a need for the crude verification he seemed to demand (20:25,27-28). It is enough to have seen (v. 29, see vv. 20,25). It is unfortunate that Thomas has been remembered for his stubbornness – 'doubting Thomas.' He ought to have been remembered for the most forthright confession of faith in the gospels: 'My Lord and my God.' It is the supreme christological conviction: Jesus may, by Christians, be addressed by the same terms in which Israel had addressed Yahweh. Thomas' confession is an acknowledgment of the God revealed in Jesus. It is, most likely, a confessional formula of the evangelist's Church.

Thomas has made the last utterance of a disciple of Jesus. The evangelist adds a comment that is crucial for all disciples of the risen Lord – those of us who live in 'that day': 'Have you believed because you have seen me? Blessed are those who have not seen and yet have come to believe' (20:29). The evangelist is writing for a generation that has not 'seen' the Lord. He would insist that Thomas and the later disciples are equal, sharing the same blessedness through their common faith in the Lord, though he be not visible. It is the tranquil assurance of union with him.

THIRD SUNDAY OF EASTER

First Reading   Acts 3:13-15, 17-19

Peter and John's healing of a cripple (3:1-9) is followed by Peter's discourse (3:12-26). It is a prophetic interpretation of that event as a fulfilment of God's plan sketched in the Scriptures. He begins by informing his hearers that the God of their fathers had raised up the Servant whom they have killed (v. 13). They requested 'a murderer' instead of 'the holy and righteous one', 'the author of life.' Yet, all had fallen within God's purpose (v. 18). Ignorance accounted for much of their past sin; now they can, like many of their people already have done, repent and be forgiven; there is an urgency in the call to conversion. The reading is an early form of explanation of the Passion and an example of the early witness to the resurrection.

Second Reading

'I am writing these things to you so that you may not sin.' Realistically, John anticipates that Christians, who, like all of humankind prone to sin (1:8-10), will sin. If we sin, Jesus Christ comes to our assistance, for he, the Righteous One, is an advocate, a counsel for the defence. He is 'the Lamb of God, who takes way the sin of the world' (Jn 1:29). From the start John sees love as the criterion of the genuine disciple: 'Whoever obeys his word, truly in this person the love of God has reached perfection' (v. 5). The message is the same as in Jn 14:15,21,23-24 – authentic love is proved by obedience, by the faithful observance of the commandments. Here we have the sign, the test, of the 'love of God,' that is, of properly divine and Christian charity. In the obedient Christian this charity exists truly.

Gospel

In v. 35, the concluding verse of the Emmaus story (24:13-35), Luke again draws attention to the 'breaking of bread' (vv. 30-31) – he is determined that his readers will not miss its significance. His breaking of bread at the start of a meal was the occasion of the two disciples' recognition of Jesus. The expression 'breaking of bread' is a technical term for the Eucharist. Luke has deliberately used eucharistic language: Jesus *took bread, blessed, broke, gave* to them. And his lesson is that as the two disciples recognized Jesus in the setting of a meal shared with them, so Christians, in the eucharistic meal, make the same real encounter with their Lord. This whole Emmaus passage, centred around the 'liturgy of the word' (vv. 19-27) and the 'eucharistic' meal (vv. 30-31), has a marked liturgical colouring. It is an early catechesis, in a liturgical setting, highlighting the encounter with the Lord in the Eucharist.

The appearance story immediately following (vv. 36-42) has quite obvious apologetic motifs: Jesus shows that he is the same person whom the disciples had known prior to the crucifixion by pointing to his body, and by eating before them. As in all the appearance stories the risen Jesus is not immediately recognizable (v. 37); a gesture or word is needed before the disciples recognize the risen Lord. This is quite a clever way of making the point that resurrection is not a return to earthly life; Jesus has risen to new life beyond death. He is the same – yet transformed. Here the point is firmly made that the risen Jesus is no 'ghost.' The assertion that he invited touching of his (wounded) hands and feet and that he ate in their presence is, in the apologetic of the time, a firm Christian rejection of any challenge to the *reality* of the new life of their Lord.

At the close of his gospel (24:44-49) Luke summarizes the last commission of Jesus to his disciples; this he repeats at the beginning of Acts (1:3-8). More pointedly, the outline and words of this gospel passage echo the apostolic *kerygma* of Acts. Jesus recalls the occasions on which he had warned the disciples that he, in fulfilment of the will of God enshrined in the Scriptures, would have to suffer, die, and rise again (cf. 9:22,44; 17:25; 18:31-33; 22:37). 'While I was still with you' (v. 44): Jesus has entered into his glory (v. 26) by his exaltation to the Father (Jn 20:17); his relations with the disciples are not what they were before his glorification.

The risen Lord gives his disciples a new understanding of the Old Testament (vv. 45-48), an insight that will enable them to see how and where it 'testifies on his behalf' (see Jn 5:39). This reinterpretation of the Old Testament is a basic element of the primitive *kerygma*: the dawning of the age of fulfilment (v. 44; see Acts 2:16; 3:18,24); the suffering of the Messiah and his resurrection on the third day (v. 46; see Acts 2:23-24; 3:13-15; 4:10). The kerygma always includes the proclamation of repentance and forgiveness of sins, a proclamation to all humankind – the universalist note is very much at home in Luke (Acts 2:38-39; 3:19-20, 4:12). The disciples are convincing witnesses and efficacious missionaries because they had seen the Lord and have believed in him; all who would, effectively, bear witness to Christ must have encountered him in personal and living faith. Today, when the call of the apostolate is urgent and the role of witness is seen as the obligation of every Christian, we are more keenly aware that religion is not the acceptance of a body of doctrine nor the adherence to a code of law, but attachment to a Person. Knowledge of Christ, in the biblical sense of acceptance and commitment, is the essence of Christian life. It is obviously the first requirement of an apostle.

FOURTH SUNDAY OF EASTER

First Reading   Acts 4:8-12

The passage 4:1-22 presents the clash of 'the apostles' and the *sanhedrin*, a little drama in three acts: arrest (1-4), discourse of Peter (5-12), and deliberation of the sanhedrin, with Peter's response (13-22). Our reading gives Peter's discourse. In the gospel, the authority of Jesus had been challenged: 'By what authority are you doing these things?' (Lk 20:2). The challenge had been uttered by 'the chief priests, the scribes, and the elders,' in other words, the sanhedrin. Now the same group challenges the apostles. And Peter responds.

By the time Luke wrote, the separation of Christianity from the Jewish religion was an accomplished fact. For Luke, too, the community he belonged to was the fulfilment of the aspirations of Israel. The resurrection of Jesus inaugurated the era of the resurrection that was the characteristic hope of Israel's strictest practitioners, the Pharisees (Acts 4:2; see 23:6). From its earliest days the Christian community encountered hostility from the leaders of Israel as Jesus himself had. The conflict surfaces in Peter's speech. For instance, the verse of Ps 118:22 'the stone which the builders rejected' was usually understood to refer to Israel, or to the temple which had been destroyed and rebuilt; Christians applied it to Jesus. Faith in Jesus finds an even more comprehensive expression in Peter's words: 'there is no other name under heaven given among mortals by which we must be saved' (v. 12). Christians are adamant that Jesus, God's only Son, is the one and only Saviour.

Second Reading

1 Jn 3:1-2

We can speak of a person being *named* to an office or a job. In a Semitic context, to be named ('called') is a more forceful expression. Our text says we are named God's children and, in case there should be any doubt, John adds: 'and that is what we are.' We *know*, that is, experience, our filial relationship to God. We have been born to a new life and share, mysteriously but really, in the life of God (1:29). The fact of being a Christian, of being born of God, is permanent assurance that one is loved by the Father; each carries in his or her person the attestation of this love. (John will, of course, insist that the Christian *live* as child of God, 3:4-23). The unbelieving world is incapable of recognising the true status of Christians because it has not come to know God. For John this means that it had failed to recognise Jesus. As for ourselves, we have to await the coming of the Lord, to see him 'as he is,' before we can arrive at full appreciation of our own Christian reality. Only then shall we see clearly that our future state will be like the glorified state of Jesus. But the process of becoming like Christ has already begun – a familiar stress in John.

Gospel

Jn 10:11-18

The passage John 10:1-18 opens with two parables: on the right way of approach to the sheep (1-3a), and on the relation between shepherd and sheep (3b-5). The first parable is explained in vv. 7-10; our reading is the explanation of the other. Jesus is the good shepherd who is willing to die to protect his sheep, his own sheep whom he knows intimately.

Our passage particularly brings to mind a passage from Ezek 34 where God promises his people, in the first place, that he himself would become their shepherd, and then that he would choose a shepherd for them in the messianic age. Jesus' assertion that he is the good shepherd indicates that this age has arrived and that he is the promised one. He is a shepherd so very different from those castigated by Ezekiel: 'You have not strengthened the weak, you have not healed the sick, you have not bound up the injured, you have not brought back the strayed, you have not sought the lost, but with force and harshness you have ruled them' (Ezek 34:4). In every point he stood in sharp contrast to them.

The second characteristic of the true shepherd is that he knows his sheep intimately and that they know him. In John the mutual knowledge of Jesus and those who belong to him is an extension of the mutual knowledge of Father and Son (see Jn 17:25-26). Knowing Jesus and the Father means being of one mind and heart with them. But the goodness of this Shepherd reaches beyond his own sheep to invite others to join his flock (v. 16) – 'I, when I am lifted up from the earth, will draw all people to myself' (12:32).

In vv 17-18 John speaks of laying down life.

Death is often seen as making a mockery of life, love, and freedom, but when Jesus speaks of his own death, he sees it otherwise. Having said earlier that the Father's love for the Son is expressed in showing him how to create and give life (5:19-21), he now states that this Father's love is particularly expressed in Jesus' dying: 'Because of this the Father loves me, that I lay down my life, in order that I may take it up again.' It is not that the Father's love is dependent on Jesus' death. Rather, that love is presupposed; but in Jesus' dying the Father's love is expressed in a special way and is grounded yet more firmly' (T. Brodie, *John*, 372).

FIFTH SUNDAY OF EASTER

First Reading   Acts 9:26-31
Paul gives his own account of his visits to Jerusalem in Gal 1:18 - 2:10.

The visit here mentioned corresponds to the first that Paul speaks of (1:18-24). Three years after his conversion he went to Jerusalem to see Peter and remained with him fifteen days. He also saw James. In our passages we are told that the Jerusalem Christians (not surprisingly, in view of his record – 8:1-3; 9:1-2) were apprehensive of any dealings with Saul – how could they trust him? Barnabas was able to persuade them that Saul the Pharisee had, indeed, become a true Christian. Once accepted, his charism was potent – so remarkable that it boomeranged on him. The hellenists (Greek-speaking Jews who had already engineered the death of Stephen) wanted to get rid of him too; in their eyes he was a traitor. The brethren had to hustle Paul to safety. In sharp contrast v. 31, a typically Lucan summary statement, sums up the situation of Christian communities able to live in peace. Luke notes in particular how the spread of the Church and the joy which filled its members are the work of the Holy Spirit.

The role of Barnabas (v. 27) is to be noted. It is thanks to this 'son of encouragement' (4:36) that Paul was accepted by the Jerusalem community. Later, it is Barnabas who again rescued Saul from oblivion in Tarsus (11:25-26) and was the first companion of him who was to become the apostle of the Gentiles (13:1-3). Paul owed much to this discerning and magnanimous Christian.

Second Reading   1 Jn 3:18-24

The passage 1 Jn 3:10-23 is a meditation on Jn 13:34-35, on the 'new commandment': to love one another mutually *as* Christ has loved us. Jesus had declared that this would be the sign of the authentic Christian ('By this everyone will know that you are my disciples,' 13:35) and John reminds the disciples themselves of the criterion. For charity is not only a sign; it is also a test which divides true Christians from those who are such in name only. Love is not an action or a series of isolated actions, it is a permanent quality, a religious state. Here, however, the accent is on the manifestation of this love which is constantly active, which proves itself, gives itself and sacrifices itself. It is love 'in truth and action' and it is by its fruits that it becomes an unmistakable criterion of divine sonship. Christ himself had set the example of unselfish love: his voluntary sacrifice is the highest example of authentic *agapé*. And so it is that the commandment of love includes faith in the Son: Christians are bidden to believe in the crucified Son of God and to love one another (v. 23).

Of course, the Christian remains a sinner and one's conscience may reproach one with many failings (v. 20) but God is 'greater than our hearts' and he will readily overlook the sins of one who is moved to pity by the plight of one's neighbour and seeks to help. Hardness of heart alone will provoke the severity of the sovereign Judge. In other words, the quality of fraternal relationship determines that of relations with God. But the sincere Christian, conscious of the disposition of God's heart – 'we know' (v. 24) – can and must approach God without fear and stand simply and even boldly before him (v. 19). We can do so because God and the person who loves one's brothers and sisters are one: one abides in the other (v. 24). Brotherly/sisterly charity is the guarantee of the most direct and intimate loving relationship between God and the Christian.

Gospel   Jn 15:1-8

The image of the vine recalls the Old Testament designation of Israel as the vine of Yahweh (see Is 15:1-7; Jer 2:21; Ezek 15:1-8; Ps 80:8-19). Jesus declares that he himself, and not the Israel of old, is the real vine of God. But from this understanding of the image, we may move still further to stress the intimate relationship of branches and stock within the Vine. And Jesus does stress the union between himself and his disciples.

'I am the vine, you are the branches.' We tend to regard this statement as no more than a figure of speech. Spontaneously, (for this is our way of thinking) we take the declaration about the vine to mean that the union of Christ with his own is *like* the link between the branches and the vine. The disciples are asked to think about a vine, to regard the vital link of branches and trunk. Jesus is thought to say, in effect: the union between us, between you and me, is something like that intimate unity of nature. What he really means is precisely the opposite! For him, the intimate union of vine and branches is a *symbol* of the infinitely closer union of Jesus with his disciples. That is why Jesus can speak of himself as the *genuine* Vine: the sublime truth which the vine symbolizes is fully realized only in him. Understood in this way, the declaration of Jesus is emphatic and clear: we live by the life of the Vine, we live by the life of Christ.

The Christian life is unthinkable except in terms of Christ. He and the Christian abide one in the other because they share a common life. The branches, however, while living by the sap of the vine, need to be tended. This is the work of the Father who, by trial and chastisement, guides and trains his children (see Heb 12:5-11). The Father tends the Vine, but its branches will bear fruit only if they are effectively attached to the Vine, only if his life flows in them: apart from him they can do nothing, they count for nothing. The Father expects the disciples, his children, to bear fruit. He is glorified in the Son, in his obedience and in the perfect accomplishment of his work. It is a short, inevitable, step to see the glorification of the Father also in the obedience and fruitfulness of those who are joined to the Son.

Important in this process is the role of Jesus. The picture of him that is given here follows one that by now is rather familiar in the gospel. At first (v. 1) he is 'the true vine'; then (v. 5) he is simply 'the vine'; and finally (v. 8) he has momentarily disappeared from view and is replaced by the fruitful emergence of the disciples. The descent, while related to that found in the prologue and foot-washing, is particularly close to that found in 10:7-18: starting with the same 'I am' formula, Jesus (in chapter 10) had gone from being the gate (10:7), to being the good shepherd (10:11), to a title-less laying down of his life (10:17). In neither text does this imply that Jesus is reduced to meaninglessness. In 10:17-18 his dying had been surrounded by his Father's love and command, and it had been used to underline his authority. And in 15:8-10 his fruit-bearing is likewise surrounded by his Father's love and commands, and his own love becomes a centre for others. But the descent does involve a diminution, and it means that if the branches are beginning to flourish, if people are developing and emerging, it is because in Jesus there has been poured out a divine love which makes people realize they have a home, a place in which to abide (T. Brodie, *John* 480).

SIXTH SUNDAY OF EASTER

First Reading   Acts 10:25-26, 34-35, 44-48

Up to this the Christian community had been exclusively Jewish. Now is a turning-point: the reception of the first Gentiles. That fact is so important that Luke has narrated it three times (10:1-48; 11:15; 15:6-18). The first of the three short excerpts from Acts 10 that make up our reading (25-26) tells of Peter's arrival at Cornelius' house and his refusal of a welcome befitting a heavenly messenger. The significance of Peter's coming to a pagan home and accepting hospitality (v. 48) is clearly brought out in the later objection of the 'circumcision party': 'Why did you go to uncircumcised men and eat with them' (11:4).

A Spirit-guided Peter is taking the first practical step in breaking down the ancient barrier between Jew and Gentile; both are one in

Christ. The verses 34-35 deal with the unlimited goodness of God. For some time now Jews had welcomed Gentiles who were prepared to take on full Mosaic observance (proselytes) and had tolerated 'God-fearers' (10:2). The Cornelius story touches on two basic problems involved in the admission of Gentiles into a Christian community. The first is whether or not they should be admitted without being obliged to the law of Moses. The other is whether a Jewish Christian might, without defilement, accept hospitality from and share table with a gentile Christian. The acuteness of this problem is evident in Gal 2:11-21. Luke's story provides answers to both of these problems.

In 44-48 we have Luke's 'Gentile Pentecost.' When Peter had finished his outline of the gospel (34-43) the Holy Spirit fell upon his Gentile hearers, and they spoke in tongues just as had the disciples at Pentecost (2:4). The amazement of the Jewish Christians (v. 45) is due to their realization that 'the gift of the Holy Spirit had been poured out even on the Gentiles.' Peter reacted to the situation by promptly baptizing these Gentiles. In a sense, this incident brings out the intimate connection between baptism and the Holy Spirit. Normally, the rite of baptism is the occasion of the gift of the Spirit, but a divine gift cannot be inexorably bound to a rite, a human element. The gift of the Spirit incorporates people into the Christian community; baptism is the external sign of this invitation. The Holy Spirit had designated these Gentiles as members of the Church; Peter had no option but to go ahead and formally enrol them.

Second Reading   1 Jn 4:7-10

Paul had told us that *agapé* is poured into the hearts of Christians (Rom 5:5). John insists that love is closely linked to the 'rebirth' of the believer, it is the proper attribute of his divine sonship: 'everyone who loves is born of God.' One loves because one has been born of God: this must be taken with great seriousness. God, in generating us, communicates to us his nature and his life. And, since 'one born of God' and 'one who loves' are equivalent designations of the Christian, we must take it that the one born of God has received a faculty of loving, a power of loving inherent in the divine nature in which one participates. This is the basis of brotherly/ sisterly love, which issues from the new nature. *Agapé* is the fruit of the divine 'seed' received at baptism.

The Christian must love because one has been born of God and because love comes from God; indeed, 'God is love' (v. 8). Is this to say that John is giving a definition of God? The context (4:7-9) is all-important. John is giving the fruit of his contemplation on the *manifestation* of God through history; above all, in the person, life and teaching of Jesus. In the Old Testament the relations of God with his people were marked by his *hesed*, his loving kindness. This characteristic is to be seen in the life and death of Jesus. As John meditates on the deeds of Jesus and on his teaching on love, he discovers that Christ is first and foremost the revealer of God as the only Son who reposes permanently in the bosom of the Father, who makes known the 'mystery' of God (Jn 1:8).

John does not say that God is loving or that he has loved, but that he is *love*. Nor does he say that love is in God, but that God is love. And if this is not, strictly speaking, a definition of God, it points to the distinctive attribute of God: love is of God's essence. If God engenders children he necessarily makes them share in his love – since he communicates to them his own life – in such a way that they also should be all love towards their brothers and sisters (vv. 7-8). It is Christ who has revealed and communicated to people the love of his Father (v. 9). Verse 10 takes up and deepens this thought. God had shown what love is by the sending of his Son into the world, in the death of his Son, and by forgiving all our sins. These three great mysteries of salvation – incarnation, redemption, grace – sum up the Gospel (Jn 3:16; 1 Jn 3:16).

Gospel   Jn 15:9-17

This is the second part of the passage of the Vine and the Branches; the first part was the gospel reading of the previous Sunday. In this second part the image of the vine has slipped into the background to reappear, momentarily, in the metaphor of fruit: 'I appointed you to go and bear fruit, fruit that will last' (v. 16). The intimate union of vine and branches, which the image had stressed, is now presented as a bond of love which should unite the disciples of Christ. His affection for them is a friendship which knows no limits; he asks that all of them should love one another as friends and bear outwardly the fruit of charity. To abide in him, to live with his life, is to abide in his love, in the love with which he loves his disciples as the Father has loved him. Jesus had loved his disciples before he had chosen them: they are to abide in that love which is his more than it is their own.

He goes on to show what abiding in his love means. The love of Jesus is modelled on that of the Father. The fidelity of the disciples, in abiding in the divine life and under the divine care, should model itself on the Son: as he has observed the commandments of his Father, so they should observe his. The parallel shows that love and obedience are mutually dependent: love arises out of obedience, obedience out of love. It follows that authentically Christian obedience can flourish only in an atmosphere of Christian love.

The 'commandments' of Jesus may be reduced to one: the commandment of love. Love is the sap of the Vine, the bond of existence within the unity of Father, Son and believers. Jesus had hitherto granted to his disciples, to his own, obvious marks of affection and that from the moment he had chosen them (see Jn 13:1). But now he is going to give them the supreme evidence of his love. Voluntary death, a life freely laid down, will be the characteristic proof of *agapé*, a force which moves one to sacrifice oneself for others. The statement that the greatest love is that which entails the supreme sacrifice is not, however, a definition of love; Jesus means that this sacrifice is the most expressive mark of it. The sense is: nobody can give a more convincing proof of love than one who offers one's life for those whom one loves. And when Jesus adds: 'You are my friends,' in effect he is telling them: Nobody has a greater love than that which I have for you. But it is also clear that this status of friend is not one which precludes obedient service.

Jesus sketches for his disciples the programme of the Christian apostolate: 'You did not choose me, but I chose you. And I appointed you to go and bear fruit, fruit that will last' (v. 16). It is he who chooses, calls, and appoints them; the initiative is entirely his. The principle of the apostolate is union with Jesus, but the disciples have a task to perform. And, by bearing the fruit that Jesus expects of them (fruit, even in the apostolate, which may well be hidden from eyes of flesh) they are true children of their heavenly Father. Then they can indeed address him as Abba; then they can pray to him with absolute confidence.

As for Jesus himself, he does not draw up for his disciples an elaborate code of laws; he has no wish to place a heavy burden on them. He desires to set them free, not to bind them. All that he commands them is reduced to one precept: 'Love one another.' But he is not thereby less demanding. The substitution of the rule of law can effectively stifle further generosity. At any rate, there is no getting away from the fact that the one thing Jesus has asked of us – the one thing that Jesus has *commanded* us to do – is to love one another.

THE ASCENSION OF THE LORD

First Reading   Acts 1:1-11

Luke follows contemporary practice when at the beginning of his second volume (Acts) he echoes the close of his gospel. The introduction to Acts passes from a brief recapitulation of the gospel (vv. 1-2) to a summary of the conversation of Jesus with his apostles after his resurrection (vv. 3-80, and a description of the Ascension (vv. 9-11).

In 1:6-8 the question of the apostles and the answer of the risen Jesus provide an answer to questions that had been asked many times before Luke wrote. Just as the conception of Jesus, 'Son of the Most High,' was due to the coming of the Holy Spirit on Mary (Lk 1:35), so the inception of the mission of the Church is brought about by a coming of the Holy Spirit on the apostles. In v. 8 Luke offers the programme his story is to follow. The phrase 'to the ends of the earth' harks back to Is 49:6, a prophecy of universal salvation. Rome, where the story will end (28:30-31), while not the end of the earth, is the centre of the Empire from which all roads lead to the end of the earth. In vv. 9-11 Luke describnes the departure of Jesus. The cloud is the vehicle which transports Jesus into the presence of God. The cloud of ascension will be the vehicle on which he will come at his parousia (v. 11). In the Gospel (24:50-51) the ascension is placed at the close of one Easter day of appearances; it comes as a solemn finale. In Acts the ascension comes at the end of forty days and has something of the flavour of a farewell. (It goes without saying that we must avoid any impression that our feast of Ascension is, or ever was, meant to mark a first return of the risen One to his Father). The ascension marks the close of an era. Jesus' journey to God has been completed by his 'being taken up' into heaven. It likewise signals the beginning of a new era, that of the mission of the Church which is about to be inaugurated.

Luke sets out to show how Jesus continues to act and teach after his resurrection through the Holy Spirit and through the followers of Jesus who will be his 'witnesses' to the ends of the earth. They are the nucleus of his Church which is the continuation of his presence and power. They no longer experience Jesus among them in the same way as before when they walked and talked with him during his earthly ministry. He is no longer earthbound; yet, while sharing in the glory of his Father, he continues to guide and direct his community. His followers receive a promise and a mission. The same Jesus, now in the glorious presence of his Father, will continue to be with them through the Spirit – a power enabling them to become Christ's 'witnesses.'

Through them the message of Jesus would reach out in ever-widening circles.

Second Reading   Eph 1:17-23

Here ascension is viewed as the logical conclusion and completion of the resurrection. The passage must be viewed against the background of the letter as a whole. The letter was occasioned by controversy over the cosmic role of Christ. There were some who claimed that he should be classed among a host of beings, intermediaries between God and humankind (v. 21). The author formulated his own view in contrast. The meaning of the resurrection-ascension event is that God has raised Jesus above those nebulous powers to his due position as crown of creation. First-born of all creation by nature, and first to be born form the dead by resurrection, he is first in every way (see Col 1:15-18). But what interests the author is the consequences of this for Christians. The Father's exaltation of Christ is evidence of 'his power for us who believe.' If Christians are baptized into Christ, they have risen with him, and with him have been exalted into heaven, and with him glorified (Rom 8:30). In another sense the transformation into the glorious Christ is still to come; at least it is yet to be revealed (Col 3:4). The basis of the christian hope in the ascension is that by it the Christ in whom we already abide is raised to the right hand of the Father and his power is at work in the Church

Second Reading *ad libitum*   Eph 4:1-13

The author of Ephesians, writing in the name of Paul, is addressing all believers. He describes himself as 'prisoner in the Lord,' as Paul had called himself 'slave of Jesus Christ' (Rom 1:1). The phrase 'the calling to which you have been called' evokes *ekklesia*, 'Church' – the assembly of those called. A life 'worthy of the calling' is one fostered by the virtues which make for peace and harmony within the community: humility, gentleness, patience, love. Unity is at the centre of God's saving plan. It is so because the one God is Father of all. The community is 'one body' (see 1 Corinthians 12:12-26), made so by the acknowledgment of one Lord, expressed in one Baptism.

Unity does not mean uniformity. There is need for a diversity of gifts within the church. Paul had stressed that fact (see 1 Corinthians 12-14 and Romans 12:3-8). Here the gifts are associated with preaching and teaching (vv. 11-12).

Obviously, this passage is chosen for Ascension-day because of vv. 8-10. The author cites Psalm 68:19 (which refers to the enthronement of God in Zion) and then interprets it as a reference to the heavenly enthronement of the ascended Christ and his subsequent bestowal of gifts on the church. Descent into 'the lower parts of the earth' (v. 9) can mean descent into the abode of the dead (see 1 Peter 3:19; 4:6) or incarnation on earth. The real significance of Christ's ascension is that he is no longer earth-bound but now fills the universe with his presence (v. 10).

Gospel Mk 16:15-20

Today it is commonly accepted that Mark ended his gospel at 16:8. It is evident, however, that even early Christians had been disconcerted by such a seemingly abrupt ending. It is, in fact, a classic example of the literary feature of unresolved conflict. Its purpose is to involve the reader who must complete the story for oneself. The most ambitious attempt to round off the gospel 'satisfactorily' is found in what is known as the Longer Ending – 16:9-20. That passage is no help to a proper understanding of Mark. It is little other than a pastiche of borrowings from the endings of the other gospels. For our reading look to Luke 14:36-49; John 20:19-23; Matthew 28:18-20.

The passage is concerned with the missionary charge of the risen Christ. The preachers of the good news are described as people at home in the world. Their preaching was to have the same effect as Jesus' own: it was to challenge people of all times and places to take a stand on the gospel, either believing (and being baptized, that is, initiated into a Christian community) or rejecting Christ in unbelief.

SEVENTH SUNDAY OF EASTER

First Reading Acts 1:15-17, 20-26

Jesus had chosen 'twelve of them, whom he also named apostles' (Lk 6:13). In the early Church 'apostle' was a broad designation and included women (see Rom 16:70. It is Luke who limits 'apostles' to the Twelve (except in Acts 14:4,14). 'The Twelve' were the nucleus of the new Israel. Just as the Jews believed that their roots could be traced back to the twelve patriarchs , so the new Israel is rooted in the Twelve. The defection of Judas had left a gap which must be filled. In vv. 21-22 we have an important statement of Luke's idea of what 'apostles' are. The chief duty of the 'apostle' – that is to say of one of the Twelve – is to witness to the resurrection; but he is also to witness to the public life of Jesus. To do this he must have been associated with

Jesus from his baptism until his ascension. Elsewhere Luke notes that knowledge of what happened in the ministry of Jesus must be allied with a clear understanding of its significance in the context of the divine plan of salvation (Lk 24:44-47).

The Twelve, therefore, provide continuity between the historical life of Jesus and the era of the Church. The role of the Twelve in the early Church is more important as symbolizing a principle of life than for their active contribution. For instance, Matthias is never again mentioned in the New Testament and, apart from Peter, we hear little, or nothing, of any of the others. Yet, the Twelve, with their specific qualifications, stand at the origin of the Christian Church and they have unique familiarity with the preaching Christ. The Twelve, as Twelve, have no successors.

Second Reading   1 Jn 4:11-16

The section 4:7-21 is on the theme of brotherly/sisterly love – vv. 7-10 form the second reading of the sixth Sunday of Easter. Today's passage introduces us to another characteristic of *agapé*: initiative. In real love, the love of God for us, it is he who takes the initiative. Jesus, in showing his love for us, laid down his life. The love of Christians, that love which is a sharing in the love of God, in the love of Christ, must have this quality of initiative. But our love of God cannot have the priority, the initiative, which is characteristic of *agapé*. God and Jesus have first loved us; we cannot love them in the same way. But we can take a loving initiative – towards our brothers and sisters. It is by loving his brethren that the Christian can love *as* God loves. In so far as one possesses, and puts into practice, love towards one's neighbour, God abides in one – as the Lord had promised (Jn 14:23).

For *agapé* does indeed mark the vital encounter of the Christian with our God: 'So we have known and believe the love that God has for us. God is love, and those who abide in love abide in God, and God abides in them' (v. 16). That 'we' refers to John's community who 'know and believe' – who are fully convinced, totally persuaded, who believe with all their being. The object of such solemn assurance is *agapé* in its biblical sense of *manifestation* of love, and especially in its Christian acceptance of a love properly divine, revealed and committed to humankind. It is the 'love which God has for us' because the manifestation of the divine love, object of the apostles' faith, is, in the concrete, the incarnate and redeeming in Christ. Faith discerns in the incarnate Word and presence and the nature of God; and it discovers that God is love. To believe in the love which God has among us is not only to confess Christ the Saviour who manifests this love; it is to accept it, to receive it, to be united to it and to live by it. It is, consequently, to incorporate the divine *agapé* to 'abide in love.' For the Christian is one who adheres to the revelation of the true God in the person of Jesus, who enters wholeheartedly into his plan of salvation and who is faithful to his commandments, especially that of brotherly/sisterly love (Jn 13:34-35).

Gospel   Jn 17:11-19

The most solemn prayer of Jesus in the New Testament is the priestly and royal prayer of Jn 17. Here, Jesus prays for himself (1-5), for his disciples (6-19) and for the community of the future who will 'believe through their word' (20-26). Our reading gives most of the prayer for the disciples. Jesus prays for his disciples present at the meal (chapter 13); he had taken care to make his Father known to them. Indeed they were the Father's gift to him in the first place – they know that the Father is the source of all that Jesus had done for them. Jesus has given them 'the word' of the Father: he has revealed the Father. Now he is the high priest.

Jesus had come into the world because God so loved the world that he gave his only Son (3:16), in order to save that world of humankind (v. 17). But the world would not face the light; the saving gift had been turned into judgment (3:18-19). Jesus who is now sending his disciples into the world to speak again his word of salvation, cannot pray for that hostile world (17:6-10). The disciples are being sent, as Jesus was sent, to challenge the world so that people might, at last, turn from darkness to light. He prays for those whom he leaves behind to carry on his work. He commits them to the Father's care and prays especially that they may know among themselves the warm communion of Father and Son. He reminds the Father that he, on earth, had kept and guarded them (vv. 11-12).

V. 13 opens the theme of Jesus' return to the Father. He speaks, while he is still with them, so that the disciples he is leaving behind may find the joy which follows on the fulfilment of the commandment of love. In bearing witness to the world they must, as he, suffer the world's hate. But that is a feature of their task, as it was of his. The Father will 'protect them from the evil one' – surely an echo of the Lord's Prayer (Mt 6:13).

The disciples will be consecrated in the truth, that is to say, in God's word – the truth that is Jesus' revelation of the unseen God. To be consecrated in the truth means to have a closer union with Jesus who is the Truth (14:6). They have accepted him and kept his word (17:6,14); now they must bring him and his word to others. Jesus sends them as he himself was sent; the mission of this community of the faith is to continue the mission of Jesus. By his death (his 'sanctification') Jesus will confirm and consecrate his disciples. His death is a sacrifice, the supreme high-priestly action on their behalf (vv. 16-19).

PENTECOST SUNDAY

First Reading
Acts 2:1-11

'When the day of Pentecost was fulfilled' – God's time has come, the beginning of the new era of the Spirit. Luke exploits Jewish tradition which characterized Pentecost as the feast of the giving of Torah on mount Sinai. According to the legend a mighty wind turned to fire and a voice proclaimed the Law. In a further refinement, the fire split into seventy tongues of fire corresponding to the seventy nations of the world: the Law was proclaimed, not only to Israel, but to all human-kind. Luke, too, has the mighty wind and tongues of fire coming upon the group of disciples.

The gift of tongues manifested the presence of the Spirit. Elsewhere (e.g. 10:46) Luke understands tongues as glossolalia, the same gift that Paul discusses in 1 Corinthians 12-14. Here he chooses to give 'tongues' another, symbolic meaning. The disciples spoke in 'other' tongues and the hearers heard them 'each of us in our own native language' (v. 8). And the hearers are 'from every nation under heaven' (v. 5). Luke asserts that the universal proclamation was not that of the Law, but is the proclamation of the Good News – a proclamation that has undone the sentence of Babel (Gen 11:1-9) and re-united the scattered nations. Here, in dramatic form, is the same assurance and the same commission to the Church as in Matthew 28:16-20. Luke's message, in this passage, is that on this day the last age begins, the time of the Church which, today, receives its life-principle, the Spirit. Present are witnesses from the whole world into which the Church is destined to spread – they see the irrestible power of God at work.

Second Reading
1 Cor 12:3-7.12-13

In chapters 12 to 14 of 1 Corinthians Paul is concerned with the charismatic gifts and especially with the Corinthians' attitude to them. Their predilection for tongues and prophecy had led to dissension – and Paul is determined to stress unity. He admits that the gifts are

manifold but inists that all have one and the same source – the Spirit.
He indicates three categories (gifts, services, activities) – his grouping
and listing are not meant to be exhaustive. The 'gifts' are those of
wisdom and knowledge and faith (v. 8); 'services' comprise prophecy,
discernment of spirits and tongues; 'activities' refer to healing and
miracles (vv. 9-10). He will insist that the purpose of these charisms
(as of any gift of the Spirit) is to 'build-up' the community (12:7;
14:4,12).

Further to underline the desired unity, he introduces the image of
the body (vv 12-13). A single body has many members, and each and
every member is part of one same body (v. 12). 'So it is with Christ'
– Paul means by 'Christ' the christian community (v. 13). Whatever
the social or religious origin of Christians, all are 'baptized into one
body'. The community has many individual members, and each
member is part of the one same community. Moreover, all are imbued
with the same Spirit (v. 13), the Spirit of unity (vv. 4-11). There is no
place for divisions within the community of Christ. Diversity is rooted
in unity.

Second Reading *ad libitum*   Gal 5:16-25

In Paul's theology Spirit and flesh are two realms standing in total
opposition to each other (see Romans 7:4-8:8). The flesh seeks to
please itself; the Spirit seeks to please God. This leads to two
contrasting lifestyles. The 'works of the flesh' (vv. 19-21) and the
'fruit of the Spirit' (v. 22) – catalogues of vices and virtues – illustrate
effectively the two lifestyles. Indeed, this passage, Galatians 5:19-23,
greatly helps a proper understanding of *sarx* ('flesh') and *pneuma*
('Spirit') throughout Paul.

After his list of the fruits of the Spirit Paul observes: 'There is no
law against such things' (v. 24). In v. 18 he declared: 'If you are led by
the Spirit you are not under the Law.' Led and guided by the Spirit of
Christ the Galatians need no law to tell them to 'do this' or 'avoid that.'
Two conclusions follow in vv. 24-25. Those who are in Christ have
crucified the flesh with its passions and desires: by association with the
crucified Christ, faithful Christians have put the power of the flesh to
death. They can no longer seriously contemplate that lifestyle. Secondly, the Galatians are reminded that if they really live by the Spirit,
then they should follow the Spirit's lead. Note v. 16 – 'Live by the
Spirit, I say, and do not gratify the desires of the flesh.' Christian
morality is not response to law, nor does it become something
automatic. It has to be actively lived under the guidance of the Spirit.

Gospel   Jn 20:19-23

Our first reading had shown Luke's version of the birth of the Church; our gospel reading gives John's version of it. On Easter Day the risen Jesus comes to his disciples, breathes the Holy Spirit upon them and sends them out on a mission of forgiveness. Note in Peter's sermon, which is a prophetic explanation of the Pentecost event, the statement: 'Repent, and be baptized every one of you in the name of Jesus Christ so that your sins may be forgiven; and you will receive the gift of the Holy Spirit' (Acts 2:38). Luke and John are saying the same thing: the risen Lord gives the gift of the Spirit and inaugurates the mission of the Church. It is a striking example of the primarily theological concern of the New Testament writers.

It is significant that in John the Church is founded by the risen Lord. When Jesus breathes upon the disciples it shows that a new creation is taking place. Just as God made 'the man' into a living being by breathing life into him (Gen 2:7) and as in Ezekiel 37 the dead bones of Israel are stirred to life by the breath of God, so the life of the Church comes from the breath of the Spirit of Jesus. This is the new or eternal life, which Jesus brings to being, which plays such a major part in John's gospel. In this sense everything is already accomplished when Jesus breathes life into his disciples.

Gospel *ad libitum*   Jn 15:26-27; 16:12-15

In the farewell discourses (Jn 14-16) we have five passages in which the Holy Spirit appears as the 'Paraclete' (or Advocate, Helper) – in the last of them (16:13-14) under the synonymous title of 'the Spirit of Truth.' This passage and 15:26-27 form our reading. The Paraclete, sent by Jesus, will not only enlighten, he will be the primary witness to Jesus, the support of all other witnesses. Jesus had been speaking (15:18-25) of the world hating his disciples in the same manner that it had hated him. Then he adds: 'When the Advocate comes, whom I will send to you from the Father ... he will testify on my behalf. You also are to testify ... ' (vv. 26-27). Here is the reason why the disciples must expect to encounter hatred and maltreatment. The Paraclete among them represents Jesus' abiding presence in humankind. And, in hating the disciples in whom the Paraclete dwells, the world is striking at Jesus' uncompromising presence. In this way the Paraclete 'bears witness' to Jesus.

In 16:12-15 we find the role of the Paraclete as teacher of the disciples. Jesus had told them, in 16:12 – 'I still have many things to say to you, but you cannot bear them now.' Only after his glorification could there be an understanding of what was said and done during the ministry. After the resurrection the Paraclete will guide them into the full meaning of what Jesus has said. If he will lead them into *all* the truth, he will not speak on his own. There is no new revelation. Jesus is *the* revelation of the Father, the Word of God. But what does it mean that the Paraclete 'will declare to you the things that are to come'? Rather than any fresh revelation this means a spelling out for successive generations of the contemporary significance of what Jesus has said and done.

In John, the Spirit – under the title of Paraclete – is presented as the divine power that continues and completes Jesus' ministry. The Spirit is the perpetuation of Jesus' presence among his followers. The activity of the Spirit is to reveal the mind of Christ, to bring out the implication of his person and his message. In John's thought, the Holy Spirit is the gift of the glorified Lord, the Paraclete who is to take the place of Christ among humankind. And if John calls the Spirit 'another Paraclete' (14:16; see 1 John 2:1) it is because he is, in a true sense, another presence of Jesus. 'As yet there was no Spirit, because Jesus was not yet glorified' (Jn 7:39). If, then, the Spirit can only come when Jesus departs, the Paraclete is the presence of the 'absent' Jesus. The risen Jesus is identified with the life-giving Spirit (see 1 Cor 15:45). His presence now among his own will not be in the figure of the Man of Galilee, but as the life-giving Spirit. As Paraclete, the glorified Lord is abidingly present in his Church. In this way, the later Christian is assured that, in a real sense, one is no further removed from the time of Jesus than the earlier Christian.

The Solemnities of the Lord

THE MOST HOLY TRINITY
SUNDAY AFTER PENTECOST

First Reading   Deut 4:32-34, 39-40

It is no easy matter to choose a fitting reading from the Old Testament for the feast of the Holy Trinity since the Old Testament has no intimation of that theology.

The chosen text speaks about the power and glory of God and of his nonetheless close relationship with his people. No other nation ever enjoyed such an intimate relationship with its gods. No other people could claim that the God who created heaven and earth involved himself in their history and remained present to them through his word.

Privilege, however, carries with it obligation and the second part of today's reading reminds the Israelites of the duties that spring from their relationship with God. They can never forget the moral standards which their status as God's people imposes on them. They can never ignore the laws and commandments which formulate the demands of their religion and which enable Israelites of all generations to discern the kind of conduct that pleases God and ensures his continued favour. This is the relationship of love which God wants to exist between himself and his children. Later revelation will show that it reflects the intimate relationship that exists between Father and Son. In and through the Son we are brought into a relationship of childhood with God, our Parent.

Second Reading   Rom 8:14-17

The whole of chapter 8 of Romans is taken up with the theme of life in the Spirit. The Christian who lives in Christ (8:1) also lives in the sphere of the work of the Spirit who reveals Christ and imparts salvation (8:9). By the indwelling Spirit, Christians are made children of God, sharing the divine life; this is the reason why they can address their Father with the intimate title used by Jesus himself: *Abba* (8:14-16). Now the undreamt-of effect of God's gift of his Spirit emerges: it is our adoption as God's children, our participation in the sonship of Christ. The Spirit who animates and activates Christians, who is the source of our new life, makes us children of God.

The 'Spirit' of God (or of Christ) is not a 'spirit' of slavery, slave-mentality – a play on the word *pneuma*. It is the Spirit who brings men and women into union with Christ and establishes them in a special filial relationship to the Father. Not surprisingly, the Spirit must bring the Christian to an awareness of this extraordinary situation, one beyond the bounds of human expectation. It is an exercise of divine condescension. The God who had adopted us as his children awakens in us an awareness of that fact, and then gently helps us in our wondering acknowledgment of that fact: Abba! It has about it something of the flavour of a mother teaching her little child to pray. There is the same quality of love that strips the exercise of any condescension. The close of v. 17 brings us firmly down to earth. True, we are indeed children of God and fellow heirs with Christ - 'if, in fact, we suffer with him.' That is his way: 'Was it not necessary that the Christ should suffer these things and then enter into his glory?' (Lk 24:26). There is no *Christian* way to glory other than his.

Gospel   Mt 28:16-20

The glorious Son of Man commissions his Church. A 'mountain' is a place of revelation – an apt setting. The 'eleven' worshipped their Lord – yet some 'doubted'. Matthew is drawing for his community a picture of every Christian community – believers caught between adoration and doubt. Jesus solemnly declares that, by his death-resurrection, he has been given, by the Father, total power over the universe. He is, therefore, in a position to launch a universal mission, and he duly commissions his representatives who are to achieve his task. Consequently, he sends them into the world to make disciples of 'all nations.' During his ministry Jesus limited his concern to Israel; in this new era the good news is for all.

One becomes a *disciple* through baptism in the name of Father, Son, Spirit – a triadic formula which doubtlessly reflects the baptismal liturgy of Matthew's Church. Disciples must be taught Jesus' commands.

> The teaching of Jesus will encompass much of what was in the Mosaic Law. But the Church teaches these commands not because they come from Moses but because they come from Jesus ... The command of Jesus – one might almost say Jesus himself – is the ultimate law of morality, the criterion for deciding what is will of God' (J. Meier, *Matthew*, 372)

Matthew skilfully rounds off his Gospel by catching up the God-with-us (1:23) of his prologue: the all-powerful Son of Man promises to be with us always. It is an encouraging word to the Church of our day – a Church seemingly floundering about.

It is important to be clear that this solemn commission, so theologically important, is *not* historically a command of Jesus to his Church at its beginning. Acts 12-15 and Galatians 2 show that reception of Gentiles and the mission to them were bitterly resisted. This commission voices the experience of a Church that had become open to all, a Church tranquilly convinced that it had become what the Lord had meant it to be.

CORPUS CHRISTI
THURSDAY AFTER HOLY TRINITY

First Reading
Ex 24:3-8

This passage describes the ratification of the Sinai covenant between God and Israel. Two dominant ideas emerge, namely the significance of the sacrificial blood, and the place of the word of God in the ceremony. The constant pattern of word and event throughout the Old Testament is well illustrated in this passage. Blood, symbol of life, belonged exclusively to God. Here the blood of the sacrificed animals is sprinkled by Moses, half of it on the altar of God and half on the people. The prophetic word spoken by Moses interpreted the event for the people. The word of the Lord is accepted by the people in their promise to observe all the commands of their God – not the acceptance of a legal system, but an acceptance in faith of the gift of life. By this response in faith the people bind themselves to God. He is their God who has manifested himself to them and has chosen them as his people.

The phrase which explains the choice of this passage for today's Mass is 'the blood of the covenant', a phrase which is repeated in the gospel reading. On Sinai the blood was, in some sort, a sacramental sign of the relationship that now existed between God and his chosen people. At the Last Supper, where a new people of God was established and a new covenant sealed, a new relationship between the Lord and his people was ratified with the sacrificial blood of Christ, and a rite was instituted which would be a perpetual reminder of the saving death of Christ and of the intimate bond of fellowship that exists between him and his covenant community.

Second Reading
Heb 9:11-15

In 9:11-28 the author of Hebrews presents the sacrifice of Christ as being efficacious and definitive. The perfection of Christ's priesthood and cult is contrasted with the imperfection of the old levitical priesthood, and, in a framework of typology and imagery drawn from the Old Testament, a theology of the saving word of Christ is propounded. The great barrier of access to God is sin and Hebrews uses details of the ritual of the Day of Atonement to draw typological parallels with the 'heavenly liturgy' of Christ – his work of salvation.

The 'greater and more perfect tent not made with hands' is either the heavens through which Christ passed in order to arrive before God in the Holy of Holies, or Christ's glorified body in which he entered heaven (v. 11). If it is by virtue of his own blood that he entered into the heavenly sanctuary once for all, it is by the same means that he has won for us an eternal salvation – 'eternal' because it belongs to the heavenly, eternal source of perfect efficacy (v. 12). Vv. 13-14 constitute an argument *a fortiori:* if the old liturgy with its animal victims could achieve a reconciliation with God which affected the 'outer person', so much more will the effects of Christ's liturgy with himself as victim reach the 'inner person.' 'Through an eternal spirit': the divine power, the principle behind Christ's work. Jesus had become priest 'through the power of indestructible life' (7:16); it is to this life which cannot be destroyed that 'the eternal spirit' corresponds.

What the statement means is that Jesus' self-offering is a heavenly, not an earthly, reality. It is offered through an eternal spirit because it is offered in that new, heavenly sphere of existence that he entered at the time of his resurrection and exaltation. And it is this same 'eternal spirit' permeating the saving work of Christ which is the ultimate reason for that work being able not only to cleanse the 'flesh' of people like the liturgy of the old 'fleshly' rituals but to bring about that internal, spiritual renovation of conscience and newness of heart (8:10) which enable us to come to heavenly glory.

Gospel   Mk 14:12-16.22-26

The account of preparation for the passover (vv. 12-16) is quite like that of preparation for the entry to Jerusalem (11:1-6). Here, as there, two disciples are sent off with a precise description of the situation they will encounter and are told exactly what to say. And here, too, all turned out as the Teacher had assured them. Here only in Mark is the last supper designated a passover meal.

The phrase 'While they were eating' (v. 22) resumes the meal episode after the warning of betrayal (vv. 17-21). Jesus 'took bread', 'blessed', 'broke', 'gave': the same actions and the very same words as in both feeding stories (6:41; 8:6). Then the disciples 'did not understand about the loaves' (6:52; see 8:17-21); now the mystery is being revealed. Jesus is the 'one loaf' (8:14) for Jews and Gentiles because, as he tells them, his body is being given and his blood poured out for Jew and Gentile (vv. 23-24).

'This is my body'; Paul (1 Cor 11:22) adds 'which is for you'. But this is already firmly implied in Mark both through the repeated references to Jesus' death since the beginning of the passion narrative and the explicit statement in the cup saying. 'This is my blood of the covenant' − Exodus 24:8 is certainly in mind: 'See the blood of the covenant that the Lord has made with you.' By the sprinkling of sacrificial blood the people of Israel shared in the blessings of the covenant given at Sinai. Likewise this blood of the cup will be poured out 'for many' (a semitism, meaning 'all'): a new covenant is being forged and sealed whose blessings are offered to all. The death of Jesus founds the new community. The Last Supper helps us to understand the meaning of Jesus' death on Calvary.

The whole of the Supper narrative (vv. 22-25) is based on the eucharistic liturgical tradition of Mark's Church. While less explicit than the Pauline tradition (1 Cor 11:23-26) it has the same meaning. In both the body and blood are given: the context is sacrificial death. In both the blood seals a new covenant. In both the eucharistic meal anticipates the eschatological banquet of the kingdom. And if Mark does not have Paul's 'Do this in remembrance of me', the eucharistic liturgy of his Church was the living fulfilment of that word.

THE MOST SACRED HEART OF JESUS
FRIDAY AFTER THE SECOND SUNDAY
AFTER PENTECOST

First Reading   Hos 11:3-4.8-9

Hosea has to warn his nation, Israel, of approaching Assyrian danger; he has to speak of judgment. But his lead idea remains the divine goodness (*hesed*) which explains the origin of Israel (11:1-9) and which will have the last word. Israel is Yahweh's own son, born to him in Egypt. In bold imagery the prophet shows the divine parent as a doting father playing with and feeding and guiding the faltering steps of his precious first-born. What he gets in return is base ingratitude (vv. 2,7). The heart of God is wounded, not in resentment but with anguished love for a people set on self-destruction. 'How can I give you up!'

Paul knew the same God as Hosea. When he, in his turn, agonised over the obduracy of his people he can ask: 'Has God rejected his people?' and answers with the whole conviction: 'God has not rejected his people whom he foreknew' (Rom 11:1-2). Hosea and Paul had taken with utmost seriousness the declaration of their God: 'I am God and no mortal ... and I will not come in wrath' (Hos 11:9). It is tragic that so much of Christian tradition has looked to a 'God' who is all too 'human'. And that despite the fact that the true humanness of God-made-man underwrites the truth of Hosea's declaration.

Second Reading   Eph 3:8-12.14-19

Ephesians 3:1-19 is a prayer of intercession. The object of the prayer is not expressed until v. 16; before that 'Paul' speaks of his apostolic role (vv. 2-13). His demand on his readers' behalf (v. 16) is similar to that of 1:17-19. It is a prayer for their progress in faith and love and their comprehension of the -'mystery' so that they may accomplish their vocation as the 'fullness' of God, that is, as Church (vv. 16-19). 'Paul' makes three petitions, as he prays for strength (v. 16), faith and love (v. 17), understanding (vv. 18-19).

'That he may grant that you may be strengthened in your inner being' (v. 16). This is a strength that comes to us as gift through the Spirit of God – 'the Spirit helps us in our weakness' (Rom 8:26). It is a strength that is an empowerment of the inner person, in the true core of one's personality, at the point where one relates directly with God. 'That Christ may dwell in your hearts through faith, as you are being rooted and grounded in love' (v. 17). Christ-faith-love: these three words belong together. Through faith and love Christ *dwells* in our hearts. That is why we may 'know the love of Christ that surpasses knowledge (v. 19). 'I am loved': that is the knowledge which surpasses all others. That love was made visible to us on the cross. And if we attain this knowledge – rather, if it is granted to us – then our response must echo that of Paul: 'I regard everything as loss because of the surpassing value of knowing Christ Jesus my Lord' (Phil 3:8).

Gospel   Jn 19 31-3

The Beloved Disciple speaks here as a witness to a revelation that is important for all the Christians whom he symbolizes. It is very probable that in this flow of water from the side of Jesus (from within him) John saw the fulfilment of Jesus' prophecy. For the flow of water coloured by Jesus' blood fulfils the promise of 7:38-39: 'As the Scripture says, "From within him shall flow rivers of living water". Now he said this about the Spirit ... ' Thus, for John the flow of water is another prophetic symbol of the giving of the Spirit, carrying on the theme of v. 30.

On a secondary level the flow of blood and water symbolizes the origin of the sacraments of Baptism and Eucharist through which the life of Jesus is communicated to the Christian. Blood and water flow from the dead Jesus. The drama of the cross does not end in death but in a flow of life that comes from death. The death of Jesus on the cross is the beginning of Christian life. Finally, reference to the passover lamb of which a bone should not be broken (Ex 12:10,46) forms an inclusion with the 'Lamb of God' heralded by the Baptist at the beginning of the gospel (1:29).

Ordinary Time

Introduction to the Liturgical Season

GOSPELS

For the second Sunday in ordinary time, every year, the Gospel is from John and continues the theme of revelation or manifestation which ran through the Christmas season. In Year B, we hear the passage about Andrew saying, 'We have found the Messiah'.

Then, beginning with the third Sunday in ordinary time, there is the semicontinuous reading of one of the synoptic gospels each year. The year of Mark, Year B, includes five readings from the sixth chapter of John.

The readings from Mark run from the beginning of the public ministry of Jesus to the eschatological passages which precede the accounts of the Passion. The aim is to enable us to appreciate the different perspectives found in each Gospel. The English lectionary (Vol. I, pp. xlviii-xlix) includes useful tables which show how the texts in the lectionary are related to the overall structure of each Gospel. These tables let us see how the lectionary takes account of the combination of narrative passages and discourses in Matthew's Gospel of the Kingdom; the gradual revelation of the mystery of the Son of Man in Mark; the journey towards Jerusalem in Luke.

FIRST READINGS

The First Readings are taken from the Old Testament, and are chosen to harmonize with the Gospels. They provide quite an amount of material, and are an invitation to become more familiar with the Old Testament.

SECOND READINGS

The Second Readings (the readings 'from an apostle') are semi-continuous, beginning on the second Sunday. They are from Paul, James, and Hebrews; Peter and John are read during Eastertide and Christmastide. The First Letter to the Corinthians is divided up between the three years. Hebrews is divided between Years B and C.

The solemnities of Trinity, Corpus Christi, and the Sacred Heart are provided with suitable readings.

The last Sunday of the year celebrates Christ the Universal King. The readings this year present quite a striking juxtaposition of texts.

There is the Gospel of the haunting encounter between Jesus and Pilate (from John). The First Reading presents the figure of the one like a son of man from Daniel, and it is the Second Reading especially which gives voice to the joy and thanksgiving of the Church, showing Christ as the Ruler of the kings of the earth (Apocalypse).

Philip Gleeson OP

Sundays of Ordinary Time

SECOND SUNDAY OF THE YEAR

First Reading   1 Sam 3:3-10.19

God always filled the major role in the Hebrew view of history. People played their part in the building up of Israel in response to a call of Yahweh. Samuel was the instrument through whom Israel received its first kings (1 Sam 8-12). Samuel, himself conservative, opened a whole new chapter in the development of Israel. Up to now there was a loose tribal confederacy; under the king the tribes were to be, for a while at least, built into a nation. This shift of history through the agency of Samuel could only happen by Yahweh's choice.

The boy Samuel, an answer to a mother's fervent prayer, had been, by her, in thankfulness, dedicated to the Lord and was brought up by the priest Eli at the sanctuary of Shiloh (1 Sam 1). Our reading gives the story of the boy's call to be a prophet. The insistent word of the Lord came through again and again until Eli was convinced that it was the Lord who called. This episode, charmingly related, is the model for all later prophetic vocations. The initiative is firmly with God; the 'call' is his. And being a call it elicits a response, to be freely given. And since God always speaks with purpose, every word will have its effect. No authentic word of his prophet will God let 'fall to the ground.'

Human response to God's call comes through willing obedience. Samuel will later remind Saul that obedience is better than sacrifice (1 Sam 15:22). The same sentiment is expressed in today's Responsorial Psalm (Ps 40). It is God's gift to furnish humans with an 'open ear' – a heart responsive to his will. Christ, true prophet, whose food was to do the will of the Father (Jn 4:34), was the model of joyous response (Heb 10:5-6). His followers are called to share in faithfulness to God's purpose. Through obedience the prophetic mission, begun in Samuel and lived perfectly by Jesus, is kept alive in the world. It is noteworthy that this first reading and responsorial psalm are read in the liturgy of religious profession. The self-dedication of religious to 'the affairs of the Lord' is a sharing in the obedience of Christ to the Father. And through this obedience their way of life bears prophetic witness.

Second Reading   1 Cor 6:13-15.17-20

Until the sixth Sunday of the year inclusively, second readings are from 1 Corinthians. Paul visited Corinth for the first time on his second missionary journey. There he founded a church and remained for eighteen months, from winter of 50 A.D. to the summer of 52. Later, at Ephesus (54-57), he was informed of rival parties and of scandals in the Corinthian church; and the Corinthians, in a letter to him, had submitted a number of questions.

In 1 Corinthians he faced up to the unsettled situation of the community and answered its questions. Notable features of his reply consider the Christian attitude to marriage and celibacy, the authentic doctrine of the Eucharist, and the first appearance of his teaching on the body of Christ. He uncompromisingly rejects the wisdom of the world, the foolish self-sufficiency of human thought. It is foolish because it ignores humankind's complete dependence on God; that is why he is desirous of knowing nothing except 'Jesus Christ and him crucified.'

While it may be that his experience of dismal failure at Athens just before his departure for Corinth (Acts 17:32-33) had influenced Paul's approach, it must be that the real motivation of his uncompromising preaching of Christ crucified was because he had come to a profound understanding of the cross. He realized that here the ornate language of Greek rhetoric would be wholly out of place. The gospel message, in its starkness, would speak for itself: God redeemed the world through the death of his Son on a cross and he, Paul, was sent by Christ to preach the Good News of this redemption. By human standards it is foolishness: it is folly to look for redemption to one who could not save himself from death. 'Theology of the cross' sounds grim. Yet, theology of the cross, as preached by Paul, is positive and full of hope. That is because his starting-point is the graciousness of God – or, as he calls it, the 'foolishness' of God. This foolishness of God, expressed in the cross of Jesus, shows God's commitment to humankind; he is indeed a God bent on the salvation of humankind.

The problem which faces Paul in 1 Corinthians 6:12-20 is that of casual copulation with a prostitute. It arises because of a conviction of some Corinthians that they, possessing a special 'wisdom', had been raised to a spiritual sphere in which everything material was irrelevant and where no corporeal action had any moral value. In their eyes, everything was permissible. They could eat what and where they pleased (even in pagan temples); they could sleep with whom they pleased. They flouted convention on principle. Paul takes up in turn, and qualifies, three slogans of the Corinthians.

He begins with the slogan: 'All things are lawful for me' (v. 12). Taken literally this is destructive of community – and, for Paul, true

Christian community is all-important. He points out that 'not all things are beneficial': what I want may be hurtful to the community. And if the community breaks apart one is back in slavery to Sin (Rom 6:17-18) and Paul will not have this enslavement (v. 12). To the slogan, 'Food is meant for the stomach and the stomach for food' (v. 13) he retorts that the body is not for immorality but for the Lord, and the Lord for the body. The proof is that God raised Jesus from the dead (v. 14): God's deed refutes the Corinthians' assertion that the body is of no concern. The body is morally relevant. With his repeated 'Do you not know' (vv. 15,16,19) Paul draws out implications of his own authentic teaching. A Christian belongs *wholly* to Christ; and casual sexual intercourse is manifestly un-Christlike conduct (v. 15).

The third Corinthian slogan: 'Every sin that a person commits is outside the body' (not 'every other sin,' RSV) (v. 18), reflects their view that sin can only be in the 'spiritual' sphere. Paul has already reinstated the body and so can firmly declare that the immoral person sins against one's own body (v. 18) because one does not use it for the purpose intended by God. In casual fornication the other person is not empowered to grow but is used, as an object, for selfish gratification.

In conclusion Paul asks: 'Do you not know that your body is a temple of the Holy Spirit within you?' (v. 19) God's presence in Jesus was in and through the physical, historical existence of Jesus. Similarly, God's presence in his members (v. 15) is in their bodily lives. Bought at a great price (v. 20), the physical death of Jesus, Christians belong to Christ (3:23). They glorify God, do God's will, by living Christian lives which cannot be lived otherwise than in the body.

Gospel
Jn 1:35-42

Before embarking on his gospel proper, John (1:19-51) brings forward a series of witnesses who bear testimony to the Messiah in a variety of messianic titles. John the Baptist calls him the 'Lamb of God' (vv. 29-36) and 'God's Chosen One' (v. 34). Andrew speaks of him as the 'Messiah' (v. 41). For Philip he is 'he about whom Moses in the Law and also the prophets wrote' (v. 45): and Nathanael exclaimed: 'You are the Son of God; you are the King of Israel' (v. 49). Jesus himself rounds off the list by adding his own designation: Son of Man (v. 51).

As John's account of the call of Andrew and Simon, this gospel reading is related to the call of Samuel (first reading). With Samuel, Israel had reached a turning-point in its history; Christ's coming was the turning-point of history itself. John the Baptist is still preaching his baptism of penance by the Jordan and points out Jesus, the Lamb of

God, to two of his followers. The designation 'Lamb of God' suggests the Passover lamb (see 1 Cor 5:7). More immediately, it seems we should look to the 'Servant of Yahweh.' In Is 53:7 the suffering servant is likened to a 'lamb led to the slaughter' and it is noteworthy that the Aramaic word *talya* can be translated 'lamb' or 'servant.' The Baptist points to the Lamb who is the Servant who suffers and dies for the sins of the world (Jn 1:29). John's fate and mission, in his own words, were that he should decrease, pass from the centre of the stage, so preparing the road for the Redeemer. Here we see him lose two of his followers to Jesus. This self-less type of witness characterizes the Baptist's testimony in the Fourth Gospel.

'What are you looking for?' Jesus asks and bids the seekers 'come and see.' To 'come to' Jesus (3:18-21) and to 'see' him (14:9) is the active movement towards the person of the Lord and the understanding in faith of who he is. Though the first who answered the call was Andrew, attention focuses on the initiative of Jesus who designated (by a significant change of name) Peter for a future supportive role in the Christian community.

THIRD SUNDAY OF THE YEAR

From this Sunday until the thirty-third Sunday inclusive, gospel readings are from the Gospel of Mark. In fact, practically the whole of Mark will be read. While we begin, here, at 1:14, we should note that the passage 1:1-8 was read on the Second Sunday of Advent (p. 15) and 1:7-11 on the Baptism of the Lord (p. 51).

THE GOSPEL OF MARK

Underestimated from early times because of its brevity (almost all of Mark is found in Matthew and Luke) in our day the gospel of Mark has come into its own. Above all, the evangelist Mark stands side by side with Paul as a stalwart proclaimer of a theology of the ctross, a *theologia crucis*. And, congenial to modern christology, the Marcan Jesus is the most human of all. Mark sets the pattern of a gospel: it is concerned with christology and discipleship. Jesus is Son of God, that is, God-appointed leader of the new covenant people; he is 'son of man', the human one who came to serve, the one faithful unto death. One who has come to terms with the cross (with the meaning of his death) can know him and can confess him – like the centurion (15:39). His disciples did not understand him before Calvary. The Christian reader of the first century, and of today, is being challenged to come to terms with the love of God shown forth in the cross of Jesus.

THE SETTING

The view that Mark had written in Rome about 65 A.D. and for people in Rome, had long been the prevalent one. But it had not gone unchallenged because the traditional data which point to this provenance and date are of uncertain worth. We are forced back to the text of the gospel: to an anonymous writing of the first Christian century. The author is not named in the gospel; the traditional name Mark was quite common. Nothing in the gospel points necessarily to a Roman origin. We can be sure that 'Mark' wrote for a specific community and in face of the actual circumstances of that community. We are left to tease out a plausible setting for, and a likely date of, his gospel.

Today we confidently set the writing of the gospel close to the events of the Jewish war of 66-70 A.D. A careful reading of Mark 13 would suggest a date soon after the Roman destruction of Jerusalem in 70 A.D.

With a growing number of recent scholars I would propose that Mark was written to and for a Christian community somewhere in the Roman province of Syria. This would offer a setting close to the tragic events of the war. The community may even have harboured Christian refugees from the conflict, making it that more immediate.

The gospel of Mark, after an introduction (1:1-13) which sets the stage for the drama that follows, is built up of two complementary parts. The first (1:14 - 8:30) is concerned with the mystery of Jesus' identity; it is dominated by the question, 'Who is Jesus?' The emphasis in this part of Mark is on Jesus' miracles; the teaching is largely parabolic. The second part (8:31-16:8) is concerned with the messianic destiny of Jesus: a way of suffering and death. The emphasis in this second half of Mark is on Jesus' teaching which, now directed at his disciples, builds upon their recognition of him as Messiah and is concerned mainly with the nature of his messiahship and with the suffering it will entail for himself and for his followers.

THE PLOT

As in most stories, the events and actions of the Marcan story involve conflict, and Jesus is the immediate cause of the conflict. We may illustrate by glancing, firstly, at conflicts between Jesus and the authorities, and then at those between Jesus and his disciples.

Jesus versus the Authorities

The authorities involved are the religious and political leaders – and in relation to them Jesus is at a disadvantage. Mark does indeed show Jesus having facile authority over evil spirits – the exorcisms – and over nature – the stilling of the storm. But Jesus' authority does not extend to lording it over people. Still, what Jesus says and does challenges directly the authorities of Israel. For their part, the authorities view themselves as defenders of God's Law. They contend that Jesus assumes unwarranted legal authority for himself, interprets the law in a manner they consider illegal, and disregards many religious customs. They respond by uttering charges against him.

Jesus, for his part, had been anointed to usher in God's rule (1:9-11). The issue for him was how to get the authorities to 'see' God's authority in his actions and teaching. The narrator skilfully created tension and suspense. By the end of the five conflict-stories (2:1-3:6) the sides are clearly established (3:6). The impending clash with the authorities is kept in sight during the journey to Jerusalem (8:27-1):52). The climactic confrontation in Jerusalem comes quickly. It is noteworthy that the first accusation against Jesus was a charge of blasphemy: 'Why does this fellow speak in this way? It is blasphemy!' (2:7) – thus, from the start of the story Jesus walks a tightrope. Nevertheless, the reader recognizes that Jesus is firmly in control. At the trial he himself volunteers the evidence his accusers need. ' "Are you the Messiah, the Son of the Blessed One?" Jesus said, "I am" ' (14:61-62). Jesus, not the authorities, determines his fate.

The narrator resolves the conflict between Jesus and the authorities only when they condemn Jesus and put him to death. It is an ironic resolution. The authorities have, unwittingly, co-operated in bringing to pass God's purpose. By means of this ironic resolution the story depicts Jesus as the real authority in Israel. The authorities condemn as blasphemy Jesus' claim to be Son of God but, since in the story world, Jesus' claim is true, they are the ones guilty of blasphemy. The irony is hidden from the authorities, but it is not hidden from the reader. The reader knows that Jesus will be established in power and the authorities condemned (8:28-9:1; 13:24-27, 30-32; 14:62).

Jesus and the Disciples

At stake in the conflict with the disciples is whether Jesus can make them good disciples. The disciples struggle at every point to follow Jesus but are simply overwhelmed by both him and his demands. Jesus' efforts to lead the disciples to understand are matched by their fear and their hardness of heart. Theirs is not the determined opposition to Jesus of the authorities – they are trying to be his followers. They do consistently misunderstand Jesus' teaching and end up by failing him utterly. Yet, they had followed him to Jerusalem.

Jesus just cannot lead his chosen disciples (effectively, the Twelve) to understand him, cannot get them to do what he expects of them. In an effort to bring them to realize how dense and blind they are, he hurls challenging questions at them (4:13, 40; 8:17-21, 33; 9:19; 14:37, 41) – and is met with silence. He tries to prepare them for his impending death and for his absence. He knows that they will fail him in Jerusalem; yet he seeks to urge them to stand by him (14:37, 41-42). The outer conflict reflects a conflict within the disciples: they want to be loyal to Jesus, but not at the cost of giving up everything, least of all their lives. The fact remains that readers of the gospel are most likely to empathize with those same disciples. By doing so the readers come to discern their own inadequacies. They find comfort in the realization that, although the disciples fail him, Jesus remains unflinchingly faithful to them.

Jesus does not, however, manage to make them faithful disciples. They failed him – and the question stands: will they learn from their failure and, beyond his death, at last become truly followers of him? When Jesus had warned his disciples of their impending failure (14:26-31) he had added a reassuring word: 'After I am raised up, I will go before you to Galilee' (14:28). That word is then caught up in the message of the 'young man' at the tomb: Go, tell his disciples and Peter that he is going ahead of you to Galilee; there you will see him, just as he told you' (16:7). Throughout the gospel 'to see' Jesus means to have faith in him. What Mark is saying is that if the community is to 'see' Jesus, now the Risen One, it must become involved in the mission to the world that 'Galilee' signified. Galilee was the place of mission, the arena where Jesus' exorcisms and healings had broken the bonds of evil. There, too, the disciples had been called and commissioned to take up Jesus' proclamation of the coming rule of God. 'Galilee' is the place of the universal mission. But no disciple is ready to proclaim the Gospel until she or he has walked the way to Jerusalem (10:32-34) and encountered the reality of the cross.

THE CHARACTERS

Characters are a central element of the story world. The narrator brings characters to life either as one 'tells' the reader directly what characters are like or as one 'shows' the characters by having them speak and act, or by having others talk about them and speak to them.

Jesus

The narrator of Mark tends to show the characters to the reader. Obviously, Jesus is the dominant character and his characterization is, not surprisingly, complex. Jesus speaks and acts: what he *says* discloses his understanding of himself and of his mission; what he *does* reveals the extent of his authority from God. In Mark's story, Jesus is proclaimed God's Son at his baptism, for it was then that God declared Jesus to be Son and anointed him with the Holy Spirit (1:9-11). This was a decisive experience for Jesus. Henceforth, he was convinced that through him 'the rule of God has come near' (1:15). But, if Jesus did have authority – *exousia* – from God, that power of his did not have any shade of domination. The hallmark of the use of his authority in relation to people (as distinct from his authority over evil and nature) is consistently, and emphatically, that of service, *diakonia*.

The death of Jesus was wholly consonant with his understanding of authority. He was the one who had come to serve. And if he *spoke* of renouncing self, being least and losing one's life (8:34-37), his *living* of all this lent unanswerable authority to his words. Mark sees clearly (as Paul, before him, had grasped) that the death of Jesus set the seal of authenticity on every single word and deed of him. Mark makes his point superbly by presenting the death of Jesus as a disaster, without any relieving feature at all. Mark does not veil the awesome nature of death. Death is abandonment, isolation and separation. Paradoxically, the *theologia crucis* of Paul and Mark is a surer ground of hope than a *theologia gloriae* which has little to answer to the harsh questions of reality.

The Minor Characters

The narrator shows the authorities in a consistently negative light. The disciples – in practice, the Twelve – are presented in an unflattering light. In contrast, the characterization of the minor characters is firmly positive. Here, indeed, is an eye-opener. One's attention is drawn to something so obvious that it had escaped our attention. The fact is that, over against opponents and disciples, minor characters in the gospel steadfastly exemplify the values of the rule of God. Mark seems to be reminding his community that the sterling Christian qualities are to be found in the 'simple faithful.'

The narrator develops these 'little people' as foils to the authorities and disciples and as parallels to Jesus. These minor characters do measure up to Jesus' standards – especially as they exemplify the values of faith, of being least, of willingness to serve. In the first half of the gospel they measure up to Jesus' opening summons: 'be converted, and believe in the good news' (e.g. 1:29-31, 40-45; 5:18-20, 21-43; 7:24-30, 31-37; 8:22-27).

In the final scenes, in Jerusalem, the minor characters exemplify especially the teaching about being 'servant of all.' Where, before, Jesus had served others now, in his time of need, others serve him. The consistent conduct of the 'little people' stands in sharp contrast to the conduct of the Twelve. In the first half of the story, while there is no direct comparison, the minor characters emerge as models of faith – more than can be said of the Twelve. In the last scenes in Jerusalem the minor characters do fulfil the functions expected of disciples. Here the 'little people' are highlighted (10:46-52; 14:3-9; 15:340-41; 16:1-8). Henceforth, any enlightened reading of Mark's gospel must acknowledge the major contribution of its minor characters.

THEOLOGY OF THE CROSS

Throughout the first half of the gospel of Mark (1:14-8:26) the question of Jesus' identity had been repeatedly raised and had met with various answers. Some, the religious leaders, had rejected the evidence of his works and of his teaching; others had been impressed and had been prepared to acknowledge him as a prophet or as an Elijah-like figure (6:14-15). The chosen disciples had failed to understand him. Only the evil spirits had recognized Jesus – and they were silenced. But now (8:27-33) we have come to the point where the disciples do, at last, proclaim him as Messiah. The passage is the hinge of Mark's work, at once climax of the first part, the secret of the Messiah (the identity of Jesus), and transition to the second part, the mystery of the Son of Man (his destiny of death and resurrection). The second half of the gospel (8:27-16:8) provides an answer to the question raised in the first half, Who is Jesus? The answer is not understood by his disciples who cannot accept his suffering messiahship. They had not come to terms with the cross. (See 'Mark's Passion Narrative', Passion Sunday, p. 71).

It is not enough to declare that Mark is a *theologia crucis;* one must, to some extent, spell out what it means. Here is an attempt to do just that. God is revealed with unwonted clarity in one human life and in one episode of human history. If Jesus is image of the invisible God (see Col 1:15), the cross is revelation of true God and true humankind. On the cross God shows what it is to be human. God's Son dramatically demonstrates the radical powerlessness of the human being. He shows us that we are truly human when we accept our humanness, when we face up to the fact that we are not masters of our fate. The cross offers the authentic definition of humanness: God's definition. There, he starkly and firmly reminds us of who and what we are. On the cross God defines the human being as creature – not to crush or humiliate, but that he may be, as Creator, wholly with his creature. On its own, humankind has indeed reason to fear. With God, in total dependence on God, there is no place for fear.

The resurrection of Jesus makes that clear. For the resurrection is God's endorsement of the definition of humankind established on the cross. And it is God's endorsement of the definition of God established there. It is here he defines himself over against all human caricatures of him. God, in the cross, is a radical challenge to our hubris, our pride. He is the God who has entered, wholly, into rejection and humiliation and suffering. He is the God present in human life where to human eyes he is absent. He is the God of humankind. He is God *for us*.

For Jesus, as for all of us, life was pilgrimage – at more than one level. What Luke had to say of the twelve-year-old is perceptively true: 'And Jesus increased in wisdom and in years, and in divine and human favour' (Lk 2:52). His journey was not only from Nazareth to the Jordan, from Galilee to Jerusalem. It was, above all, a journey of faith. Jesus, who knew the Father as no other did, still had to learn what it was the Father asked of him at the end of all. He found himself face to face with the stark reality of the cross: '... not what I want, but what you want.' While fully aware that, in everything he did and said, he revealed the true God, he was to find that his last word was to be the revelation of what Paul would call the 'foolishness' of God (see 1 Cor 1:18-25). The man himself was the revelation; his life and his death the medium of his message.

The pilgrimage of Jesus – *the* representative of our God – from a ministry of uninhibited love of humankind to death on a human-provided cross, is the great and ultimate human pilgrimage. No banners there, no colourful procession – despite an ephemeral welcome (Mk 11:1-10). Just disillusionment, shared by followers: 'Jesus was walking ahead of them; and they were amazed, and those who followed were afraid' (10:32). They had caught the smell of disaster; the whiff was clear enough. Popular enthusiasm had waned: Jesus was no messsianic warrior but a pacifist for the cause of God. Yet, he had fearlessly challenged the religious establishment by his criticism of Temple and of the 'tradition of the elders' (7:1-13). He was a heretic.

He had implicitly challenged Rome – by his subversive view of authority (10:42-44). He was a rebel. It did not matter that his challenge was totally peaceful and wholly marked by love. He was walking the most precarious walk of all: the walk of one who holds for love in face of those who acknowledge only power – whether naked or subtly disguised. That awesome, and awful, journey to the cross is comfort to all who have seen in Jesus of Nazareth the image of the invisible God. It is the consolation of all who have found in him the ultimate assurance that God is on *our* side.

Jesus had 'set his face to go to Jerusalem' (Lk 9:51). Mark's Gethsemane-scene (14:32-42) shows that he did not fully understand God's way, shows that he did not seek to die this gruesome death. His Gethsemane decision was to trust God despite the darkness of his situation. He entrusted to the Father his own experience of failure: his endeavour to renew Israel was being brutally thwarted. His people had rejected him as they had, formerly, rejected his Father. The cross was the lonely goal of his journey. We have sanitized the Way of the Cross and the Cross itself. The reality was sordid. And here we should remind ourselves that, as Christians, we know about God through the humanity of Jesus. We need to accommodate ourselves to the idea of a Supreme Being who can fully reveal himself in this manner.

Throughout his ministry Jesus had preached the rule of God – God as salvation for humankind. His last sermon was the most eloquent of all. The close of his earthly pilgrimage was to be his unequivocal proclamation of true humanity and of true divinity. For the cross of Jesus is God's revelation of himself. There he is seen to be the *Deus humanissimus* – the God wholly bent on the salvation of humankind. No wonder that Paul can ask, in awe: 'He who did not withhold his own Son, but gave him up for all of us, will he not with him also give us everything else?' (Rom 8:32). This is the God revealed in the *theologia crucis* of Paul – and of Mark.

First Reading   Jon 3:1-5,10

The book of Jonah is post-exilic, written likely in the fifth century B.C. Far from being a naive story of a man-eating 'great fish,' it is a sophisticated satire. It hits out at Jewish exclusiveness and boldly asserts that God is the God of all peoples. A Hebrew prophet is sent by God to Nineveh, capital of the Assyrian oppressor. The prophet, knowing the mercy of his God, and fearing that the Ninevites may repent and escape their fate (the last thing he wants) seeks to evade the task (chapter 1). There is no escaping God and, the second time, Jonah obeys (chapter 3). His worst fears and realised: the king of Nineveh and his people at once believe the word of the prophet and do penance (3:5-9). The irony is unmistakable: the preaching of the reluctant Jonah meets with an immediate and universal response in the pagan city, whereas the great prophets had, over the centuries, preached to the chosen people in vain!

The book may be regarded as a dramatization of Jeremiah 18:8 (alluded to in Jonah 3:10): 'If that nation concerning which I have spoken turns from its evil, I will change my mind about the disaster that I intended to bring on it.' The author not only demonstrates the possibility of a heathen city repenting and turning to God but draws attention also to the love, mercy, and forgiveness of God and, in the person of Jonah, strongly rebukes (4:9-11) those who would be unwilling to see God's mercy beyond Israel.

Jonah is story. The literal-minded will question the 'fish', will challenge, on archaeological grounds, the size and population of Nineveh (3:3; 4:11) and, on historical grounds, the conversion of the Assyrians. One who listens to story will take all in one's stride. For one will see in it the God who is caring Father of all – and hear in it a stark challenge. The challenge is that of Jesus himself: 'Love your enemy!' *Story* is dangerous. We are adept at pulling its teeth.

Second Reading   1 Cor 7:29-31

In the second part of this letter (7:1-11:1) Paul answers the queries raised in the letter of the Corinthian community; in the first place (chapter 7) the merits of marriage and celibacy. He favours the celibate state but he acknowledges that marriage is good and he insists on the mutual conferring of conjugal rights (7:1-9). Concerning divorce, he reiterates the Lord's teaching (vv. 10-11) but, nevertheless, gives his own view on mixed marriages (vv. 12-16). Then, by association of ideas, he turns to exhort Christians to remain in the way of life which the Lord has assigned to each (vv. 17-24).

In 7:25-40 he passes to a new question on 'spiritual' marriages, that is, marriages in which the partners committed themselves to a celibate life-style. Paul is being asked what he thinks of the practice. He begins by stating his conviction that the Parousia of Christ was imminent (vv. 29,31; see 1 Thessalonians 4:13-18), and he assumes that the Corinthians share that view. They cannot, then, imagine that the realities of their present lives are going to go on for long.

This is the central thrust of vv. 29b-31a whose individual phrases should not be taken out of this context. Paul is not recommending that husbands should cease to love their wives (v. 29b), nor that they should put on a hypocritical show of sorrow or rejoicing, nor that they stop all commercial activity. His concern is to prepare them for the day when all these will change. He is asking for an attitude of detachment from the dear, familiar things which tend to absorb humanity. It is foolish to give too much importance to the imperma-nent (J. Murphy-O'Connor, *1 Corinthians*, 73).

Two things should be kept in mind for properly understanding this chapter of Paul: the eschatological perspective; and the fact that not marriage as such is being considered but marriage within a troubled Corinthian setting.

Gospel   Mk 1:14-20

Mark intersperses his gospel with a series of summary statements which succinctly describe a period of activity and trace the course of events. His first summary (1:14-15) opens the public ministry and covers the initial period. The opening words are ominous: 'after John was arrested (lit. delivered up).' The fate of the Baptist was to be delivered up to his enemies in accordance with the divine will (6:17-29) – he is a type of the suffering Messiah. The long shadow of the cross reaches to the beginning.

And now begins the preaching of 'the good news of peace' and Mark's sentence, 'the kingdom (reign) of God has come near; repent, and believe in the good news' is an admirable summing-up of the preaching and message of Jesus. Like the Baptist, Jesus calls for a thorough-going conversion; but, more urgently, he calls on people to embrace the Good News. The evangelist intended the words 'believe in the gospel' to be taken in the Christian sense of faith in the good news of salvation through Jesus Christ. (See First Sunday of Lent).

The expression 'kingdom of God' was not current in Judaism at the time of Jesus. There was, however, an expectation that approximated to that of Jesus. In general one might say that the vision which fuelled expectation was of Israel as a 'kingdom of priests and a holy nation' (Ex 19:6). And the conviction was that God's intervention on behalf of his people could be prepared for and hastened by their efforts to become the kingly and priestly people of God. In the main it was believed that the desired result could be achieved by faithful observ-ance of Torah and through the Temple cult. The various groups within Judaism each had its own manner of hastening the coming of the 'kingdom'. Thus, the Pharisees relied mainly on meticulous observ-ance of Torah; the Essenes of Qumran, though they had distanced themselves from the official priesthood (in their book an illegitimate priesthood), saw themselves as the priestly elect of the nation; the Zealots would defend the Law and tradition with the sword. In the midst of this diverse concern for the renewal of the people of Israel as God's holy elect stood Jesus who shared that concern. But he would not define the holiness of God's people in cultic terms. He redefined it in terms of wholeness.

And where all other groups were, in their various ways, exclusive, the Jesus movement was inclusive. His challenge and his invitation were to all. What Jesus claimed was that this decisive intervention of God was happening in his ministry. The kingdom is here and now present in history in that the power of evil spirits is broken, sins are forgiven, sinners are gathered into Jesus' friendship. The kingdom comes as a present offer, in actual gift, through the proclamation of the gospel. But it only fully arrives on condition of the positive response of the hearer.

The call of the first disciples (v. 16-20) is a passage shaped to bring out the nature of Christ's call and the Christian response, to show what 'following Jesus' means. The decisive factor is the person of Jesus himself. In order to become a disciple of Jesus it is not necessary to be an exceptional person. It is the mighty, immediate impression of Jesus on Peter and his companions, reinforced by his personal word of call, which brought them into his following and made them his disciples. Mark is not intent on describing a scene from the ministry of Jesus. Rather, he is more concerned with the theological dimension of a typical call to discipleship.

FOURTH SUNDAY OF THE YEAR

First Reading   Deut 18:15-20

In Deuteronomy 18:10-14 the Lord had warned the Israelites against the use of various magical techniques for discovering the will of God. Prophecy, Yahweh's gift to his people, is Israel's special means of communication with God (v. 15). The Israelites on Sinai had begged to be spared the awesome ordeal of hearing the divine voice directly. They asked Moses to represent them in God's presence and to convey God's word to them. Yahweh granted their request and the office of prophetic mediator came into being.

'The Lord will raise up for you a prophet like me' (v. 15); the verb implies 'continually raise up' and refers to a line of prophets in succession to Moses. Biblical tradition represents Moses as the ideal prophet. Exodus 33:11 tells us that 'the Lord used to speak to Moses face to face, as one speaks to a friend.' The prophet can never speak on his own authority. The prophet who proclaims as a divine word something that has not come from God is threatened with death (v. 20). The prophet of lying vision and deceit is no successor of Moses.

Later Jewish tradition saw in v. 18 not a promise of a line of prophets but a promise of a figure of the last days, a Prophet-like-Moses. It seems clear from Acts 3:22-23 (which quotes Deut 18:15-16,23) that the early Christians regarded Jesus as the awaited prophet. Jn 6:14 and 7:40 also make reference to the people's expectation of the Prophet-like-Moses.

Second Reading   1 Cor 7:32-35

Today's reading follows directly on last Sunday's excerpt from 1 Corinthians 7. It is clear that Paul himself believed that his celibate state was better than the married state (vv. 7-8); it enabled him to give his undivided attention to the Lord (vv. 32-35). He is clear that it is gift (v. 7) and he will not impose practical acceptance of the ideal on all. This is what some at Corinth wanted to do.

Again, properly to evaluate vv. 32-35, one must appreciate the strained Corinthian situation; otherwise one must think Paul's remarks banal. There were some in that community who had committed themselves to celibacy in marriage. They would have sought to persuade married couples to forego sexual relations and would have tried to convince engaged couples to enter into a 'spiritual' marriage. Those who did marry would come under pressure from these ascetics and have 'worldly troubles.' Paul stresses *anxieties* and wants Christians to be free of them. And he realistically notes the total absorption of the newly married (vv. 33-34). His care to describe the unmarried man/woman as '*anxious* about the affairs of the Lord' would seem to hold a smack of irony, a challenge to the ascetics: are they really as concerned 'to please the Lord' as they claim to be? When the whole of chapter 7 is taken into account, it is clear that though Paul regarded the single state (which was his own, v. 7) as best, he did not glorify it, and finally refused to make it mandatory for any other (v. 35). Throughout, his fundamental objection is to the presumption of those who claim to know what is best for others.

Gospel   Mk 1:21-28

'A day in the life of Jesus' (1:21-34) illustrates a feature of the early ministry: the authority of Jesus in terms of teaching and exorcism and healing. Two distinct episodes are set in the Capernaum synagogue: a teaching of Jesus which provokes the admiration of his hearers, and the expulsion of an unclean spirit which awakens reverential fear in the bystanders.

Later, in 3:22-30, we learn that exorcisms are to be seen in terms of the struggle between the Spirit and Satan begun in the temptation (1:12-13). Each specific exorcism is a particular instance of the unrelenting hostility between Jesus and the spirits of evil, a struggle continued in the life of every Christian. Jesus' word of command (and a word is enough, v. 25) produces convulsions and shouting (v. 26). This is not only a manifestation of spiteful anger: the exorcism stories show a contrast (implicit here) between the demons' violence and hurtfulness towards the person possessed and the gentleness of Jesus and his communion with the liberated person (see 9:26-27; 5:2-5,15). In this case (v. 22) what 'amazes' is the note of assurance and authority in Jesus' teaching. He speaks with prophetic authority in a manner very different from the traditionalism of the scribes. The spirit of the gospel stands out firmly against the spirit of legalism.

The extreme amazement (v. 27) of those present was occasioned by the authoritative teaching and the effortless exorcism. 'With authority' is best taken along with 'a new teaching' to mean 'a new teaching with authority behind it.' Expressions of astonishment at the actions of, or before the person of, Jesus are frequent throughout Mark. It is the evangelist's way of drawing the attention of the reader to a manifestation of Jesus' true nature. The crowds are amazed because they do not understand what is really taking place and who it is that stands before them. The Christian reader should not miss the full message of the text.

A Note on Exorcisms

In the first century A.D. (and before) belief in demonic possession and in the efficacy of exorcism existed in both Judaism and pagan religions. In this context, it is not surprising to find exorcism among Jesus' activities. John P. Meier comments:

> However disconcerting it may be to modern sensibilities, it is fairly certain that Jesus was, among other things, a 1st-century Jewish exorcist and probably won not a little of his fame and following by practising exorcisms (along with the claim of performing other types of miracles). Perhaps in no other aspect of Jesus' ministry does his distance from modern Western culture and scientific

technology loom so large and the facile programme of making the historical Jesus instantly relevant to present-day men and women seem so ill-conceived. One can approach his exorcisms with greater sympathy if one remembers that Jesus no doubt saw them as part of his overall ministry of healing and liberating the people of Israel from the illnesses and other physical and spiritual evils that beset them. Granted the primitive state of medical knowledge in the 1st-century Mediterranean world, mental illness, psychosomatic diseases, and such afflictions as epilepsy were often attributed to demonic possession. If Jesus saw himself called to battle against these evils, which diminished the lives of his fellow Israelites, it was quite natural for him, as a 1st-century Jew, to understand this specific dimension of his ministry in terms of exorcism. All of this simply underscores the obvious: Jesus was a man and a Jew of his times. (*A Marginal Jew*, Vol. 2, 406f).

FIFTH SUNDAY OF THE YEAR

First Reading   Job 7:1-4.6-7

The book of Job (probably dating from the beginning of the fifth century B.C.) belongs to the stage when the idea of individual retribution (the traditional doctrine of retribution, in its simplest form, is that the good are rewarded and the wicked punished *in this life*) palpably ran up against insoluble practical difficulties. It is important to have in mind that, until the first half of the second century B.C., the Hebrews had a very vague notion of the afterlife. At death a person did not quite disappear, one continued to exist in some dim, undefined way in Sheol; but in that dismal abode of the dead all, rich and poor, good and bad, were equal.

Given this situation it is inevitable that throughout most of the Old Testament, retribution of good and evil was seen in an exclusively earthly perspective, strictly within the confines of this life. In the dialogues Job wrestles with a tormenting problem: he is suffering, yet knows himself to be innocent. The inadequacy of the traditional position has become apparent, but people can close their eyes to a disturbing new truth. Here the three friends are the champions of 'orthodoxy'; they have accepted the classic teaching without question and quite refuse to admit that it will not fit the facts of the present case. Their position is very direct: suffering is punishment for sin; if a person suffers it is because one is a sinner – the facts must be made to fit the traditional viewpoint! Hence they proceed to comfort the sufferer by pointing out that he must be a sinner and a great sinner at that, judging by his sufferings – and they grow insistent as he protests his innocence.

Our reading is a brief extract from Job's anguished response (chapters 6-7) to Eliphaz's (the senior of the friends) assured insistence that Job is being rightfully punished for his sin. It is not surprising that, in face of his atrocious suffering and such cold comfort, Job takes a dim view of life. Later, in chapter 29, he nostalgically paints a glowing picture of his former life. Manifestly, the author of Job is sensitive to the tragic predicament of humanity and he gives poignant expression to the pain and confusion that baffles the person who grapples with the problem of suffering and tragedy. We should not allow ourselves to forget the happy times. For, normally, life is not all drudgery and is something better than a dreary passing from hopeless night to weary day, as Job paints it. But we may surely ask what is the ultimate meaning of our transitory life and how we may give it meaning.

Second Reading   1 Cor 9:16-19.22-23

In 1 Corinthians 8 Paul has told his readers that it may be necessary to forego one's rights in order to avoid leading others astray. In our reading he shows how he himself lives it out; he does not insist on his right as an apostle to be supported by the Corinthians to whom he preaches. Though he had the support of the Law and the word of the Lord (1 Cor 9:13-14) to back up his claim to be supported by his converts, he did not wish to insist on his right. He preaches because he cannot resist the overwhelming power of Christ who has called him to be an apostle. He feels that by taking a reward from others he would be putting an obstacle in the way of the gospel. Paul finds the Corinthians jealous of their rights and wants to make the point that renunciation of rights can readily become a Christian duty.

To add further muscle to his own example, he carefully refrains from stressing that he had no objection to accepting support from a community *after* he had left it (see 2 Cor 11:7-9; 12:11-6; Phil 4:15-16). But he did make a principle of being independent of the community to which he ministered. In v. 14 Paul had noted: 'The Lord commanded that those who proclaim the gospel should get their living by the gospel.' Yet, in v. 15 he waived the obligation imposed by the command of the Lord.

This is not an isolated incident, because Paul exhibits the same reaction to the commandment concerning divorce (see 7:10,15).

His practice shows conclusively that he considered the commands of Jesus, not as binding precepts, but as guidelines to be used critically (1 Thess 5:21). His respect for the value of the guideline is proved by the fact that he quotes it even when he intends to do the opposite, but the ultimate criterion on which Paul relies is his own assessment of the concrete situation' (J. Murphy-O'Connor, *1 Corinthians*, 87).

Paul, who was so proud of his freedom as a Roman citizen (see Acts 21:39) and as a Christian (1 Cor 9:1) was prepared to become a slave of all for the sake of the gospel. His aim is to make himself 'all things to all people,' to be at the service of all, to meet people on their own ground. He has special interest in the 'weak.' These were in the first place, the scrupulous brethren of chapter 8, converts from paganism, who wanted to remain free of their pagan past. But Paul's concern was wider and reached to others who laboured under any sort of weakness. He desired to help, but, above all, to be heard; and he knew that the preacher must win a sympathetic hearing.

Gospel   Mk 1:29-39

In healing Peter's mother-in-law (1:29-31) Jesus, who had cast out a demon (vv. 23-26), is shown to have power over sickness. Like the exorcisms, the miracles of healing, too, are signs of salvation. The early Christian community was not interested in miracles of Jesus as brute facts. It regarded them in a twofold light: as a manifestation of the power of God active in Jesus and as signs of the redemption which Jesus had wrought. Here the phrase, 'he raised her up' (*egeiró*, 'to lift up' also means 'raise from the dead'), has symbolic meaning. The woman 'lifted up' from 'fever' symbolises one formerly prostrate beneath the power of sin now raised up by the Lord and called upon to serve him.

At the close of this specimen day (1:21-34), 'all' the sick and possessed of the town are brought to Jesus (vv. 32-34). This summarizing passage describes Jesus' mission up to now and marks a transition to the further spread of his work. The demons (v. 34) understood, as the crowds and the disciples do not, that Jesus is the envoy of God and are bidden to keep silent. This 'secret' has to do with the true status of Jesus. Mark is sure that what 'Son of God' means can be understood only when Jesus had shown, through suffering and death, what it means. That is why Jesus cannot be proclaimed 'until after the Son of man had risen from the dead' (9:9).

Reference to the prayer of Jesus (v. 35) may give us a proper understanding of the episode of 1:35-39. Mark mentions Jesus' prayer on two further occasions: after the multiplication of loaves (6:46) and in Gethsemane (14:35.39). Each time the true nature of Jesus' messiahship is in question and he has to contend with the incomprehension of his disciples (6:52; 14:10). So, here, the disciples have 'hunted him out' because they feel that he, the wonder-worker, was missing a golden opportunity. This is not the attitude of true disciples; this is not the following of Jesus to which they had been called.

SIXTH SUNDAY OF THE YEAR

First Reading   Lev 13:1-2, 45-46

The whole of chapter 13 of Leviticus is concerned with 'leprosy' – a term not confined to Hansen's disease but which includes different kinds of infectious skin diseases. Whatever the actual nature of the disease may have been the person afflicted with it was considered ritually unclean, as was anybody or anything that came into contact with the person. It was the duty of the priests to diagnose the disease. Once they had confirmed that someone was a leper no compassion was shown the unfortunate sufferer. The person was forbidden to live in any town or village. His clothes were to be distinctive and he had to let his hair grow loose. Since contact with a leper rendered a person 'unclean,' the leper was obliged to cry out: 'Unclean!' when he saw anybody approach.

Although the rabbis maintained that the healing of leprosy was 'as difficult as raising the dead,' it was believed that the disease sometimes healed spontaneously. When a leper was pronounced cured and had undergone a purification rite, he was readmitted to the community (Lev 14). Since lepers were such outcasts and their disease so feared, we can imagine how surprised and even shocked the people were when they saw Jesus go so far as to touch them in the manner described in today's Gospel reading.

Second Reading   1 Cor 10:31-11:1

In 1 Corinthians 10:23-11:1 Paul turns his attention to 'the weak.' Coming from a pagan background, they could not as readily come to terms with the eating of idol-meat (8:7) as could 'the strong,' mostly Jewish converts with supreme contempt for 'idols' (8:4). Where in chapter 8 he had urged on the Strong their obligation of delicate

Christian consideration for the weak, he now (10:23-30) reminds the Weak that they should show consideration for the Strong and strive to appreciate their viewpoint. Our reading gives Paul's conclusion to the whole lengthy (and, for our day, rather tiresome) debate. This conclusion is a thoroughly positive principle, one susceptible of very wide application indeed: 'do everything for the glory of God' (v. 31).

A Christian gives glory to God by being what he or she is meant to be: a manifestation of the love of Christ. Hence one must give no offence to any*one*. One must never do anything that would make it difficult for the Jew or the pagan to see the beauty of Christianity. One's action should never lead a Christian to reject the Church or be the reason of one's failure to grow in holiness. Paul himself had always been guided by his consideration for the good of others and be urges the Corinthians to follow his example. The ultimate norm, for him and for them, is Christ 'who did not please himself' (Rom 15:3). In order to assure them that the ideal is not beyond the reach of humankind Paul can say to the Corinthians: 'Be imitators of me, as I am of Christ' (11:1). The implication is awesome. To demonstrate to others that the love of God in Christ is a present reality a preacher should be able to point to oneself. Paul, at least, would hold that, if one cannot do so, if one cannot show forth in one's person 'the life of Jesus' (2 Cor 4:10), one really has no right to speak.

Gospel   Mk 1:40-45

The significance of the cure of a leper lies in the fact that (as we have seen in our first reading) leprosy is the ultimate uncleanness which made one socially, and in the religious sphere, wholly an outcast. The Law was helpless in face of leprosy; it could only defend the community against the leper. But what the law could not achieve, Jesus accomplishes. See Romans 8:3.

In v. 41 'moved with anger' – read in significant manuscripts – (and not 'moved with pity') should be taken as the original reading. (It is inconceivable that Christian scribes would have changed 'moved with pity' into 'moved with anger' – the reverse process is readily understandable). The anger of Jesus is his reaction to the disease which brings him face to face with the power of evil. He is shocked by the fact that the community has to defend itself against this poor wretch and does so by branding him as a pariah. He reaches out to the man a loving and healing hand. This is how a Christian community should deal with sinners and down-and-outs. In v. 45 we read that the former leper began to tell his tale to everyone he met. Significantly, 'to talk' also means 'to proclaim' and 'the news' is *ho logos*, 'the word.' These terms carry Christian overtones which Mark's readers would not have missed. A Christian is one 'cleansed' by Christ in baptism; one who then ought to 'preach' and 'spread abroad the Good News.'

The evangelist will have placed the passage here, after his summary account of Jesus' ministry, because of the strong light it throws on the salvation now accessible to all people. It is also notable that the conflict-stories (2:1-3:6) which follow immediately contain charges against Jesus as a violator of the Law. The present story shows that Jesus respected the Law: he commanded the healed leper to carry out the requirements of the Law (v. 44). Mark could have felt that the story at this point would establish the falsehood of the subsequent charges.

SEVENTH SUNDAY OF THE YEAR

First Reading   Is 43:18-19.21-22.24-25

In Isaiah 40-48 we have a series of hymns to the Lord Redeemer. Today's reading is taken from one of them, on the redemption and restoration of Israel (43:1 -44:23). The author is encouraging the exiles in Babylon, assuring them that all is not lost despite the recent disaster of the destruction of Jerusalem and of the exile. On the contrary, there is prospect of a glorious future. Israel was conscious of its past, of the great things that the Lord had done for it from the time of the Exodus onwards. These great deeds were recalled in song and story. Now, the prophet proclaims, a greater deed was about to be performed in comparison with which past history would appear a small thing. There would be a new exodus (this time from Babylon), a new journey through the desert, a new settlement in the homeland. This new age would be a pure act of grace, totally unmerited by an Israel which had only burdened its God with its sins.

The new order of things would be characterized by the forgiveness of sins, thus ensuring reconciliation and friendship between God and humankind. In making the forgiveness of sin a characteristic of the new age, second Isaiah is in the tradition of Jeremiah: 'I will forgive their iniquity, and remember their sin no more' (Jer 31:31-34) and Ezekiel: 'I will sprinkle clean water upon you, and you shall be clean...' (Ezek 36:25-29).

Second Reading   2 Cor 1:18-22

From today until the fourteenth Sunday inclusive second readings are from 2 Corinthians. In Macedonia, towards the close of 57 A.D., Paul learned from Titus (2 Cor 2:12-13; 7:5-16) that the turbulent Corinthian community, in the meantime shaken by further crises, was at last reasonably tranquil. Second Corinthians expresses his satisfaction at this turn, but is also very much of an apologia.

The writing is, in large measure, a defence of the apostolic ministry and reveals the deeply human side of Paul. In 1 Corinthians (1:18-30) Paul had spoken of the folly of the cross; the same idea runs through 2 Cor 4:6-11 – God works through human weakness so that the success of the apostolate and the advance of the kingdom of God will be seen as the work of God not of humankind. The message is preached by weak 'servants of the word' like himself to show that it is the power of God and not anything in themselves that brings it to fruition.

Paul seeks to re-establish the warm relationship that had existed between the Corinthian community and himself (see 1 Cor 4:14-16). Rivals of his, 'travelling preachers,' more eloquent than he, less demanding in their moral standards, had attempted to come between him and the community. They accused Paul of promising a great deal by letter and doing little in person. He had been accused of vacillating; of saying one thing to them and of doing (or meaning) something else. They instanced his failure to visit Corinth as arranged. He explains why he had changed his travel plans. It was to spare the feelings of the community that he had not come: one painful visit was more than enough (1:23- 2:1)

Refuting the charge of duplicity, he declares himself to be not a man who answers 'yes' and 'no' in the same breath. He is very conscious that he is a sign of Christ, and Christ was fidelity itself. Paul plays on the fundamental idea behind the Hebrew word 'Amen' ('to stand,' 'to be [or make] firm') and on the meanings of the word itself: 'So it is, 'Yes''. The word brings to mind fidelity. Christ is the Amen, the Faithful One (Rev 3:14; 19:11). He is God's 'Amen' to his promises, he fulfils them. He is the seed of Abraham (Gal 3:16), the Davidic Messiah (Rom 1:4), the last Adam (1 Cor 15:45). We make our Amen through him. It is an Amen which says 'yes' to all that God has done for us, which expresses a conviction that he will continue to help us and ensures a constancy in our own Christian living.

Such confidence gives glory to the Father. It is he who has brought about our union with Jesus and has anointed us for mission. He has sealed us as his very own and given us his Spirit who is the pledge of future fulfilment.

Gospel   Mk 2:1-12

Up until now Jesus had been carrying out his mission in Galilee, teaching, healing, casting out demons. At this point (chapter 2) comes his first explicit confrontation with official Judaism. It is documented in a series of five controversies: on forgiveness of sins (2:1-12), on eating with tax-collectors and sinners (2:13-17), on fasting (2:18-22), on grain fields and the sabbath (2:23-28), and concerning healing on the sabbath (3:1-6). At the same time, the section sets the teaching of Jesus in relief: the section is not only apologetic but is markedly catechetical as well.

The fact is that each of the separate units which make up the complex is not only a conflict story, a debate with adversaries, but is, too a pronouncement story. We can see that the saving message of each is to be found in a saying of the Lord – the stories are so many illustrations of that 'new teaching with authority behind it' (1:27). If we set out the five climactic sayings one after another we can readily perceive how valuable they are for an understanding of the Christian gospel:

The Son of Man has authority on earth to forgive sins.

I have come to call not the righteous but sinners.

Can the wedding guests fast while the bridegroom is with them?

The Son of man is Lord even of the sabbath.

Is it lawful to do good or to do harm on the sabbath, to save life or to kill?

These sayings – all of them in part or in whole Christian formulations – have a vital bearing on the content of the gospel message and on the early Church's understanding of its Lord.

Today's reading (2:1-12) is the first of the conflict-stories. The passage is composite, with vv. 1-5a, 11-12 forming a coherent miracle-story, augmented by a section on the remission of sins (vv. 5b-10). Mark has converted a miracle story into a controversy story. The evangelist is telling us that the cure of a paralytic was intended to manifest the sin-forgiving power of the Son of Man. In the early kerygma the remission of sins was regarded as intrinsic to the experience of being a Christian. Thus Acts 10:43 states, 'All the prophets testify about him (Jesus) that everyone who believes in him receives forgiveness of sins through his name.' In the light of this and similar texts it is evident that the early Christians proclaimed the forgiveness of sins as a present fact. This meant a head-on clash with Jewish belief which regarded forgiveness as a future benefit to be hoped for.

The very presence of the forgiveness of sins debate in the gospel is an indication that it was a live issue for Mark's community. Their assertion of forgiveness of sins on earth was blasphemy to their Jewish adversaries. Their defence is their claim of a share of the authority of the eschatological Son of man (v. 10). For Mark the full revelation of the Son of man is in his suffering, death and resurrection and so is accessible only to believers. When, however, those who believe in Jesus seek to live and act in the Spirit of Jesus, they participate in his power to forgive sins. The story is a vindication of the Church's claim to declare the forgiveness of sins in the name of Jesus (see John 20:23), a forgiveness achieved in baptism.

EIGHTH SUNDAY OF THE YEAR

First Reading   Hos 2:16-17.21-22

Hosea, a younger contemporary of Amos, preached in the northern kingdom of Israel during the latter years of Jeroboam II (783-743 B.C.) and during the turbulent years that preceded the fall of Samaria in 721 B.C. Hosea was the first to represent the covenant relation of Yahweh with his people as a marriage. It is out of his own personal experience (Hos chapters 1,3) that the marriage image came to the prophet and that he realized its aptness in describing the relations between Yahweh and his people. He understood that the psychology of human love can wonderfully illustrate the mystery of God's relations with humankind, the reality and depth of his love. The divine Husband has been betrayed by his spouse who has given herself to adultery (to Baal worship). Yet he seeks only to win her again to him and if he chastises her it is with that sole end in view. As a last resort he determines to bring her back once more to the conditions of the Exodus, the honeymoon period of their love (2:16-17). In fact, he ultimately goes beyond this and promises to bring her into the harmony of a new garden of Eden (2:18) where their love will be the crowning and fulfilment of the mutual love of the first human couple (2:21-22). In Hosea's view, what God is calling for is a restoration of his people's first fervour and simplicity. His people had been led from this first love through over-concern with human affairs.

Second Reading   2 Cor 3:1-6

Things had gone so badly between the Corinthians and Paul that he, who had brought the faith to them, was now expected to produce a letter of introduction! Paul is at his most deadly when he is being ironical. The itinerant evangelists, his opponents, press their charge: 'This man commends *himself*, but we can show *our* letters of recommendation from other communities.' Paul, devastatingly, can retort that the Corinthian Church itself, every man, woman and child of it, is *his* letter of recommendation. The Christians of Corinth are a sufficient recommendation of Paul's authenticity. Christ delivers this letter, through his work, with the help of the Spirit. It is not written on stone like the old law. It is the 'letter' of their faith in Christ, written by the Spirit on their hearts.

Paul is confident of the success of his work – because success comes from God. Of himself he can do nothing. He takes up now a key-idea which surfaced in Galatians and will run through Romans: he has been appointed minister of a new covenant, not based on a written law, but on the Spirit. The law showed what was wrong but could not, of itself, provide the dynamism which leads to right conduct. The Spirit is a principle of life which effects a new way of living. It is a transforming power.

Gospel
Mk 2:18-22

Today's reading is made up of a pronouncement story (2:18-20) to which two sayings, on patches and wineskins, have been added (2:21-22). The fact that the disciples of Jesus did not fast brings home to those who can understand that the Bridegroom is with them. But those who do not recognize the signs of the times (see Matthew 16:2-3) are scandalized by such conduct.

The two appended sayings (vv. 21-22) are designed to make clear that the new movement which Jesus inaugurated cannot be confined within the limits of the old religion. The bridegroom is manifestly Jesus and his being 'taken away' (v. 30) is a veiled reference to his impending death. Like the disciples of John (see 6:29) the disciples of Jesus, too, will have their time of mourning (see Jn 16:20). The qualification 'and they will fast in that day' would suggest that fasting had become a practice in the Marcan community.

Though the parabolic sayings (vv. 21-22) certainly had an independent existence, it is clear that in their Marcan context they will illustrate a contrast between the old spirit and the new. A patch of unshrunk cloth will shrink at the first wash and tear apart the weakened fabric of the old garment. Old wineskins become thin and brittle; the new fermenting wine would burst the skins and wine and skins would be lost. The new spirit is not a piece added to the old nor a new element poured into the old: it is a vivifying power which transforms the abiding teachings of the old revelation. This is what Jesus outlines in the Sermon on the Mount, the Gospel which Paul develops in his turn.

NINTH SUNDAY OF THE YEAR

First Reading   Deut 5:12-15

We have two versions of the ten commandments, the 'ten words' (Ex 20:2-17; Deut 5:6-21). Today's reading gives the Deuteronomical text of the sabbath commandment. The sabbath probably goes back to the very origins of Yahwism. It was prescribed in the Code of the Covenant (Ex 23:12) and in the Yahwistic 'ritual decalogue' (Ex 34:21). In both texts a settled, agrarian way of life is presupposed, but they are both adaptations of an earlier law. The sabbath is also found in both forms of the decalogue as the central commandment and the most developed. The developments date from a period when the sabbath had become one of the leading religious observances.

The reasons given for the sabbath law are different in Exodus and in Deuteronomy. In the first the sabbath is said to be an initiation of Yahweh, who rested after his work of creation (Ex 20:11). In the other it serves to remind the people of deliverance from slavery in Egypt (Deut 5:15). The fact that there are two different explanations shows that the law was very old. In its simple form, every seventh day was 'sanctified' and a day of rest. It was not a feast nor was it marked by any special rite. It was simply a day when everyday activities ceased.

In Jewish religion of the post-exilic period the sabbath became one of the great signs of the covenant, and its observance was more and more emphasized. This in turn led to meticulous discussion of what constituted the sabbath rest and of what kind of work was forbidden on the sabbath. Sabbath observance became an end in itself. It was against this attitude and such casuistry that Jesus spoke and acted.

Second Reading   2 Cor 4:6-11

In his first letter to the Corinthians (1:18-30) Paul had spoken of the folly of the cross. The same idea runs through the present reading: God works through human weakness so that the success of the apostolate and the advance of the Kingdom of God will be seen as the work of God, not of humans. In v. 6 it would seem that Paul refers not only to the creation of earthly light but also to the heavenly light of revelation granted him on the Damascus road (see Acts 26:13,18). Through this experience he recognized that the glory of God was to be seen rather on the face of Christ than on the face of Moses (3:7).

This message is preached by weak 'servants of the word' like himself to show that it is the power of God, and not themselves, which brings it to fruition. Their lives are paradox, revealing the intimate nature of their ministry which is to prolong in time the paschal mystery, the death and resurrection of Jesus. They may be worn down by the tribulations of the ministry but the life of Jesus flows from them to others. What was true of the apostolate in Paul's day remains true of the Church in every generation. The all too human character of Christian ministers is no indication that the Church's mission will fail.

Gospel   Mk 2:23-3:6

Today's reading contains the last two of the five conflict stories. The passage 2:23-28 is made up of a pronouncement story (vv. 23-26) to which the sayings of vv. 27-28 have been appended. In Mark's version (unlike Matthew and Luke) what is at issue is not 'work' on the sabbath but a comparison of David and Jesus. The intent is christological: Jesus, as God's Anointed, has the same freedom as David in respect of the law.

The wisdom saying of v. 27 has a rather close rabbinical parallel, 'The sabbath is delivered unto you, and ye are not delivered to the sabbath.' The meaning of the saying is that God ordained the sabbath for the benefit of humankind; it is a reaction against a false evaluation of the sabbath whereby people become slaves to sabbath observance. Jesus uttered his word, at once criterion and critique: 'The sabbath was made for humankind, and not humankind for the sabbath.' Paraphrased, it runs: 'Religion is in the service of men and women; men and women are not slaves of religion.' Wherever religion is burden, it has become oppressor, not servant. Authentic religion must foster freedom. Mark's christological point is made in v. 28: in the light of vv. 23-27 ('so then') the Son of man is lord of the sabbath. Christians had begun to observe not the Jewish sabbath but the day of the resurrection, 'the Lord's day' (Rev 1:10). They maintained that their Lord had set the sabbath free and their distinctive observance was traced back to his authority.

The fifth conflict-story (3:1-6) is the climax of the series. Here Jesus himself is more aggressive and the plot against him (v. 6) points to the inevitable end of this persistent hostility. But this issue is, too, of immediate interest to Mark's community. If Christians had chosen to observe the Lord's day rather than the Jewish sabbath, they had thereby opted for some form of sabbath observance. The question then remained as to how far to push that observance and in what spirit. The challenge of Jesus (v. 4) and his deed of mercy will have given them their principle and their pattern.

The Pharisees accuse Jesus of a breach of sabbath observance. He views the matter in a wholly different light and he challenges their attitude. To heal a person is to 'do good'; to leave one in one's infirmity is to 'do evil.' In forbidding healing on the sabbath the rabbis would equivalently admit that, on this day, moral values are reversed: it is forbidden 'do good' and proscribed to 'do evil'! The real issue is no longer what one is permitted to do; it is the obligation of doing good at all times and in all circumstances. Jesus asks, 'Is it lawful to do good or to do harm on the sabbath, to save life or to kill?' How sad it is that the spirit of legalism has so often and so firmly asserted itself in the Christian Church. We had been so eager to observe rules, as well as to impose them, anxious to measure our Christianity by the punctiliousness of our 'observance.'

TENTH SUNDAY OF THE YEAR

First Reading   Gen 3:9-15

Genesis 3:1-7 tells the tragic story of Temptation; then (3:8-19) comes judgment on the fateful human decision. In v. 8 we see that the former familiarity with Yahweh (chapter 2) is now gone. True, he comes as before, strolling in the garden, eminently accessible – but *they* are changed. The man and woman flee the very sound of God and hide, or attempt to hide, from him. He has come, as before, but because of *their* conduct he must now be Judge. They must face the consequence of responsibility. Humans cannot remain hidden from God, from the God they now fear (vv. 9-10). So far, man and woman had experienced shame within themselves and fear before God. Fear and shame will henceforth be the common experience of humankind.

The man's reply to the second question of Yahweh witnesses to his desperate attempt to clear himself of guilt, to place responsibility for the results of his actions anywhere than at his own door (vv. 11-12). First he blames the woman. Ultimately, he seeks to pin the blame on God: she is the woman 'whom you gave to be with me.' The attempt to involve God is pathetic (but it is still the way of humankind). More tragic is the breakdown between man and woman – here the man betrays the woman. Somehow – and it is perhaps the intent of the

Yahwist who had already shown himself to be unconventional by his insistence on the importance of woman (2:18-25) – the woman emerges from this sorry episode with more dignity than the man.

Humans are called to responsibility for their conduct: 'Where are you?' (Gen 3:9). While humans cannot be made responsible for the origin of evil, humans remain answerable. The primeval story of Genesis looks to the human state as it exists in the lives of real men and women. The question faced there is: why is the human being, created by God, limited by death, suffering, toil, and sin? The question is not answered. The mystery of evil is left hanging – a mystery. The fact is that humankind is alienated from God – alienated but not cut off from God. Sin and death are part of human existence. Consciousness of nakedness had followed awareness of rebellion, awareness of guilt (3:7). God 'clothed them' (3:21). The feeling of guilt is removed. God sent man and woman out into the world free of guilt feeling.

Second Reading   2 Cor 4:3 - 5:1

In the preceding passage read last Sunday, Paul spoke of the trials and tribulations of his apostolic mission. In v. 13 he gives the reason why he should submit to these sufferings. He is far from daunted because he has that faith which made the psalmist exclaim: 'I believed, and so I spoke' (Ps 116:10). Paul's interpretation of his sufferings (vv 10-1) is rooted in faith, not in reason. For him faith consists in the knowledge that God who has raised Jesus from the dead will raise the apostle to be with Jesus – and raise up, too, his Corinthian brethren. All, together, will come into the presence of God. Paul's apostolic concern is to bring more and more people within the influence of God's grace so that God may be more and more glorified as people acknowledge his graciousness.

'So we do not lose heart' (v. 16) looks back to 4:1. Paul admits that his 'outer nature,' his self as subject to suffering, is being worn down, but he asserts that his 'inner nature,' open to God, is being renewed all the time. With his eyes on the parousia and all that it entails his present suffering is a matter of small moment – because his present brief tribulation will be followed by eternal glory. Logically, then, his eyes are fixed not on the things and values of this world but on the age to come and its reality. He looks not to the present, visible, changeable world but to that which is future, invisible, eternal where God will provide us with a permanent dwelling in place of a temporary tent (5:1).

Gospel

Mk 3:20-35

Our reading aptly illustrates a statement in the prologue of the Fourth Gospel: 'He came to his own home, and his own people did not accept him' (Jn 1:11). Here, the family of Jesus, and the religious leaders of his people, fail to recognize him and the true source of his activity. His relatives are not his real kindred, those who do the will of God; and the scribes who accuse him of being in league with the devil are guilty of the gravest sin of all – sin against the light. In his own way, Mark wrestles with the problem that tormented John: that people could choose darkness rather than light (Jn 3:19).

Mark's distinctive 'sandwich' technique points us, unerringly, to a true understanding of the passage 3:20-35 – the episode of the scribes is 'sandwiched' between the two sections (vv. 20-21 and 31-35) on the family of Jesus. It is his pointer to us that the 'slices' and the 'filling' have been blended into one. In v. 21 'friends' (RSV) should read 'family' – the Nazareth family, concerned for Jesus, had come to 'seize' him. They wanted to save him for himself: 'he has gone out of his mind.' Then emerge the Jerusalem scribes: official Jewish reaction. Verse 20 contains two accusations: he is possessed by Beelzebul, an evil spirit; his exorcisms are wrought by the power of 'the prince of the demons,' that is, Satan.

The accusations are taken up in turn in vv. 28-29 and v. 27. The charge that Jesus casts out demons by the power of Satan is answered by a denial that Satan is divided against himself (vv. 24-26) – there are no signs of the alleged civil war. The explanatory editorial comment of the evangelist in v. 30 shows that the saying on blasphemy against the Holy Spirit (vv. 28-29) is to be taken as Jesus' response to the accusation of being possessed by Beelzebul. The meaning of 'blasphemy against the Holy Spirit' is shown in v. 30. It is the act of attributing the exorcisms of Jesus (and, by implication, his whole ministry), wrought by the power of the Spirit, to the agency of Satan. The unpardonable gravity of the sin comes from the fact that, in attributing the activity of Jesus to a demonic influence (3:22a), one refuses to admit that the kingdom of God has come. One thus puts oneself outside of it, rejecting the kingdom. The 'sin' or 'blasphemy' is not so much an offence against the Spirit as humankind's refusal of the salvation which God offers by the Spirit active in Jesus. The whole presence and teaching of Jesus make abundantly clear that, from God's side, there is no such thing as an unforgivable sin.

The pronouncement story (3:31-35) preserves the saying of Jesus that his true kindred are those who do the will of God. For Mark it is a continuation of vv. 20-21. His insertion of the Beelzebul dispute establishes a relationship between the attitude of the family of Jesus and the attitude of the religious authorities – his own did not receive him. The mother of Jesus (v. 31) does not appear again in Mark, but she is mentioned in 6:3. Those who are sitting around Jesus are in the process of listening to his teaching and thus of placing themselves in his 'family.' Jesus subordinates the bond of kinship to the higher bond of brotherhood. The will of the Father is the motive power and guide of all Jesus' activity: 'My food is to do the will of him who sent me' (Jn 4:34). Those who similarly do the will of God enter into a real relationship with Jesus, they belong to the family of God. But the first requirement in doing God's will is to know it. One must learn at the school of Jesus.

ELEVENTH SUNDAY OF THE YEAR

First Reading   Ezek 17:22-24

The allegory of the eagles (Ezek 17:1-10) is aimed at Zedekiah who had violated his oath of allegiance to Nebuchadnezzar; his punishment will be defeat and deportation (vv. 16,20-21). A great eagle (Nebuchadnezzar) has broken off the top-most branch (Jehoiachim) of the cedar (Judah) and carried it off to Babylon – Jehoiachin was, in 597 B.C., taken into permanent exile. The 'vine' set in his place was Zedekiah, now vassal of Nebuchadnezzar. He turned to another eagle (Egypt); the result was disaster. The riddle ends with the query: 'Can the Davidic dynasty survive?'

In today's reading Yahweh promises that he will plant in Zion a twig from the top (*semereth*) of the cedar (v. 22). The same term designates Zedekiah in v. 3: Ezekiel hopes that God will raise up a Messiah from the descendants of Jehoiachin. It must have seemed to his contemporaries that the transplanted twig could only shrivel and die. But that would be to ignore the protective power of God, the God who puts down the mighty from their thrones and raises up the lowly, the God who destroys mighty kings and nations ('the high tree') and raises up the weak ('the low tree'). The God of Israel would transplant the people of Israel in the land of their fathers. There would be a messianic age and a new Davidic dynasty – the 'noble cedar' offering shelter to birds of every sort. The nations of the earth ('all the trees of the field') would recognize the presence of the might of God in this turn of events. The immediate restoration was not as Ezekiel had dreamed. But he had glimpsed a future son of David whose kingdom would be universal.

Second Reading   2 Cor 5:6-10

The corresponding reading of last Sunday concluded with Paul's conviction that the death of the body will yield to resurrection and transformation (5:1-2). In today's section he switches to the image of being 'at home' or 'away from home.' First of all, he acknowledges that earthly existence is separation from the Lord; he lives his life by faith. And, of course, he would prefer to be at home with the Lord. This is strikingly like Philippians 1:23 'My desire is to depart and be with Christ, for that is far better.' Still, in his present exile, Paul is steadfastly 'confident.' His one and only object is to please the Lord. Again note the close parallel in Philippians. Though his ardent desire was to be with the Lord he declares: 'To remain in the flesh is more necessary for you' (Phil 1:24) – in other words, he is pleasing the Lord. That is why he has no fear of appearing before Christ.

Gospel   Mk 4:26-34

The nucleus of Mark's parable section (4:1-34) is a group of three parables: the sower (3-9), the seed growing to harvest (26-29) and the mustard seed (30-32); the two latter comprise today's reading.

The parable of the seed growing to harvest (26-29) is peculiar to Mark. It seems best to take it as a parable of contrast between the inactivity of the sower and the certainty of the harvest. The sower goes his way; the seed sprouts and grows without his taking anxious thought. It is God who brings about the growth of the Kingdom. Paul had learned the lesson of the parable: 'I planted, Apollos watered, but God gave the growth' (1 Cor 3:6). It may be that, originally, it was Jesus' reply to those who looked, impatiently, for a forceful intervention of God; or it may have been meant to give assurance to those of the disciples who were discouraged because nothing seemed to be happening. Mark, at least, takes it in the latter sense. Jesus encourages his disciples: in spite of hindrance and apathy the seed was being sown. Its growth is the work of God who will bring it to harvest.

The parable of the mustard seed (30-32) is another parable of contrast; but again the idea of growth must be given due weight. The contrast between insignificant beginning and mighty achievement is primary – but the seed does grow into a plant. The detail of branches in which the birds of the air nest (v. 32) manifestly recalls Ezek 17:23

(first reading). In Mark's view, the proclamation of the kingdom will bring all nations within its scope. The parable would have been the reply of Jesus to an objection, latent or expressed: could the kingdom really come from such inauspicious beginnings? His reply is that the little cell of disciples will indeed become a kingdom. And, in the last analysis, if the kingdom does reach its full dimension, that is not due to anything in the men and women who are the seed of the kingdom; the growth is due solely to the power of God. That is why Jesus can speak with utter confidence of the final stage of the kingdom. And that is why the parable is a call for patience.

TWELFTH SUNDAY OF THE YEAR

First Reading
Job 38:1,8-11

The dialogues of Job (chapters 3-31) were necessarily inconclusive (the speeches of Elihu, chapters 32-37, are a later attempt to restate the traditional theology maintained by the friends). The answer to Job's problem is given by Yahweh himself (chapters. 38-39). Job had not understood the ways of God in his regard; the long litany of questions presents him with the transcendence of the mystery of God. In highly dramatic form these chapters are a restatement of Is 55:9 – 'As the heavens are higher than the earth, so are my ways higher than your ways.' It is not for humans to question the wisdom or the justice of God's behaviour. God understands the workings of the world which he himself has created. Humankind is in the dark.

Today's passage (chosen with the gospel reading in mind) stresses God's mastery of the watery chaos. It reflects the old Semitic myths of the origin of the world – the world was created out of primeval watery chaos, an evil force which would withstand God. With this background in mind we can better appreciate the force of the poetic imagery where the violent power of the sea is so overwhelmed by God's might that he treats it as a new-born baby ('swaddling band') and places it securely within its play-pen (v. 11). From this image of effortless authority we may gain a deepened sense of God's creative might which implies his unlimited and effective concern for the world.

Second Reading
2 Cor 5:14-17

Our appreciation of Paul will be increased when we understand that what is central to him is not so much a doctrinal position as his experience of the boundless love of Christ. This is the driving force behind his passionate, at times polemical, interest in the Christian communities for which he feels himself responsible. Today's reading brings us close to the heart of Paul. The love of God stirs him and he, in his turn, proclaims Christ, dead and risen again. Here he gives the reason for Jesus' death not in cultic terms (a sacrifice for sin) but in terms of human existence: Christ died so that we should live a Christ-centred and no longer self-centred life. In v. 17 he uses a stronger expression: accepting Christ means entering a new creation. This radical newness is a here-and-now reality for those who are 'in Christ,' that is to say, for those who have accepted Christ and the outgoing power of his love as the norm of their existence.

Paul mentions one result of this new life in his own case; he no longer judges anyone by worldly standards and conventions. This goes, supremely, for his understanding of Christ (v. 16). Before his conversion Paul would have looked upon Jesus as a man among people, 'according to the flesh.' On the Damascus road he encountered the risen Saviour. Within the context of the situation in the Corinthian Church of the time there is a polemical note to Paul's remark about 'a human point of view.' He implies that the rival preachers who operate in Corinth do in fact follow worldly standards of prestige-seeking and are not permeated by a vivid realization of the all-embracing love of Christ.

Gospel   Mk 4:35-41

Certain Old Testament ideas and passages form the background of this miracle-story. Control over the sea and the calming of storms are characteristic signs of divine power (Job 7:12; 38:8-11; Pss 74:13; 89:8-9; Is 51:9-10). Calming of a storm at sea is a major proof of God's loving care (Ps 107:23-32). It is also noteworthy that calm and untroubled sleep is a mark of perfect trust in God (see Prov 3:23-24; Pss 3:5; 4:8; Job 11:18-19). Mark's narrative is a miracle-story with a catechetical point.

The reproach of v. 40 transforms the miracle story into a catechetical lesson; though from the beginning, doubtless, the episode was seen as one which raised the question of the identity of Jesus, and as a teaching on faith. Jesus blames the disciples for their lack of confidence. The term translated 'afraid', *deiloi*, is very strong, expressing total disarray. During the storm the disciples had failed in that confidence in God of which the tranquil sleep of the Master was a visible sign. However, Jesus accuses them especially of lack of confidence in his person (see Jn 14:1). By his tranquil sleep, his reproach, and his stilling of the storm, Jesus exhorts his disciples to have trust in him at all times and in all circumstances.

When all is said and done, it is not the little handful of disciples in that lake drama who are chiefly in question. The cry, 'Master, are we to perish for all you care?' (v. 38) suggesting that the disciples are awake and in danger while their Master 'sleeps' reflects the post-Easter experience of the Church. Christians may feel that the Lord has no care for them, has abandoned them, and the Church may seem to be at the mercy of forces pitted against it. Individuals and communities who feel so earn the rebuke: 'Have you still no faith?' It is enough that he should 'awaken,' that they should have faith and trust in his presence, for the storm of their fear to be stilled. Mark has painted an episode in the life of Jesus in colours of early Christianity.

THIRTEENTH SUNDAY OF THE YEAR

First Reading
Wis 1:13-15; 2:23-24

This reading has been chosen to give background to the message of the Gospel today: that Jesus' saving power can dominate death itself. The author of the Book of Wisdom lived in the middle of the first century B.C., almost certainly in the hellenistic city of Alexandria in Egypt. He had fully assimilated the insight that some had reached about a century earlier, that of the blessed immortality of the just with God beyond death. For the author of Wisdom, humans are mortal by virtue of their earthly origin (7:1) and he takes physical death for granted. In our reading, then, he is not speaking of physical death but of 'spiritual' death, what Revelation calls 'the second death' (Rev 2:11; 21:8), definitive separation from God. He asserts that God is good and wants human happiness. V. 14 does little more than spell out the conviction of Gen 1:31 'God saw everything that he had made, and indeed, it was very good.'

One of the precious lessons of the Old Testament that we Christians could take wholly to heart is that God's world is good. The rather enigmatic v. 15 ('for righteousness is immortal') means that righteousness leads to immortality. When the author takes up the 'image of God' of Gen 1:26, he connects it with the blessed immortality for which humankind is destined, but which can be forfeited by sin (2:23). And 2:24 makes very clear that he understands 'death' not as physical death but as spiritual death. Still looking to Genesis, this time Gen 3:1-7, he interprets the 'serpent' there as the 'devil' – Satan – of later Jewish speculation, and he states that 'death' is something that the wicked ('those who belong to his company') experience.

What our reading says, in short, is this: (1) God's plan is that humankind should enjoy a blessed immortality which is God's gift; God did not create humans in order to destroy them. (2) The full bitterness of death as the total wreck of human existence will be experienced by those who are 'of the devil's company.'

Second Reading
2 Cor 8:7.9.13-15

Chapters 8 and 9 of 2 Corinthians are, each of them, concerned with a collection for the Jerusalem Church. This matter of a collection on behalf of the 'saints' of Jerusalem was of great importance in Paul's eyes (See Gal 2:10; 1 Cor 16:1-3; 2 Cor 8-9; Rom 15:25-27). Since, for him, the Christian is a member of the Body, and life in Christ is the life of the people of God, the unity of the Church is essential. He developed his theology of unity especially in the face of differences between Judaeo-Christian and Gentile converts and under the impetus of internal strife in the Corinthian community. In view of this, and of his high regard for Jerusalem, the collection was much more than a work of charity.

Two preoccupations dominate his appeal in 2 Cor 8: (1) that the Corinthians be as generous as can reasonably be expected and (2) that they feel themselves entirely free, not under pressure of Paul's authority, for 'God loves a cheerful giver' (9:7). Christian generosity is appealed to in a context of Christian maturity.

Paul offers two reasons why the Corinthians should respond generously. Firstly, the Corinthians obviously prided themselves on the abundance of charismatic gifts which they enjoyed (v. 7; see 1 Cor 12-14); all the more reason that they should excel in generosity too. Charismatic gifts, if genuinely from the Holy Spirit, must give their recipients an even greater sensitivity to the practical needs of fellow-Christians. Secondly, Paul sets before the Corinthians the example of the Lord Jesus (v. 9) who emptied himself in his incarnation (see Phil 2:5-11) in order to full up our emptiness. This must surely serve as a stimulus to them. While the Corinthians are not expected to impoverish themselves they ought give generously whatever they can spare. Christian love should find it intolerable that one community could live in affluence while another is in material need.

Gospel
Mk 5:21-43

The dovetailing of one story with another is a feature of Mark's style;

it is his 'sandwich' technique. But nowhere else does an insertion so clearly separate two parts of a single story as it does here (5:21-24a [24b-34], 35-43). Each 'sandwich' is a carefully constructed unit and should be read as such. The ideas of salvation and faith are the major themes of our twin narrative. Jairus is persuaded that at Jesus' touch his daughter will be 'made well' (v. 23) and the woman is convinced that if she touches Jesus' garments she will be 'made well' (v. 28). Each time the verb is *sózó* which means also 'to save.'

More pointedly still, in v. 34, Jesus reassures the woman, telling her, 'your faith has made you well – has saved you.' Mark has in mind more than bodily healing. Salvation stands in close relation to faith. Jesus, then, exhorts the father of the dead girl, 'Do not fear, only believe' (v. 36). Furthermore, the evangelist lets it be understood that the narrative of the daughter of Jairus has to do with resurrection. The verbs 'to arise' and 'to rise up' in 5:41-42 are used to describe the resurrection of Jesus (14:28; 16:6 and 8:31; 9:9-10; 10:34).

A confirmation of the theological significance of the raising accomplished by Jesus is the exclusive presence of the three privileged witnesses, Peter, James and John (5:37) who are also alone with Jesus at the Transfiguration (9:2), in Gethsemane (14:33) and (with Andrew) on the Mount of Olives as hearers of the farewell discourse (13:3). Each time their presence is a pointer to the reader: here is something especially significant. Jesus raises the dead girl to life because he is 'the resurrection and the life' (Jn 11:25). For Mark and his readers he is the Lord, the source of saving power (Mk 5:30). And the narrative is a lesson in salvation by faith.

Faith comes to fulfilment only in personal encounter with Jesus, only when one enters into dialogue with him. Jairus believed that Jesus has power to heal one at the point of death, when all earthly means had failed. But Jesus looks for a deeper faith: faith in him as one who could raise from the dead, a faith that must find expression in the midst of unbelief. The woman, too, had faith in the power of Jesus. She, too, is asked to have a deeper, fuller faith in him; she meets his gaze and comes to kneel at his feet. And through faith in Jesus she and the little girl are *saved*.

The lesson cannot be missed. The Christian is asked to recognize that faith in Jesus can transform life and is a victory over death. But this faith is not something vague or impersonal. One must come to him, seek him out. One must kneel at his feet, not abjectly, but in the intensity of one's pleading (v. 22) or in humble thankfulness (v. 33). This Jesus will give to one who believes that peace the world cannot give (v. 34). He will assure that person of life beyond death (v. 41).

FOURTEENTH SUNDAY OF THE YEAR

First Reading
Ezek 2:2-5

The typical Israelite prophet is a man who has received a divine call to be a messenger and interpreter of the word of God. He is a man who has met with God; the word which comes to him *is* word of God. Armed with this conviction, the prophet was outspoken, a merciless critic of the people and of the establishment. Ezekiel was called to be a 'watcher' for the house of Israel, a pastor of his people (Ezek 33:1-9). He had not only to deliver the divine 'word' of prophecy; he was also like a sentinel on a city wall who must warn the people of approaching danger, who would give Israel a chance to 'turn,' to repent. The verses of our reading, from the account of his call, underline what an uphill task was his.

When, in 597 B.C., Nebuchadnezzar had, after a short siege of Jerusalem, accepted Jehoiachin's surrender, he had the king, together with leading citizens, deported to Babylon. Among those exiles was Ezekiel. In Babylon (chapter 11) he received his call. The word of the Lord to him is a hard word (2:1-5) for the hearts of the people are far from God. God will not abandon his people. Whether they listen or refuse to listen, the prophet will be sent.

Ezekiel had to become wholly indifferent to public opinion, 'like the hardest stone, harder than flint' (3:9), as he uncompromisingly delivered God's word. What mattered was that the people should know without possibility of evasion that 'there has been a prophet among them,' that their God was still concerned over them. Ezekiel's life and mission hold the abiding lesson that the proclaiming of God's word is a serious and demanding task. God's spokespersons must be prepared for misunderstanding, opposition and rejection. It was so for the Old Testament prophets, it was so for Jesus himself (see today's gospel), it must be so for the prophets of our time. The call and the sending come from God and he gives his Spirit to enlighten and strengthen those who accept the task.

Second Reading
2 Cor 12:7-10

Chapters 10-13 of 2 Corinthians is Paul's letter written 'out of much distress and anguish of heart and with many tears' (2:4) – a stirring and emotional defence of his apostolate and gospel. The Lord has called him to the apostolic ministry; this is approbation and praise enough; self-praise would sound foolish beside it (chapter 10). Much of chapter 11, is bitingly sarcastic. Paul had been called a 'fool'; let them put up with his 'folly' then! He had been driven to self-defence by the fickleness of the Corinthians who were ready to accept a different gospel.

Although boasting about visions is out of place, Paul is compelled to recall an extraordinary experience he had: he had found himself caught up the divine presence (12:1-4). A keen reminder of his human weakness kept him from being carried away by the experience (vv. 5-7). We do not know the nature of the 'thorn in the flesh'; most likely it was a recurring illness. He regarded his infirmity as an impediment to the effectiveness of his ministry and prayed to be rid of it. This was not to be and Paul realized that God's mysterious ways of salvation were at work in his own person. What was important to him above all was the Lord's answer to his prayer: 'My grace is sufficient for you, for power is made perfect in weakness' (v. 9).

When he continues 'whenever I am weak, then I am strong' (v. 10) Paul does not mean that weakness is power, or that the weak will become powerful. He means that the human limitations and disabilities of the sincere and generous apostle are not an obstacle to apostolic work because the power of Christ within one 'is able to accomplish abundantly far more than all we can ask or imagine' (Eph 3:20). Indeed, insult, persecution, even calamity, may be vehicles of that power, a power all the more manifest because it works through the frailty of the apostle.

These are comforting words and challenging words for Christians and especially for those entrusted with the ongoing proclamation of Christ's message. To acknowledge our human weakness should not be an excuse for lapsing into a comfortable mediocrity. The love of Christ must be a driving force (see 2 Corinthians 5:14) for his power is at its best in weakness. Paul's words proclaim to Christians that the enemy of the apostle is not humbling self-knowledge but thoughtless self-sufficiency.

Gospel   Mk 6:1-6

The episode of the rejection of Jesus at Nazareth (6:1-6a) has deep meaning for Mark and he has placed it deliberately at this point in his gospel. A poignant problem in the early days of the Church was the fact that while many Gentiles were accepting the Good News, the Jewish people resisted it (see Romans 9-11). Already, in Mark, the bitter opposition of the authorities has been demonstrated (2:1-3:6); and Jesus was misunderstood even by his own family (3:20-35). Now, at the close of the Galilean ministry, his own townspeople are challenged to make up their minds about his claim, and they take offence at him. Their rejection of him is an anticipation of his rejection by the Jewish nation (15:11-15). That final rejection of him is possible because the blindness of people to God's revelation had been present from the start (see John 1:10-11). The issue is one of faith or unfaith in Jesus; or, in Christian terms, faith in or rejection of the Lord.

Today's reading lays bear one of the roots of this unbelief. Jesus' fellow-townsfolk react in astonishment to his teaching. They wonder at the origin ('where') of his wisdom. They had heard of his mighty works. They are on the verge of asking the right question about him. But they make the mistake of imagining that they already have all the answers to their own questions. That attitude is fatal to faith. Besides, they cannot bring themselves to believe in the greatness or in the mission of a man who is one of themselves. They 'took offence' at him: by Mark's time *skandalon* had practically become a technical term to describe the obstacle which some found in Christ and which prevented them from passing on to full Christian faith and discipleship (see Romans 9:32-33; 1 Peter 2:8; 1 Corinthians 1:23).

The proverb of v. 4, in one form or another, was current in the ancient world; Jesus implicitly assumes the role of prophet. His word must have fortified the early Church against the enigmatic refusal of the chosen people as a whole to accept the message of Jesus. Christian communities down the ages must beware that the proverb does not fit them. Prophets are never comfortable people to have around and we are adept at finding ways of discrediting them.

'He could do no deed of power there': Jesus always demanded faith in himself when he worked a miracle – because a miracle is a sign of the kingdom and without faith would lack significance. Want of faith in Nazareth meant that an opportunity of doing a 'deed of power' was not there. The decisive thing is that a person bow in acceptance before the mystery of the person of Jesus. The people of Nazareth failed to do this because they thought their own natural knowledge of Jesus was adequate. Their unbelief was, humanly speaking, so surprising that Jesus' amazement is stressed by the evangelist. His message seems to be that if Christians of his day were understandably troubled by Israel's lack of faith, they must remember that their Master, too, had marvelled at this unbelief.

Christians today may often be amazed and puzzled at the unbelief of people who have heard the message of Jesus. More important than seeking reasons is not to be discouraged by disbelief. Jesus continued his work after the Nazareth disappointment.

FIFTEENTH SUNDAY OF THE YEAR

First Reading   Amos 7:12-15

Amos was the great champion of justice. He castigated the disorders that prevailed in an era of hectic prosperity (the reign of Jeroboam II in Israel – 783-743 B.C.). To his eyes the symptoms of social decay were glaring. Wealth, concentrated in the hands of a few, and these the leaders of the people, had corrupted its possessors; oppression of the poor was rife; the richly-endowed national religion, with its elaborate ritual, provided a comfortable, self-righteous atmosphere. It was this dangerous complacency that the prophet set out to shatter. His preoccupation sounds sharply in a ringing declaration like the following: 'Take away from me the noise of your sings; to the melody of your harps I will not listen. But let justice roll down like waters, and righteousness like an ever-flowing stream' (5:23-24).

Our reading is an historical interlude between visions of the prophet (7:1-9:15). Amos, a native of Judah, was preaching in the northern kingdom of Israel. He does not pull his punches; his warnings reach a climax in the verse immediately preceding our passage: 'The high places of Isaac shall be made desolate, and the sanctuaries of Israel shall be laid waste, and I will rise against the house of Jeroboam with the sword' (7:9). This is too much for Amaziah, chief priest of the shrine of Bethel; he peremptorily ordered Amos to get back to his own country.

Amos' reply, which underlines the clash of charismatic prophethood and institutional priesthood, is a definition of the true prophet. He is not a court prophet nor one of a group of 'ecstatic' prophets – he is prophet by divine call. In his case the call had come to a poor, unsophisticated shepherd and 'dresser of sycamore trees,' a total outsider to the ranks of the professional prophets. Choice of such as he has its own wisdom. Such a one enjoys the freedom to be honest to a degree that one identified with an institution can rarely manage. It is in its attempt to suppress the cry of honesty that the institution sins most grievously.

Second Reading
Eph 1:3-14

Today it is widely held that Ephesians (read until the Twenty-first Sunday inclusive) is the work of a disciple of Paul (and not necessarily an immediate disciple) who sought to develop the ideas of his master in a markedly ecclesiological direction. It is agreed that the writing cannot be by Paul himself because of the direction of its theology, its unusual vocabulary, and its curious literary contacts with other New Testament epistles and with Colossians in particular. The title 'to the Ephesians' is not original; it seems likely that the letter was, in fact, addressed not to one Church but to a group of Churches. A date about 90 A.D. has been proposed.

The leading themes of Ephesians are the cosmic dimension of Christ's salvation, the Church, and the divine mystery (in their measure, too, the themes of Colossians). The cosmic supremacy of Christ, head of the universe and master of the angels, had been so firmly established in Colossians that Ephesians does not have to dwell on it at length. At most, the theme is recalled in some striking formulas (Eph 1:10,21; 4:10).

What is truly specific in Ephesians is that the idea of Christ's cosmic supremacy has influenced the notion of the Church. The Church is not only the body of Christ, it is his *pléróma*, his 'fullness' (1:23). Beyond Christians who are the 'body' properly so called, the Church embraces, in some manner, all the forces of the new creation. The cosmic breadth of view of Colossians is maintained in Ephesians but always in relation to the concept of the Church. Contemplation of cosmic salvation, which embraces Jews and Gentiles alike and touches the whole of creation, leads the author to see here the 'mystery', that is, a secret long hidden in God but now revealed; he insists on the need for supernatural wisdom in order to attain true knowledge of the divine plan (Col 1:26-28; Eph 1:3-14). For the author, the whole structure of the Church is founded in unity and leads to unity (4:1-6). And he has brought out, more clearly than in Colossians, the distinction of Head and Body (seen in the subjection of one to the other) and their union (achieved through love) when he presents the Church as the Spouse of Christ (5:23-32).

After addressing his readers (1:1-2), the author pronounces a long prayer or blessing in which he thanks God for the blessing which he has bestowed on us in Christ. Like the Jewish *berakah* ('blessing') on which it is based, it is also an announcement of God's great works in favour of his people. It is a veritable summary of God's plan of salvation, beginning before the foundation of the world and looking forward to the fullness of time when the universe will be reconciled in Christ. Throughout the prayer the emphasis is on God's initiative and Christ's mediation. The prayer is built around four themes: election, adoption, redemption, and revelation.

Election (vv. 1:4). God's choice of his elect is an act of love ('in love' should be attached to v. 4), a choice that obliges them to live holy and blameless lives. 'Before the foundation of the world': the choice is not casual but is God's plan from the beginning.

Adoption (vv. 5-6). Through Christ the elect become children of God; and this divine filiation, like the other blessings of God, has its source in the divine goodness and its end in the exaltation of his glory by his creatures. In this plan everything comes from him and returns to him. A recurrent theme in Ephesians is that men and women, understanding God's plan, should praise him and give thanks.

Redemption (vv. 7-8). Redemption is achieved by the blood of the beloved Son shed on the cross. Redemption is the setting free of an individual or a group held in bondage; in the New Testament Christ is the liberator who sets people free from the bondage of sin. So, here, 'redemption' is to be understood as 'the forgiveness of our trespasses.'

Revelation (vv. 9-10). The fourth blessing is the revelation to the apostles, and by them to all humankind, of the 'mystery,' of the universal supremacy of Christ. In Ephesians the divine plan of salvation is presented as the 'mystery,' that is, a secret long hidden in God but now revealed: the mystery is God's plan to create a community of men and women in Christ. Further, that plan is the re-capitulation of all things in Christ – in other words the unification of all things and their submission to Christ as to their head.

In Christ, Israel, a chosen people, had been set apart in order to keep alive in a fallen world the expectation of the Messiah and the hope of salvation through him – the fifth blessing (vv. 11-12). The sixth stage is the call of the Gentiles to share the salvation formerly reserved for Israel, a salvation assured by the gift of the Holy spirit long ago promised by the prophets (vv. 13-14). The motifs of this blessing will recur throughout the rest of the letter.

Gospel   Mk 6:7-13

Jesus had been rejected by his own people (gospel of last Sunday). Now he turns his attention to the twelve. He had chosen them 'to be with him' (3:14) and so he had concentrated on instructing them. But he had chosen them, too, 'to be sent out to proclaim the message'; the time has come for them to take an active part in the ministry. Mark evidently meant the incident, though preparatory and provisional, to be seen as the basis of Christian missionary activity. He carefully avoids the statement, present in Matthew and Luke, that the disciples proclaimed the kingdom of God because, in Mark's perspective, the disciples have not yet understood the true nature of the kingdom. Like the Baptist (1:4) they preached 'that all should repent.'

The sending out the disciples 'two by two' follows Jewish practice. They are to take nothing with them for the journey. If they are not received in a village they will give a solemn warning. 'Shake off the dust that is on your feet.': this is a symbolic action indicating that the place is as good as heathen. Jews shook off heathen dust on re-entering Palestine. 'As a testimony against them,' that is, as a warning to them: the gesture is intended to make them think again and lead them to repentance.

In a summarizing passage (12-13) Mark's reference to a preaching of repentance is deliberate: in his plan the preaching of the imminence of the kingdom is reserved to Jesus; the disciples, like the Baptist, prepare for Jesus' proclamation. Besides, Mark may wish to distinguish their 'preaching' from the full Christian gospel which can be proclaimed only after the Easter event. They also shared in the exorcising and healing work of Jesus. Oil was used in medical treatment (see Lk 10:34), hence its symbolical value in miraculous healing. James (5:14-15) shows that healing by anointing was known in the early Church. The practice attested here may well be at the origin of the later practice, and eventually of the sacrament of the anointing of the sick.

SIXTEENTH SUNDAY OF THE YEAR

First Reading   Jer 23:1-6

The book of Jeremiah is complex. The great bulk of the material is authentic but some passages are later than the prophet's time. This seems to be the case with the first of the two brief oracles (23:1-4,5-6) that make up this first reading. In its present form, at least, it seems to presuppose the Babylonian Exile (v. 3). At the same time, the oracle squares with Jeremiah's view that the radical reason for his people's disastrous course is the culpable irresponsibility of its leaders. Having the role of guides or 'shepherds,' they have failed to keep the people together; they will be punished for their infidelity. But God will not let his people languish in exile. A faithful shepherd himself, he will gather his flock together again and entrust it to good and faithful shepherds. See Ezekiel 34.

The second oracle (vv. 5-6) announcing the future (ideal) king of David's line is authentic. Its date in the reign of Zedekiah is assured by the play on the name of the king. The term 'Branch,' derived from Is 11:1, designates the ideal (Messianic) king (see Zechariah 3:8, 6:12). The new reign will be marked, in an eminent degree, by wisdom, justice, and righteousness, and in the days of the new king the reunited land will again know peace. The name of the promised king, *Yahweh-sidqenu* ('Yahweh is our righteousness') is almost the same as Zedekiah (*Sidqiyahu* – 'Yahweh is my vindication'). Jeremiah is only too well aware that Zedekiah is a living contradiction of the promise of his name. But he is sure that the Lord will raise up one who will worthily bear that reassuring name.

Second Reading   Eph 2:13-18

Addressing himself mainly to the Gentile members of the community (2:11-12), the author reminds them that they were previously separated from Israel and, therefore, from all the hopes and ambitions associated with God's people (vv. 11-12). Christ's death on the cross, however, has served as a peace offering between the two factions of humankind (v. 13). Moreover, this death represents an end to the Jewish law and cult which constituted a division within humankind. In Christ all humankind – Jews and Gentiles alike – is united through one body and in one body. God's plan for humankind, realised in Christ, is a unity so profound that it can be described in terms of 'one new humanity' (13-17). This unity is assured by our access to the one Father (v. 18).

The reconciling of Jew and Gentile had not in fact taken place during the author's lifetime – it cannot be said to have ever happened to any significant extent. What is here stated is a matter of principle – and of hope. The heritage of the Old Testament belongs to the Church, but the Church goes beyond the narrow bounds of that heritage to gather all humankind and so 'reconcile them to God' (v. 16). The point is that it is the Church which is the focus of unity. Throughout the reading the author typifies this ecclesial unity in one word – peace (vv. 14,15,17). And peace is no mere absence of conflict; it is the dynamic reconciliation of people in one community. Reconciliation is a costly business; sacrifices have to be made. We are united 'by the blood of Christ' (v. 13), 'through the cross' (v. 15). All who truly work for reconciliation will know the cost – but will not count the cost.

Gospel
Mk 6:30-34

In this short passage Mark first rounds off (vv. 30-31) his account of the mission of the Twelve (last Sunday's reading). Emphasis has shifted to the instruction of the disciples and Jesus' desire to be alone with them. The desire prepares for the retiral to a 'desert place' where the miracle of the loaves will take place. Here only in Mark are the Twelve called 'apostles.'

It might seem that the missionary journey had achieved their advancement from discipleship to apostolate. But they will be fully apostles only when they are sent out by the risen Lord. After their missionary labours the Twelve needed to rest. More significant is the fact that Jesus wants them to be 'by themselves.' This Greek expression (*kat'idian*) occurs seven times in Mark (4:34; 6:31,32; 7:33; 9:2,28; 13:3) always in a redactional passage and is each time used in reference to a revelation or an instruction reserved for the disciples. Each time the *reader* is being nudged towards special attention.

The details of vv. 32-34 are quite vague and the destination is unknown. For the evangelist the important factor is that the disciples reach a 'desert' place (a fitting Exodus setting for the bread miracle) and that they are 'by themselves.' Jesus' attempt to seek solitude for himself is frustrated, but he is not annoyed. Instead, he is deeply moved by the earnestness of the crowd and by their need. The image of a shepherdless people is found in Numbers 27:17; 1 Kings 22:17. Jesus sees himself in their regard as the messianic shepherd (Ezek 34; Jn 10:1-18) who will find his sheep (Ezek 34:13-14; Jn 10:9; see Jer 23:1-4).

The motif of the sheep without a shepherd foreshadows the moment when the shepherd will be stricken and his sheep scattered (Mk 14:27). The people's most pressing hunger was spiritual and Jesus began to teach them. It is interesting that in John' first discourse on the bread of life (Jn 6:35-50) the 'bread' is Jesus' teaching, his revelation.

SEVENTEENTH SUNDAY OF THE YEAR

First Reading
2 Kgs 4:42-44

The Elisha cycle of stories (2 Kgs 2-13) is an anthology, popular in style, and with complacent stress on the miraculous. Today's anecdote is typical and, obviously, prepares for the gospel story of the multiplication of loaves. The setting of the miracle is the famine mentioned in 4:38.

The core of the prophetic message (for it is as such that the miracle must be seen) is that the feeding of a hundred men with a few loaves is a token of the concern of God for his people – a point underlined by the fact that the bread which Elisha distributes is the bread of the first-fruits. He does not offer it to God but gives it to the people as a sign that God is truly with his people in the person of his prophet. The doubts of the servant are overcome by the assurance that it is the Lord who wishes to provide. The left-overs stress the Lord's generosity.

Ever since the manna in the desert the people of Israel believed that God would provide bread for the hungry, bread from heaven. In the course of time this bread came to be understood in a metaphorical sense and the bread of heaven was taken to be the word of God. Such is the history of the expression as it journeyed through the Wisdom literature and into John's gospel.

Second Reading   Eph 4:1-6

Having opened his heart to his readers in his prayer to God (1:3 - 3:21) The author now begs them to lead a life which corresponds to the gospel which they have heard. Particular stress is laid upon unity and harmony within the community which should correspond to the unity of God himself. Again it is by a dynamic peace that this unity is achieved (see last Sunday's second reading, Eph 3:13-18), a peace which is typified not by any grand gestures but by the 'ordinary' charities of 'humility and gentleness, with patience' (v. 2). The context is that of simple daily life. But we touch the hem of a great mystery – for it is not just a matter of people living together harmoniously, but of preserving 'the unity of the Spirit' (v. 3).

The Holy Spirit is the principle of unity for the Church as he is the principle of unity between humankind and God (2:18,22). The author underscores his teaching by heaping up expression after expression of this fundamental Christian oneness: 'one body, one Spirit ... one Lord, one faith, one baptism ... ' (vv. 4-5). All comes from 'one God and Father of all, who is above all and through all and in all' (v. 6). The pattern is an emphatic expression of Christian unity.

Gospel   Jn 6:1-15

Last Sunday's gospel reading brought us to Mark's introduction to his narrative of the feeding of the five thousand. The Lectionary switches to John's gospel, and his chapter six is read over Sundays Eighteen through Twenty-One. All four gospels carry the story of the multiplication of loaves: Mark (6:32-44; 8:1-10; see Lk 9:10-17) and Matthew

(14:13-21; 15:29-38) have two accounts of a miraculous feeding.

There are several arguments for regarding these two accounts in Matthew and Mark as variant forms of the same incident. And it seems best to take it that the fourth evangelist (Jn 6:1-15) drew on an independent tradition quite like that of Mark's and Matthew's second account. We deal, then, with variant versions of one incident.

Like Elisha, the prophet of the old covenant, Jesus, the prophet of the new, feeds the hungry crowds, only more astonishingly. The introductory sentences (6:1-3) bring together motifs which belong to the common substance of the Gospel tradition: a journey across the Sea of Galilee, the pressure of the crowd, the reputation of Jesus as a healer, his withdrawal to 'the mountain' with his disciples. In v. 4 we meet a distinctively Johannine trait: the reference to the festival of Passover. The Christian reader could hardly miss this hint of the eucharistic significance of the following narrative. In the question ,'How are we to buy bread ... ?' (v. 5) we find a reaction like that of Moses (Num 11:13; 21-22; see 2 Kgs 4:43).

While in the synoptic gospels the disciples distribute the bread, John has Jesus himself do it, which reminds us of the circumstances of the Last Supper. Only in John is the gathering of the fragments given as a command of Jesus, and in the *Didache* the same word *synagein*, is used for the gathering of the Eucharist. John is again introducing the theme of the Eucharist which will be dealt with explicitly in 6:51-58.

The crowds, however, do not understand the proper meaning of Jesus' sign (vv. 14-15). They take Jesus to be the prophet and king who will fulfil their material hopes and ambitions. This is a view of his miracles which Jesus violently rejects as he retires from the scene. He is God's spokesman and the true Messiah but not as understood by his contemporaries. Christians must beware that our understanding of Christ is not tainted by triumphalism.

EIGHTEENTH SUNDAY OF THE YEAR

First Reading   Ex 16:2-4.12-15

This reading is about the murmuring of the people of Israel in the desert and God's promise of manna and quails. In Numbers 11:4:34 we are told that the people had grown tired of the monotonous manna and longed for meat whereupon God sent the quails; in Exodus 16 quails and manna are provided together. Focus, however, is on the manna, with the quails getting only a brief mention.

The story of quails and manna is probably based on phenomena which may still be observed in the Sinai peninsula. Quail, in the course of their long migrations between Africa and Europe are frequently forced down to rest there and are then easily caught. The manna is probably a sweet resinous substance exuded by the desert tree called *tamarix mannifera* – though it appears only in small quantities. Memory of this food, found and eaten occasionally in the desert, was built up in Hebrew tradition into the classic instance of God's care for his people (see Ps 78:24-25 – 'the grain of heaven ... the bread of angels'; Ps 105:40 – 'food from heaven'; Wis 16:20 – 'the food of angels ... providing every pleasure').

God had heard his people's cry in Egypt. He hears them still, even though they, ungraciously, hankered after the fleshpots of Egypt. In the wilderness, a place universally associated with the absence of life and life-giving resources, he provides bread and meat for his people. This feeding with quail and manna is much more than a mere satisfying of hunger. It is one aspect of the covenant relationship set up between Yahweh and his people and is a sign and promise of his abiding concern.

Second Reading   Eph 4:17.20-24

The author of Ephesians has already assured his largely Gentile readers that, in Christ, they have become co-heirs with the Jews in God's promises.

Now he exhorts them to live accordingly. In the first place they must break with their pagan past (v. 17). Throughout the section 4:17-5:20 the radical conversion of those who have been re-created in Christ is described and quite specific demands are made. The demands will, of course, be lived out only if Christians had grasped the transforming truth – the truth that is Christ and not some teaching about him (20-21). If Christ, by his death, has created in himself (of Jew and Gentile) one new humanity (2:15), the Christian, in accepting the work of Christ, must 'clothe oneself' in this new humanity by a fresh moral behaviour. The 'new humanity' is none other than Christ. The particular value of the metaphor of clothing

> is that it expresses *our* participation in the work of our salvation: we really do change our whole way of life. This is a real renewal in our minds. This conversion is symbolized by the changing of clothes connected with baptism. Paul is probably referring to this practice while intimating that what is being changed is not so much a garment as a whole way of life. It is when we 'put on' Christ in this

way that we achieve our true destiny as the image of God (Gen 1:26) (L. Swain, *Ephesians*, pp. 89-90).

Gospel   Jn 6:24-35

In John 6 we have two discourses on the Bread of Life: vv. 35-50 in which 'bread of life' is primarily the revelation of Jesus and vv. 51-59 in which 'bread of life' is now the Eucharist. Our reading (vv. 25-34) is a preface to the present two-fold discourse. Jesus begins (v. 26) by pointing out the difference between a 'miracle' and a 'sign': the multitude may have eaten the miraculous bread but unless they realized its underlying signification it had no lasting effect for them. In v. 27 he begins to press the lesson home in terms of familiar Johannine dualism: perishable food and the food that lasts for eternal life – that abiding food should be the object of their striving. Striving, literally 'working,' for the abiding food leads to a play on 'work.'

The crowd wants to know what works they should do; Jesus puts the emphasis on faith (v. 29) – having faith is a 'work'; it is the all-important work of God. The crowd still thinks in terms of works and begins to question Jesus' claims on that basis. They had seen in him the prophet-like-Moses (6:14); now they challenge him to produce manna: a sign of the End-time (vv. 30-31). Jesus' reply is that he himself is the true bread of heaven prefigured in the manna. It was not Moses who *gave*; it is the Father who *gives* the genuine (*aléthinos*) heavenly bread. And that bread is Jesus himself. Therein lies his power to feed the multitude (6:15-13): he gives bread because he is the bread of life. The crowd asks for this bread (v. 34) but in typically Johannine fashion – like the Samaritan woman, 4:15 – without understanding what it is they really ask for. In that they are not unlike a goodly number of Christians.

NINETEENTH SUNDAY OF THE YEAR

First Reading   1 Kgs 19:4-8

In his zeal for Yahweh, Elijah had confronted and defeated the prophets of Baal at Mount Carmel (1 Kgs 18:20-40) and even had the whole band of them put to death (v. 40). This won for him the implacable hostility of Ahab's queen, Jezebel, a formidable woman fanatically attached to her native Phoenician Baal religion. She vowed to have the prophet's life (19:2).

We find Elijah resting in the desert as he flees for his life (vv. 4-7).

ind him, the erstwhile bold champion of Yahweh, a broken,
rited man (v. 4); but his journey of despair will end in a meeting
with his God (vv. 9-13). In the meantime, he is sustained by his God.
Like the Israelites of the Exodus he fled into the desert and like them
his flagging hope was restored by 'bread from heaven.' In the strength
of this food he can continue his journey to the holy mountain for his
meeting with God (v. 8).

Second Reading   Eph 4:30-5:2

Christian life is not all plain sailing; that is made abundantly clear in
the candid passage, Ephesians 4:25-32. Unsocial behaviour is a lack
of respect and reverence for the Spirit who dwells in the Christian (v.
30) – the Spirit who is the pledge of future glory. There is no place for
bitterness in Christian life; Christians should be remarkable for
generous forgiveness. That is not only because of a word of Jesus (Mt
18:21-22); it is, more fundamentally, because of God's forgiveness:
'God proves his love for us in that while we were still sinners Christ
died for us' (Rom 5:8); the whole of Christian morality can be summed
up in the imitation of God. God's way has been brought near to us in
the loving example of Christ. We are to walk in love and that means
as Christ has shown, self-giving service to the point of death (5:2).
Christ's self-giving love was the sacrifice wholly pleasing to God; our
first worship of God is in the service of our fellows.

> This is not just *a* form of worship among several others. It is the *only*
> form suitable for a God who *is* Father, that is, who is himself totally
> 'for' the others who are his children. (L. Swain, *Ephesians*, 91).

Gospel   Jn 6:41-51

The Constitution on the Liturgy has stipulated that there should be a
homily 'at those Masses which are celebrated with the assistance of the
people on Sundays and holidays of obligation' (art. 52).

Our gospel reading today already is a homily! We know that later
Palestinian homiletic preaching followed a clearly-defined pattern.
The starting-point always was a Scripture text, usually from the
Pentateuch – followed by a paraphrase of the text. Then came the
homily, which took account not only of the text but of the whole
passage which formed its context. Commonly, within the homily there
was a subordinate quotation (usually from the Prophets or Writings)
to which a few lines of commentary were devoted – the whole by way
of a development of the main commentary. The closing statements

referred back to the main statement at the beginning and at the same time summed up points from the homily. Jn 6:31-50 is a typical example of this homiletic pattern.

The Scripture quotation which forms the starting-point of the Johannine homily is: 'He gave them bread from heaven to eat' (v. 31), which contains elements from Ex 16:4,15, in accordance with the practice of employing the whole context. Verses 32-33 constitute Jesus' paraphrase of the citation: 'Very truly, I tell you, it was not Moses who gave you the bread from heaven, but it is my Father who gives you the true bread from heaven. For the bread of God is that which comes down from heaven and gives life to the world.' In vv. 35-50, we find his homily on this Scripture text: first on the theme of 'bread' (vv. 35-40), then on the theme 'from heaven' (vv. 44-48), and finally, on the theme of eating (vv. 49-50).

The subordinate quotation ('They will all be taught by God' – Is 54:13), with its brief commentary, occurs in v. 45. And, according to the homiletic rules, the statement which opened the homily (v. 35) is repeated at the end (v. 48): 'I am the bread of life.' For that matter, even the Scripture quotation and its paraphrase are taken up again (in vv. 49-50). Significantly, Jesus is represented as speaking in a synagogue in Capernaum (v. 59). Fittingly, John has him following the accepted homiletic style of synagogue preachers.

In vv. 35-50 the fundamental reaction to Jesus' presentation of himself as bread is that of belief (35,36,40,47) or of coming to him, which is a synonym of belief (35,37,44-45). Only once (v. 50) is it said that anyone must eat the bread of life; it is in vv. 51-58 that 'eating' appears insistently. In vv. 35-50 'the bread of life' is, primarily, the revelation given to people by Jesus; at a secondary level, it does envisage the Eucharist.

TWENTIETH SUNDAY OF THE YEAR

First Reading   Prov 9:1-6

Chapter 9 of Proverbs contrasts Dame Wisdom (1-6) with Dame Folly (13-18) – the diptych is upset by the insertion of six independent proverbs (7-12). Personified Wisdom and Folly each has prepared her banquet and each is on the lookout for the 'simple'. Proverbs conceives a world divided into two distinct categories: the wise and the foolish. An intermediate category is that of the uncommitted, the simple or inexperienced who have yet to fall under the influence of one of the two groups and join one or other of them.

The contrast 'wise-foolish' (and not 'wise-ignorant') is significant: even the highly-skilled, cultured man is a 'fool' if he does not grasp the true meaning and purpose of life. Today's reading tells us what Wisdom offers: a splendid mansion in which a sumptuous banquet has been prepared. 'Seven' is the traditional figure for completeness and perfection. Spices were mixed with wine (v. 2) to make it more pleasant to the palate. Meat and wine are festive foods and the bread and wine of v. 5 are symbols of the teaching and experience offered by Wisdom. To a Jew the text would suggest the eschatological banquet promised by Yahweh (Is 25:6; 55:1-5), but a Christian will readily see here a foreshadowing of the eucharistic invitation (Lk 22:15).

Second Reading   Eph 5:15-20

In 5:3-20 the author of Ephesians bids Christians live as children of light – there are some kinds of behaviour which are not compatible with holiness. Though, in a sense, we stand in the 'fullness of time' (1:10), the Church is still waiting for the final accomplishment of God's saving plan. The wise Christian will make the most of this present time. One will not be a 'fool' (see first reading) but will be alert to the will of the Lord, and shape one's conduct accordingly. The further exhortation: 'do not get drunk with wine ... but be filled with the Spirit' (v. 18) might well be rendered, in modern terms: 'do not get high on spirits, but on the Spirit.' And, in the setting of Christian fellowship (19-20) it is firmly suggested that the Spirit is the source of joyful fellowship.

Gospel   Jn 6:51-58

This is a duplicate of the preceding discourse on the bread of life (35-50 – see previous Sunday); but now the theme is exclusively eucharistic. The discourse begins (v. 51) with a reiteration of the statement, 'I am the living bread that came down from heaven' (see v. 41) and goes on to draw out its logical consequence. If Jesus is both the Bread and the Giver of bread, then what he gives is himself – his flesh and blood.

The question, 'How can this man give us his flesh to eat?' receives no direct answer, any more than did Nicodemus' question, 'How can a man be born again?' The instructed Christian reader cannot miss the reference to the sacrament of the Eucharist. Indeed, the Johannine expression, 'I am the bread of life ... the bread which I shall give for the life of the world is my flesh', amounts to an expanded transcription of the words of institution, 'this is my body which is for you' as we have it in 1 Corinthians 11:24 (written at Ephesus), and John's ultimate answer to the question 'How?' would undoubtedly have been given in sacramental terms' (C. H. Dodd, *The Interpretation of the Fourth Gospel*, 338 f).

In 53-55 the language is very realistic. 'Flesh ... blood' the Hebrew idiom 'flesh and blood' means the whole person: it is necessary to reveal the whole Christ. The word 'to eat' (*trógein*) had a crude connotation – something like 'gnaw' or 'munch.' Used in a metaphorical sense, 'to eat someone's flesh' implies hostile action (Ps 27:2; Zech 11:9). The drinking of blood was strictly forbidden (Gen 9:4; Lev 3:17; Deut 22:23); its transferred meaning was that of brutal murder (Jer 46:10). If Jesus' words are to have a favourable meaning – as in the context they should have – they must refer to the Eucharist.

Throughout his words on the bread of life, John does not overlook the sacrificial aspect of the Eucharist. Jesus tells us that 'the bread that I will give for the life of the world is my flesh' (v. 51). The food of eternal life is the flesh of Christ offered in sacrifice for the world. Likewise, reference to his blood which must be drunk evokes the 'blood poured out for many' of Paul and the synoptists.

Nor is John unaware of the eschatological aspect of the sacrament. Indeed, for him, the Eucharist is *par excellence* the sacrament of eternal life; in it the Christian finds, in anticipation, the gift of life, and has the gage of final resurrection: 'those who eat my flesh and drink my blood abide in me, and I in them.' Yet, in relation to this idea of life, John organizes everything around the notions of food and of bread: the Eucharist is 'the bread of life: or 'the bread which came down from heaven.' And, all the while, the mystery of the living bread is only one aspect of the mystery of the Incarnation itself. It is significant that John does not speak of 'body' but of 'flesh' – we must eat the 'flesh' of Jesus. We are reminded of the evangelist's description of the Incarnation: 'the Word became flesh and lived among us' (1:14). The Eucharist is the memorial of the redemptive Incarnation.

TWENTY-FIRST SUNDAY OF THE YEAR

First Reading   Jos 24:1-2, 15-18

Chapter 24 stands as an epilogue to the book of Joshua. It deals with a covenant-renewal ceremony that took place at Shechem shortly after the Hebrews from Egypt had entered the promised land. Moses had led the people to the borders of Canaan; it was left to Joshua to bring them into the land (Jos 1:2-3). More significant than the idealized picture of Joshua 10-11 (which casts back into the age of Joshua the conquest of David) is the account of the Shechem assembly (Jos 24).

The Shechem covenant covers a vital stage of the development of Israel: groups who did not experience the exodus or Sinai joined the Yahwistic group at Shechem. A study of the narrative of the exodus from Egypt reveals two distinct episodes involving two groups: an exodus-flight and an exodus-expulsion, and the situation may have been more involved. Those who entered Canaan would have found groups who had never been in Egypt. Some of these were willing to acknowledge the God, Yahweh, of the Moses-group. The Shechem assembly marks the amalgamation of these groups.

While the account of the Shechem covenant is overlaid with deuteronomic theology, it is not a creation of the deuteronomists but is far older. At Shechem 'all the tribes of Israel' made the solemn declaration: 'We also will serve Yahweh, for he is our God' (24:18,24) 'So Joshua made a covenant with the people that day, and made statutes and ordinances with them at Shechem' (24:25). The 'people of Yahweh' of Moses had grown into the people of Israel. In the excerpts from the chapter that form our reading, the main emphasis is on the vital decision that the people are called upon to make – the decision whether or not to serve Yahweh. Being reminded of everything he has done for them since the Exodus, they make a decision for the Lord. They commit themselves to serve Yahweh in covenant relationship.

Second Reading   Eph 5:21-32

Here is a reading that is sure to raise hackles – understandably so. I propose that one should 'come clean.' There is no point in trying to convince women that it somehow enhances the status of women – it does not! It is a text which does not reflect the known attitude of Jesus nor of the authentic Paul.

We might profitably look at this text in the context of other passages in the New Testament. The passage Colossians 3:18-4:1 is a typical domestic code (other New Testament examples are Eph 5:22-6:9; 1 Pet 2;18-3:7) dealing with the relationship between wife and husband, children and father, slaves and master. In each case the onus of obedience is imposed on the subordinate second partner. Noteworthy is the elaboration of the master-slave relationship (Col 3:22-4:1): the text is in favour of a propertied, slave-owning class. Significant is the insistence on 'the Lord' (in 3:24 identified as 'the Lord Christ') throughout the passage.

What has happened is that the Graeco-Roman ethic of the patriarchal household has been taken and imposed on a Christian community – without regard to the Paul and Jesus traditions. What has happened is that a political and social *status quo* (as in the Pastorals) has been brought under the aegis of the Lord Jesus. The change is rough on slaves but may not, at first, have impinged too much on free women. That will change.

The change happens in Ephesians. Here the emphasis is no longer on slave/master but on the relationship of wife and husband in patriarchal marriage (Eph 5:21-33). The shift from Colossians is eloquent. The exhortation: 'Wives, be subject to your husbands, as you are to the Lord' (Eph 5:22) is not at all the same as: 'Wives, be subject to your husbands, as is fitting in the Lord' (Col 3:18). 'In the Lord' of Colossians is the element that 'christianizes' a Graeco-Roman domestic code; 'subject … as you are to the Lord' of Ephesians means something different. In the Colossian situation one might still make a case for equality of wife and husband; in Ephesians that is quite ruled out. Christ/husband … Church/wife: there is no equality between equals here (see vv. 22-24). And the last thing the author of Ephesians wants is any such equality.

The passage had opened, innocuously: 'Be subject to one another out of reverence for Christ' (5:21) – the sort of general statement that Paul could have approved. But the Ephesian author, without more ado, focuses on wives. Colossians had bidden children and slaves to 'obey in everything' (Col 3:20, 22); Ephesians extends the admonition to wives: 'wives ought to be in everything subject to their husbands' – an admonition copper-fastened by the parallel: 'as the Church is subject to Christ' (Eph 5:24). Already, in v. 22 ('be subject to your husbands, as you are to the Lord'), the wife's submission to her husband is set on a par with her religious submission to Christ. The inferior position of the wife – and consequently the inferior position of women – has been given christological justification. Nor is the situation retrieved by such statements as: 'Husbands, love your wives, just as Christ loved the Church and gave himself up for her' (5:25), 'husbands should love their wives as they do their own bodies' (v. 33). For there is no gainsaying the import of the opening and closing verses: 'Wives, be subject to your husbands … a wife should respect her husband' (vv. 22, 33). There is no longer equality in the household of the Lord.

Obviously, if this passage is to be read in a Sunday liturgy, it should be introduced with circumspection, and with great sensitivity.

Gospel   Jn 6:60-69

The long chapter 6 of John is rounded off by reactions to the discourse on the Bread of Life. The first thing one must determine is whether the passage (vv. 60-71) refers to the whole discourse (vv. 35-58). Always, v. 63 has been seen to raise a problem: it would seem that 'flesh' there must refer to the eucharistic flesh of vv. 51-58 and thus involve a contradiction. Let us suppose that v. 60 followed immediately on v. 50 (in other words acknowledge that vv. 51-59 is another, parallel discourse, inserted, later, into the complex). In v. 50 Jesus claimed to be the bread come down from heaven; in v. 60 the disciples murmur about this as the Jews murmured about the same claim (v. 41). The disciples refuse to *listen:* all the references in vv. 60-71 concern hearing or believing Jesus' doctrine. There is not a single reference to refusal to eat his flesh or drink his blood which must surprise after the great emphasis on eating and drinking in vv. 51-59. Reference to the 'ascending' of the Son of Man evidently envisages the claim that he has 'come down from heaven' (vv. 41.50). All in all, one agrees with Raymond E. Brown:

> We have interpreted 60-71 as if these verses had no reference to 51-58; it is a later editorial insertion of Johannine material breaking up the unity that once existed between 35-50 and 60-71. But one may ask, even if this theory is correct, does not the final form of the chapter where 60-71 *now* follow 51-58 require that 60-71 have some secondary reference to the Eucharist? We are not convinced that it does; for we believe that the editor or final redactor added 51-58 to bring out the secondary eucharistic motifs of 35-50, but did not make any real attempt to give a new orientation to 60-71 in light of this addition (*The Gospel according to John*, p. 302).

When then does v. 63 mean? The first notable feature is the reappearance of *pneuma* ('spirit'). In the Nicodemus passage of chapter 3 we are told that the realm of 'the above' is the sphere of 'spirit' and that rebirth into the eternal life of the higher realm is birth 'of the Spirit' (3:3-8). And there is the forceful statement: 'What is born of the flesh is flesh, and what is born of the Spirit is spirit' (v. 6). Similarly here (6:33) the point is made that only one 'born of spirit' can accept that Jesus has come from heaven and can receive his revelation. One 'born of the flesh,' and so open only to the merely human, cannot know him or his teaching. If 'flesh' here has nothing to do with the

Eucharist, neither does the emphasis on Spirit have anythiɪ,
a spiritual interpretation of the eucharistic presence of Jes
    Just as the synoptic account of the ministry in Galilee eᵪ
note of disbelief (see Mk 6:1-6) so, here, the final reactioᵢ
disciples is one of unbelief (v. 66). In the passage 67-69, whic   ₋₁ɪs
out attention to the different reaction of the Twelve who believe in
Jesus, we have John's parallel to the synoptic scene at Caesarea
Philippi (Mk 8:27-32, parr.). The chapter ends on a sombre note (70-
71): Jesus, Bread of Life – the life-giver – will be brought to death by
unbelief and betrayal.

TWENTY-SECOND SUNDAY OF THE YEAR

First Reading   Deut 4:1-2.6-8

The Book of Deuteronomy purports to offer three addresses of Moses
just before the entry of Israel into the promised land (the book is, in
fact, very much later than Moses). The first address comprises 1:1-
4:43; our reading, taken from the close of it, opens a prologue to the
promulgation of the Law to all Israel (4:1-34). Two motives urge
obedience to the law: it is a source of *life*, and it is a *teaching* of divine
origin. Israel's distinguishing trait in the world's eyes will be its
wisdom and discernment derived from the Law. Thus it is crucial that
Israel never forget what happened at Horeb (Sinai). The words 'law,'
'commands,' 'statutes,' 'ordinances' are all synonymous in Deuteronomy: they represent the full expression of God's will. The law is not
seen as a burden to be suffered but as a gift, a source of life and wisdom
and righteousness. It is not easy to maintain such an open and
sophisticated attitude to law and doctrine. A drift to legalism and
stifling orthodoxy is fatally easy.

Second Reading   Jas 1:17-18.21-22.27

The letter of James will be read over five Sundays, beginning today.
It was traditionally accepted that the James named in the address as
author of this writing is James 'the brother of the Lord,' leader of the
Jewish Christian community of Jerusalem. Against that attribution
there is the excellent Greek style and the remarkable affinity of James
with the first epistle of Clement (c. 96-98). James, then, is a pseudony-
mous writing and dates from the last decade of the first century. The
letter is addressed to a milieu in which social differences are marked.
There are the rich who expect, and receive, deferential treatment even

in the liturgical assemblies (2:1-3), people who are prodigal of generous words that cost them nothing (2:16). Entirely absorbed in their business affairs (4:13-17), they do not hesitate to cheat their workers and to squeeze the poor (5:1-6).

These same poor receive scant attention even from those who are supposed to be their shepherds and ought to be their servants (2:2-6). Such conduct cannot but give rise to dissension: jealousy (3:14; 4:2), anger (1:19), murmuring (5:9), and cursing (4:11). The exasperated poor may be driven to rebel against their lot (4:2), or they may, enviously, be seized by the desire for worldly possessions. All James' sympathy goes to the afflicted and to the weak; he has written mainly for them. Like the Old Testament prophets, he takes issue with social injustice; at the same time, however, he considers poverty to have a religious value which makes of the unfortunate the privileged friends of God – the *anawim*. And if he could, and did, turn to the sages and the psalmists to find expression of this outlook, his words have a fresh vigour from the practice and teaching of Jesus.

In our reading (and the whole passage, 16-27, should be read) James firmly asserts that God is the giver of good and perfect gifts (16-18). His greatest gift to humanity is rebirth through the Gospel; v. 18 (see 1 Pet 1:22-23) seems to refer to a baptismal liturgy. Nevertheless, one must be prepared to listen, to check hasty speech, to put away wickedness, and to attend with docility to the word of the Law written on the heart (1:19-21). In Judaism, the Law was not regarded as a burden; in a much truer sense the Gospel, fulfilment of the Old Testament, is a law of liberty which is gladly obeyed (1:22-25). It is all too easy to imagine oneself a 'religious' person; failure to control one's tongue (see 3:1-12) gives the lie to such an illusion. Genuine religion shows itself in the service of those in need and in repudiation of the life-style of the world, that is, of those who make pleasure and self-seeking their goal.

Gospel   Mk 7:18.14-15.21-23

Having completed the reading of John 6, we return to the gospel of Mark. (See Sixteenth Sunday). A precise incident lies behind Jesus' dispute with the Pharisees and scribes (Mk 7:1-23): they had observed that the disciples of Jesus did not practise the ritual washing of hands before meals. In their eyes this constituted a transgression of the 'tradition of the elders,' the oral law. (These Pharisaic traditions claimed to interpret and complete the Mosaic law and were considered equally authoritative and binding. Later rabbis would claim that 'the ancestral' laws constituted a second, oral law, given, together with the written law, to Moses on Sinai).

In responding to their criticism of neglecting one observance (v. 5), Jesus turns the debate on to the wider issue: the relative worth of oral law and the Mosaic law. He cites Isaiah 29:13 (in its Greek form!) against the Pharisees, drawing a parallel between 'human precepts' of which Isaiah spoke and the 'human tradition' on which the Pharisees count. Jesus rejects the oral law because it is the work of men (not word of God) and because it can and does conflict with the law of God. The oral law had put casuistry above love. He instances (9-13) the manner in which a son could avoid all obligations to his parents by fictitiously dedicating to the Temple treasury the money that should go to their support; this was an overturning of a precept of the Decalogue. Thus, by their tradition, the Pharisees had 'made void the word of God.'

The principle of clean and unclean was at the root of Pharisaic preoccupation with ritual purification. A saying of Jesus: 'There is *nothing* outside a person which by going in can defile, but the things that come out are what defile' (v. 15) strikes at the very distinction of clean and unclean, of sacred and secular. It is a flat denial that any external things or circumstances can separate one from God (see Rom 8:38-39). We can be separated from God only by our own attitude and behaviour. In a Gentile-Christian setting this saying was provided with a commentary. The first half of v. 15 – nothing outside a person can defile – is explained in verses 18b-19, and the second part of the verse – it is what comes out of a person that makes one unclean – is developed in vv. 20-23. In this way it is made clear to Gentile Christians that being followers of Christ does not involve them in the observance of Jewish practices. 'The Way' (see Acts 9:2, 19:9,23) is truly open to all men and women.

TWENTY-THIRD SUNDAY OF THE YEAR

First Reading   Is 35:4-7

Though it is found in the first part of the Isaiah-book (1-39) which consists, predominantly, of oracles of the eighth-century prophet, the triumphant poem of Isaiah 35 dates from the Exile and describes, in idyllic terms, Israel's return from exile. It is shot through with the joy of restoration, of good fortune, felt by one who was absolutely certain that, in the end, God would not sell his people short. Our reading bids those who were losing heart to take courage. For God will come to vindicate and save his people. And his coming will reverse their situation of suffering and oppression. As the prophet puts it: 'Then the eyes of the blind shall be opened, and the ears of the deaf unstopped ... and the tongue of the speechless sing for joy.'

Mark, in his account of the cure of a man who 'had an impediment in his speech' (Gospel reading) had this Isaian passage in mind. He uses the rare word *mogilalos* ('stammerer') – taken, surely, from the Greek text of Isaiah 35:6. For that matter, the Isaian reference to the opening of the eyes of the blind will be developed by the evangelist in the parallel miracle of 8:22-26, the cure of a blind man.

Second Reading   Jas 2:1-5

The passage 2:1-13 is concerned with class distinction: it deplores a favouring of the rich and a slighting of the poor. 'Partiality' towards the rich is the wisdom of the 'world' (1:27), whereas God's wisdom (that is, his way of acting) is partiality towards the oppressed and the poor (see Is 35; Ps 145:7-9). The Christian standard is to reflect God's standard, otherwise Christians become 'judges with evil thoughts' (v. 4). The different treatment meted out to rich and poor is especially reprehensible in liturgical assemblies (see 1 Cor 11). Besides, the *anawim* (the 'poor') are the heirs of God's promise.

The Bible's emphasis on God's concern for the poor does not imply that God loves them simply because they are poor, as if poverty were a virtue. Here, as elsewhere, the background is that of the law-court in which justice was perverted and the poor were abused by the wealthy (v. 6). The Bible (apart from Luke) sees the rich man and the poor man as oppressor and oppressed respectively. And God is determined to vindicate the oppressed. This is the only passage in James (apart from the address 1:1) in which Jesus is named and his title here is solemn: 'Our glorious Lord Jesus Christ' (v. 1). It is a confession of Christian faith based on the early credal liturgical acclamation: 'Jesus Christ is Lord!' It proclaims the Christian belief that Jesus of Nazareth who was crucified is the promised Messiah (Christ) and the Lord who has been glorified through resurrection from the dead.

Gospel   Mk 7:31-37

Mark has set the healing of a deaf-mute in the region of Decapolis; as in the previous episode (the healing of a Gentile woman's daughter [7:24-30]), he is concerned with Jesus' attitude to the Gentiles. In that story, the casting out of the unclean spirit which possessed the Gentile girl shows Jesus hearkening to the Gentiles and setting them free. This time the spirit (see 9:17) not only departs but the man recovers his faculty of hearing and speaking. The healing has the symbolic intent of showing that the Gentiles, once deaf and dumb towards God, are now capable of hearing God and paying him homage. They, too, have become heirs of the eschatological promise to Israel: 'The ears of the deaf will be unstopped ... and the tongue of the speechless sing for joy' (Is 35:5-6).

Jesus' action of putting his fingers into the man's ears and touching his tongue with spittle are common to the technique of Greek and Jewish healers. Here the gestures have a certain 'sacramental' quality (see 8:23). 'Looking up to heaven,' as in 6:41, implies Jesus' intimacy with God. 'Sigh' expresses his deep feeling for the sufferer (see 1:41). 'Be opened': characteristically, Mark translates the Aramaic word *ephphata*. (Noteworthy is Ezekiel 24:27: 'Your mouth will be opened ... and you shall speak and no longer be silent,' where the same Greek verb occurs). Both the word *ephphata* and the use of saliva passed at an early date into the baptismal ritual.

The description of this cure (v. 35) is given a solemn cast (the parallel cure in chapter 8 will be described, too, in three clauses [8:25]). The fact that the injunction to preserve silence is disobeyed is put very strongly (v. 36). As in 1:45 the deed is 'proclaimed': the deeds of Jesus cannot but speak the good news. Astonishment is 'beyond measure,' the strongest statement of astonishment in Mark. The miracle has exceptional significance. 'He has done everything well' recalls Gen 1:31. We may also see in the Greek chorus of the crowd (v. 37) the response in faith of the Christian community who perceive in the works of Jesus the time of fulfilment announced by the prophet.

TWENTY-FOURTH SUNDAY OF THE YEAR

First Reading   Is 50-5-9

This reading is an excerpt from the third of Isaiah's four Servant Songs. In this song the Servant speaks of the suffering and persecution he encountered in his effort to bring about justice on earth and to teach people the ways of God. Despite the opposition and the persecution of his fellows the Servant knows (because he is the Servant *of the Lord*) that the Lord will vindicate and deliver him – all the more because he suffers not in spite of his innocence but precisely because of it and, further, because of his preaching and teaching mission. With courageous gentleness, he offers no resistance.

Although it is not possible to identify the Servant with any historical figure, he is clearly a type of the suffering just man, the person who
is oppressed by others. The New Testament sees Jesus as this servant.
For us, in our time, he is too a type of many suffering just people. (See
Passion Sunday, p. 70).

Second Reading   Jas 2:14-18

'You see that a person is justified by faith apart from works prescribed
by the law' (Rom 3:28; see Gal 2:16). So speak James and Paul and,
at the same time, offer apparently diametrically opposed interpreta-
tions of the justification of Abraham. James asks: 'Was not our
ancestor Abraham justified by works, when he offered his son Isaac on
the altar?' (2:21); and Paul flatly asserts that Abraham was justified not
by works but by his faith (Gal 15:6; Rom 4:2-3). It can hardly be
doubted that James is challenging the Pauline slogan 'faith apart from
works.' It is evident that he has not read Paul's letters and is opposing
the use of Paul's slogan by teachers who were promoting moral
permissiveness on the basis of the apostle's thesis of justification by
faith.

We find that while James and Paul use the same words, the meaning
of the words is different in each case. When Paul put his readers on
their guard against a vain confidence in works, he has in view specific
works, those of the Mosaic law. He states emphatically that justification is an absolutely free gift of God which cannot be merited by works
of the Law – or by any works. The works envisaged by James are of
a different order; they are good deeds which sanctify Christian life
(2:15-17,25,22). Paul sets just as much store by the practice of these
virtues (see Rom 11:9-12; Gal 5:22). And when James seems to
minimize faith to the profit of works, he has in view a merely
speculative assent without repercussion on daily living, a faith that is
incapable of saving (2:14), that is dead (2:17-18); the demons believe
in this manner (2:19). Unlike Paul, he does not consider the gratuitous-
ness of faith. His concern is to encourage Christians to observe the
commandments and to lead lives that conform to the divine will. Paul
is concerned to demonstrate that at the moment of his conversion, the
unjustified person is justified independently of observance of the
Mosaic law or of one's personal merits.

Although he has no conflict with Paul, the fact remains that James
does insist on the value and necessity of works. Authentic religion
consists just as much in help given to orphans and widows in their need
(1:27) as in cultic practices; otherwise, ritual observance is a vain and

empty thing. James wants to prevent just that. He is concerned with liturgy and with the common life of the Christian assembly; this is why he insists on the need of social justice and works of mercy. An economic divide split the members of the community; hence the need for insisting on the dignity of the poor before God (2:5) and for censuring the attitude of the rich (2:6-7) – all in a liturgical context. Similarly, the liturgical salutation, 'Go in peace,' is cruel derision when not accompanied by effective help (2:14-16). James' no-nonsense approach proposes a lesson that cannot be driven home too often. It is a message that John has formulated with characteristic directness: 'Little children, let us love, not in word or speech, but in truth and action' (1 Jn 3:18).

Gospel   Mk 8:27-35

In the evangelist's eyes, the unique significance of Peter's confession (8:27-30) rests upon the fact that here, for the *first* time, the disciples speak with Jesus as to what he is in their estimation. Jesus takes the initiative and asks the disciples about the opinion of 'those outside' (4:11) – and learns that they would regard him not as a messianic figure but, at most, as a forerunner of the Messiah. It is very clear that not only was his teaching full of riddles for them but they had missed, too, the import of his works. Peter, however, has at last begun to see: 'You are the Messiah.'

The sequel will show that this is but the first stage of his enlightenment; it is the risen Lord who will open his eyes fully. Again the disciples are bidden to keep silence but now, for the first time, the prohibition is related to Jesus' own person. Mark, indeed, looks beyond Peter and the disciples to the Christian community of his concern and bids his Christians take care that they really understand who their Christ is. And they are reminded that only the Lord can grant understanding.

The passage, in truth, is occupied not primarily with the historical situation of the ministry of Jesus but with the historical situation of the Church for which Mark is writing. Historically, Jesus and Peter engage in dialogue. At a deeper level, 'Jesus' is the Lord addressing his Church and 'Peter' represents fallible believers who confess correctly but then interpret their confession mistakenly. Similarly, the 'multitude' (v. 34) is the people of God for whom the general teaching (8:34 - 9:1) is meant. Thus, a story about Jesus and his disciples has a further purpose in terms of the risen Lord and his Church.

'Peter ... began to rebuke him.' Peter has spoken for all of us. Jesus confirms this: 'You are setting your mind ... on human things.' Not the thoughts of the proud, the arrogant, but the natural reaction of those who shrink from a way of suffering.

Have we, at bottom, any different idea of salvation from that of Peter? Can we really conceive of salvation other than in categories of victory? We experience the saying of Jesus again and again as contradiction. The word of Jesus asserts, unequivocally, that the disciples of the Son of man (v. 31) must necessarily walk on his path. Only one who is willing to be called as a disciple and truly answers that call really understands Jesus. The loyal disciple cannot be preoccupied with one's personal interests but will be faithful unto death in a sustained faithfulness to Jesus (v. 34). The way of discipleship is not easy and one may be tempted to shrink from what it entails. But to seek thus to evade the risk and save one's life is to suffer the loss of one's true self. Only one who is prepared and willing to risk all for Jesus and for his gospel will attain to authentic selfhood (v. 35).

TWENTY-FIFTH SUNDAY OF THE YEAR

First Reading   Wis 2:12.17-20

Wisdom 1-5 represents the climax of Old Testament thought on the suffering and righteous man at the hands of the wicked. The setting is the life of the faithful Jew in Alexandria surrounded by pagans, and by Jews who have turned from their Jewish ways. The 'ungodly men' here are such Jews, disenchanted with traditional wisdom, who have resorted to hedonism: 'Come, therefore, let us enjoy the good things that exist, and make use of the creation to the full as in youth' (2:6). The 'righteous' are those who, despite the problems that the tradition must have raised for them, nevertheless (like Job) hold on to their faith in God and obey his commandments. Their faithfulness cuts the ungodly to the quick and threatens their existence: 'Let us lie in wait for the righteous man, because he is inconvenient to us and opposes our actions' (2:12).

Vv. 17-20 present suffering as a test or trial, primarily for the benefit of the ungodly who want to prove their own thesis, but also for the righteous whose true mettle is revealed in their affliction: 'Having been disciplined a little, they will receive great good, because God tested them, and found them worthy of himself' (3:5). The passage has been seen in Christian tradition as anticipating hostility to Jesus, the suffering just one *par excellence*. It forms a unified theme with the

Gospel reading and with the reading from James.

Second Reading   Jas 3:16-4:3

From the start of his letter, James has insisted that true wisdom (1:5) comes from God (1:17) and is modelled on Jesus' behaviour. True wisdom is the leading of a Christian life. 'Who is wise and understanding among you? Show by your good life that your works are done with gentleness born of wisdom' (3:13). This is clearly the wisdom of the righteous, depicted in Wis 1-5, as opposed to the 'wisdom' of the ungodly, and is necessarily translated into action: peace, gentleness, reasonableness, mercy, certainty and sincerity (3:17). The 'harvest' or righteousness (3:18), which is the expression of God's righteousness (1:20), is the effect of peace (3:18). True justice can be based only on peace. By contrast, James turns from peace to warfare (4:1-12). Strife is caused by unruly passions and uncontrolled desires; even prayer can be wrongly motivated (4:1-3). In short, the 'wisdom' which is human only gives rise to wars, ambitious rivalry, cut-throat competition, and injustices of all kinds. This is so because humans are basically selfish and self-seeking. We need to open our hearts to God in prayer, and submit our desires to God's purifying word.

Gospel   Mk 9:30-37

Mark 9:30-32 presents Jesus' second prediction of his suffering, death and resurrection (see 8:31-32; 10:33-34). On the fateful journey to Jerusalem Jesus 'was teaching' his disciples; Mark thus stresses both the importance of the lesson and the difficulty which the hearers experienced in grasping it. The disciples are warned of the fate that awaits their Master in the city. It is a revelation granted to them alone, but they do not understand and are afraid. 'The Son of Man is to be delivered into human hands': this is likely to be close to the form of the original passion-saying which underlines the developed version of the three passion-predictions. In Aramaic it would run something like: 'God will (soon) deliver up the son of man to the sons of men.' The disciples' thoughts are still human thoughts (see 8:33) and they cannot understand this teaching which is a revelation of God.

In vv. 33-34 their lack of understanding appears at its most blatant. They, disciples of a master so soon to suffer bitter humiliation and death are all too humanly involved in petty squabbling over precedence. The caressing of the child – 'taking it in his arms,' is proper to Mark, a vivid touch in his style – it is a symbolic gesture in the manner of the prophets; but it also tells us much of the delicate sensitivity of Jesus. 'Welcomes': the loving service of the weaker members of the community, those who stand in greatest need of being served. A Christian is one baptized 'into the name of' Jesus (Mt 28:19; 1 Cor 1:13,15), so becoming his. That is why one meets (serves) Christ himself in the disciple, and the Father in Christ. This, then, is the dignity of Christian service. Mark has made the point that the revelation of Jesus cannot be received by one who is not ready to enter into the spirit of discipleship and thereby become 'last' and 'servant.' Perhaps the reader of today is once again attuned to the unambiguous message of this word of Jesus: greatness in his Church is found in *diakonia*, service, and only there. Our first step is to have relearned this. It is high time for us to act accordingly, at all times, and at all levels.

TWENTY-SIXTH SUNDAY OF THE YEAR

First Reading   Num 11:25-29

This passage tells of the institution of seventy elders who were to assist Moses in ruling the people of Israel (see 11:14). They were endowed with the spirit of leadership, a participation in Moses' charism of leadership, and with the spirit of prophecy, that they might speak on behalf of the Lord. Though Eldad and Medad were not in the group thus commissioned they, too, were inspired by God to exercise leadership and to speak on his behalf. Joshua objects to these 'interlopers.' This leads Moses to underline what is the main point of the reading: God's choice is not a personal privilege to be jealousy guarded. It is rather a call to serve his people. Would that as many as possible were engaged in that service! And Moses fervently wishes: 'Would that all the Lord's people were prophets!'

Second Reading   Jas 5:1-6

In chapters four and five James turns to two groups of rich persons: merchants and big landowners. The passage 4:13-17 is aimed at the arrogant businessman (merchant). Somewhat in the line of Sirach 11:19 he describes the presumption of the rich – that sense of power and security that comes with wealth. He depicts them as arrogantly boastful. Their cleverness and self-confidence will not profit them, for these lie outside God's will – a will which favours the poor and rejects the arrogance of the rich.

The harshly rhetorical language is in the style of the Old Testament prophets. James views the rich as an ungodly social class; there is no hope for a rich person as long as one remains a member of that class. James accuses the rich of two crimes: luxurious living and oppression. 'Your riches have rotted ... your gold and silver have rusted ... you have laid up treasure for the last days' (5:2-3). He is clearly influenced by a saying of Jesus: 'Do not store up for yourselves treasures on earth, where moth and rust consume and where thieves break in and steal, but store up for yourselves treasures in heaven' (Mt 6:19-20).

James has in mind rich landowners: 'the wages of the labourers who mowed your fields ... the cries of the harvesters' (5:4). The concentration of ownership in a few hands was part of first-century Palestinian economic life. These capitalists were the aristocracy and upper priestly class – the Sadducees. James, acutely conscious that a parallel attitude could flourish within the Christian community, takes up the cause of the exploited and oppressed agricultural labourers. In his eyes this exploitation is equivalent to murder: 'You have condemned and murdered the righteous one' (5:6). There is the evident influence of ben Sirach:

> The bread of the needy is the life of the poor;
> whoever deprives them of it is a murderer.
> To take away a neighbour's living is to commit murder;
> to deprive an employee of wages is to shed blood. (Sir 24:21-22)

James' judgment on the rich is the harshest in the New Testament. And he is opposing the structures – which he would surely regard as sinful – that enable the rich to increase their wealth at the expense of the poor. His condemnation of unjust situations reaches beyond his own age to all similar situations. While his principal purpose is to give consolation to and comfort the poor, he takes a strong social justice stance. But he does not advocate violent overthrow of the rich; judgment is in the hands of the Lord, who hears the cries of the poor. The oppressed have the right to cry out and demand justice.

Gospel   Mk 9:38-43.45.47-48

As a correlative of a belief in demons, the practice of exorcism was widespread in the hellenistic period among Jews and gentiles. The apostolic Church found itself faced with the problem of its attitude to non-Christian exorcists who invoked the name of Jesus (see Acts 19:13-16).

Mark 9:38-43 gives one answer. The fact of casting out demons 'in the name of Jesus' shows that the exorcist recognized the power of

Jesus; he is not against Jesus and his disciples even if he is not joined to them. The saying of Jesus (v. 39) offers his disciples a directive: they are not to forbid one who acts so. The presumption is that one who does a good deed in the name of Jesus cannot be an enemy of his; the saying of v. 40 suits the context perfectly. In a Christian setting the statement means that one is a member of Jesus' Church as long as one does not categorically separate oneself from him. Linked by the catchword 'in the name of', v. 41 asserts that the smallest act of kindness shown to a disciple on the ground of one's connection with Christ will not fail to have its reward. Presupposed is God's kindness which will not overlook the slightest deed of generosity. 'Reward' is not something we win for ourselves; it is always a free gift of a generous God.

Jesus had come to seek out and save the lost. Now he utters a grim warning against any who would hurt those 'little ones,' who would shake their faith in him. Deliberately to lead others astray, to snatch from them the hope that he has given them, is seen by Jesus as the blackest sin: the very denial of his demand of love (9:42). But a person's own enemy, one's stumbling-block, may lie in oneself (see 7:20-23). Occasions of sin are to be ruthlessly cut off (vv. 43-48).

With the compelling emphasis of startling metaphor and threefold repetition the Lord urges people to make the costliest sacrifices in order to avoid sin and enter into life. 'Hell,' is, literally, 'gehenna.' Gehenna was a ravine south of Jerusalem, where infants were offered in sacrifice to Moloch (Jer 7:31; 19:5-6; 39:35). It was desecrated by Josiah (2 Kgs 23:10) and was henceforth used as a dump for offal and refuse. Jeremiah warned that there the faithless ones of Israel would be destroyed by fire. As a site of ill-omen, it came to symbolize the place of future punishment.

All of this has to be read in the context of exuberant Semitic imagery. Only crass literalism could have led to the later notion of hell as a place of fiery torment. And the notion of a God who condemns sinners to that hell has to be acknowledged for what it objectively is: blasphemy.

TWENTY-SEVENTH SUNDAY OF THE YEAR

First Reading   Gen 2:18-24

The Yahwist's charming, and theologically important, story of the creation of woman. God recognizes that solitude is 'not good' for the man; he is determined to provide 'a helper as his partner.' (In contrast to Genesis 1:26-27, where *adam* is humankind, man-and-woman, in Genesis 2 *adam* is male only until the formation of woman in 2:18-24. But not until the emergence of woman is there whole humankind.) Thus, something more than solitude is involved: there is helplessness too. See Sirach 36:29-30 – 'He who acquires a wife gets his best possession, a helper fit for him and a pillar of support. Where there is no wife, a man will wander about and sigh.' 'A helper as his partner': the word *ezer*, 'helper,' 'stand-by,' is normally applied to God himself – as in many of the psalms. The name-giving in vv. 19-20 expresses the dominion over the animal kingdom that is explicitly attributed to man in 1:26-28. But the fact that man and the animals are made from a common clay has not sufficed to establish any real bond between them; man's helpmate must be more intimately bound to him: she will be formed from part of him. This alone will assure the desired conformity between them (21-22).

Yahweh himself, 'like a father of the bride,' leads the woman to the man. As she stands before his delighted gaze, the man bursts into song – the first love song! Her very name *ishsha* (woman) indicates her relationship to *ish* (man). This is typical Hebrew word-play; the etymology is popular only, it is not exact.

'This at last is bone of my bones and flesh of my flesh' (2:23). The man now has a companion, a partner sharing life to the full. Now there is community – and now there is whole humanity. 'It is not good that the man should be alone.' Human living cannot be understood only in relationship to God. Community, a harmonious relationship between men and women, is God's purpose for humankind. The community of man and woman is the basic shape of community.

The underlying story in v. 24 is aetiological: it is told to answer a definite question: whence this attraction of man and woman, this drive of the sexes to each other; why do a man and woman now leave home and cleave to each other to become one flesh with each other and·in the child?

The story gives the answer. Man, who has lost his rib, feels incomplete and will feel so until he gets his 'rib' back, until he finds a woman. Obviously, the woman, too, yearns for the man from which she, the 'rib,' was taken. The Yahwist, as usual, goes beyond the ancient story and stresses the complementary nature of man and woman in relation to marriage: it is because Yahweh made them for each other from the beginning that man and woman will break all other ties and join in marriage. Centuries later a greater than the Yahwist will add his comment and bring out the full implication of the earlier text:

'So they are no longer two, but one flesh. Therefore what God has joined together, let no one separate' (Mt 19:6). See 1 Corinthians 6:16; Ephesians 5:31.

Second Reading   Heb 2:9-11

From today until the Thirty-Third Sunday inclusive, second readings on Sundays are from the Letter to the Hebrews.

Introduction to Hebrews

This magnificent work was written by an unknown, immensely gifted, Hellenistic Christian to encourage Jewish Christians who, in face of difficulties and persecution, were tempted to drift from Christianity. The author exhorts them to cling to the word of God as unveiled in Christ and to persevere in faith. The force of the argument rests altogether on the person and work of Jesus: Son of God, eternal high priest, offering a perfect sacrifice. It is most likely a document of the second Christian generation and may be reasonably dated in the 80s A.D.

The central theme of Hebrews, the priesthood of Christ, is formulated by reference to Jewish theological categories: Christ is superior to angels, to Moses, to the levitical priesthood and Christ's sacrifice is superior even to the high-priestly liturgy of the Day of Atonement. Such Old Testament concepts were well appreciated by first-century Jewish converts though not, even then, by all; inevitably, they lose something of their relevance after twenty centuries. Despite this, we meet throughout the letter religious truths of perennial validity. The author intended his treatise to be a 'word of exhortation' (13:22). The whole is a splendid statement of the saving work of Christ and constitutes for us today a moving word of exhortation when we may be tempted to 'fall away from the living God' (3:12).

A special worth of Hebrews is its contribution to christology. For the author Jesus is Son of God; but he is the Son who 'had to become like his brothers and sisters in every respect' (2:17), a Son who 'in every respect has been tested as we are, yet without sin' (4:15). He is the human being who stands in a relationship of obedient faithfulness towards God (3:16) and who stands in solidarity with human suffering. Thereby he is a mediator: a true priest who can bring humankind to God. If he bears 'the exact imprint of God's very being' (1:3) it is because we see in him what makes God God; he shows us that God is God of humankind.

The consistently negative evaluation of the whole levitical system might suggest that, for the author of Hebrews, the Old Testament holds nothing of value for Christians. Not so: there is, among other things, the inspiring example of faith of the great men and women of Israel, with the reminder that faith is necessary for those who would move onward to draw close to God. Faith is the firm assurance of the fulfilment of our hope. For, faith is oriented to the future and reaches out to the invisible. Grounded on the word of God, it is a guarantee of heavenly blessedness; it persuades us of the reality of what is not seen as yet and enables us to act upon it. See Chapter 11.

The realization that the saints of the Old Testament, their noble ancestors in the faith, are witnesses of the great race which Christians must run, will give them heart and encourage them to persevere. Nor are these merely interested onlookers. As in a relay race, the first runners have passed on the baton of faith – they are deeply involved in the outcome of this race run by Christians. But the example that is best calculated to sustain the patience and courage of Christians is that of their Lord who was humiliated and crucified only to rise again and enter into his glory. Jesus is the 'pioneer' – that is, chief and leader – offering the example of a faith strong enough to enable us to endure the sufferings of a whole life (12:1-11).

Commentary on Hebrews 2:9-11
The author begins his work by demonstrating that Jesus, Son of God, is superior to the angels (1:5-2:18). In 2:5-18 he faces up to the paradox that Jesus, as brother of humankind, was for a time less than the angels.

Our reading begins with his exegesis of Psalm 8:4-6 (cited by him in 2:6-8). While noting that the universe, though in principle subject to the dominion of Christ, is not yet totally subjected to him, he argues that Christ's humiliation is a necessary step towards his exaltation. By entering fully into human life, by calling all men and women his brothers and sisters (v. 11), and by experiencing the bitterness of death like them (v. 9), he became the source of their salvation and sanctification. It was 'by the grace of God' (v. 9), that is, by God's purpose of grace and love, that Jesus suffered and died for humankind. The same idea is implied in the phrase 'it was fitting' (v. 10): by God's freely ordained plan of salvation. The death of Jesus was not accidental; it was part of God's plan for him and it was through obedience and suffering that he became perfect. Jesus is the pioneer and leader of our salvation: pointing the way and leading the way along his road of obedience and suffering.

Hebrews' theology sees a thorough correspondence between Saviour and saved, Son and 'sons,' Sanctifier and sanctified. Jesus is happy to call all men and women his brothers and sisters.

Gospel   Mk 10:2-16

New Testament teaching on divorce has come under special scrutiny in recent times and Mark 10:2-12 figures prominently in all studies of the subject. In rabbinical style, question (v. 2) is matched by counter-question (v. 3). Nowhere in the written Torah is the permission of divorce explicitly spelled out; rather it seems to have been a custom taken for granted, a right given only to the husband to repudiate his wife without her having any redress (see Deut 24:1-4).

Jesus (v. 5) does not question their interpretation of the Law; but he does declare that Moses had written the 'commandment' on divorce on account of human *sklérokardia*, 'hardness of heart' our unteachableness, our failure to acknowledge God's moral demands and to obey the higher law contained in Genesis. Jesus carries his argument further (vv. 6-9) by asserting that, from the beginning, God had no divorce in mind; by creating male and female God intended marriage to be for one man and one woman bound together in the indissoluble union implied by 'one flesh' (Gen 1:27; 2:24). This monogamous union, moreover, was indeed indissoluble and unbreakable not only by reason of the two being one, but also because God himself brings the partners together and is the author of the marriage union: 'Therefore what God has joined together, let no one separate' v. 9).

An appendix (vv. 10-12) to the pronouncement story is presented as an exposition which Jesus gives his disciples in private. V. 11 declares that not only is divorce forbidden but also that marriage following divorce constitutes adultery because the first marriage bond has never been broken. The words 'against her,' referring to a man's first wife, go beyond Jewish law which did not consider that a man could commit adultery against his own wife. The statement in v. 12 goes quite beyond Jewish law since a woman was not allowed to divorce her husband. Mark has expanded the teaching of Jesus so as to meet the needs of gentile Christians living under Graeco-Roman law. And, in any treatment of New Testament attitude to divorce one must give full weight to Paul's position in 1 Cor 7:10-16.

The passage Mark 10:13-16 is a pronouncement story showing Jesus' attitude to children; its place here is on topical grounds, due, very likely, to the preceding teaching on marriage. Mark has delightfully brought the little scene to life: mothers anxious to present their children to the renowned Rabbi and wonder-worker; the disciples officiously intervening; Jesus indignant at their rebuff to children; his taking them into his arms.

The point of the narrative lies in the sayings: children, better than any other, are suited for the kingdom since the kingdom is a gift which must be received with simplicity. Jesus himself, in a true sense, is the kingdom; that is why children have right of access to him. No one can enter upon the blessings of the kingdom who is not open and willing to receive the kingdom as a gift. It is probable that the story may have been influential in determining the early Church's attitude to the practice of infant baptism.

TWENTY-EIGHTH SUNDAY OF THE YEAR

First Reading   Wis 7:7-11

The long passage 7:1-8:21, presented as a speech of Solomon, is a hymn in praise of wisdom. The inspiration of the poem is the prayer which Solomon made when he began his reign (see 1 Kgs 3:6-9; 2 Chr 1:8-10). He had asked for wisdom: 'Give your servant an understanding mind to govern your people, able to discern between good and evil' (1 Kgs 3:9). The wisdom Solomon prayed for and was granted in abundance is a vision of the way things really are. It is gained not by intense intellectual exercise but by total dedication to God. It is a revelation of God's goodness, present in the act of creation and manifest in the world of men and women. And it engenders in the 'wise' person an attitude of mind and heart that enables one to feel at home with divine and created reality. Since the fear of the Lord was regarded as the beginning of wisdom (see Proverbs 1:7), true wisdom was impossible without right relationship with God and without submission to his will.

Second Reading   Heb 4:12-13

The author of Hebrews frequently refers to the word of God, a word which covers the whole range of God's activities in relation to humankind. It is God's word which creates, reveals, makes demands, strengthens and saves. Ultimately, it was spoken, perfectly and completely, for human benefit, in the person of God's Son, Jesus Christ (1:1-3). And it continues to be spoken in our day. Our reading makes use of a cluster of images and metaphors to describe the vital force of that word of God. This word is 'living and active': *living* in the sense that through the power of the Spirit it gives life and leads to eternal life;

active in that it inspires those who hear it to live Christian lives. The word is 'sharp' and 'piercing' in that it penetrates to one's intimate being. The word discerns 'the thoughts and intentions of the heart': it tests one's moral worth because it evaluates one's dispositions.

The qualities of the word of God are such that there is no escape from its authority, no hope of shirking one's responsibility towards it. The *logos* is boldly personified, and though the context is against the view of its being identified with the personal Logos, yet the word of God's revelation is so authoritative as to be ultimately interchangeable (v. 13) with the God who speaks it. He is the one 'with whom we have to do' in the long run. We ought, hear and now, if we are wise, regulate our lives according to his word so that we may stand with confidence before his throne of grace (4:16).

Gospel   Mk 10:17-30

This is the saddest story in the gospel, this story (10:17-22) of the refusal of one whom Jesus loved to answer his call.

Entry into the kingdom is the matter at issue as Jesus is asked what one must do to inherit eternal life. He begins to answer the question by pointing to the duties towards one's neighbour prescribed in the decalogue; but he knows that observance of the law is not the whole answer. He was drawn to the man and invited him to become his disciple. But this aspiring disciple has to learn that discipleship is costly: he, a wealthy man, is asked to surrender the former basis of his security and find his security in Jesus' word. He cannot see that following Jesus is the true treasure, the one pearl of great price (Mt 13:44,46) beyond all his great possessions. He cannot face the stern challenge of loving in deed and in truth by opening his heart to his brother in need (see 1 Jn 3:17-18).

The rich man's sad departure (v. 22) was dramatic witness that riches could come between a person and the following of Jesus; the words of Jesus (23-27) drive the message home. Jesus begins by stressing the difficulty of access to the kingdom for the wealthy (v. 23) and passes quickly to the difficulty of entering the kingdom at all (v. 24). The vivid example of the impossible (v. 25) – contrast of the largest beast of burden known in Palestine with the smallest of domestic apertures – applied as it is to the rich, would come more logically before v. 24.

The point is that salvation is ever God's achievement, never that of humans (v. 27). It is the only answer, the confident answer, to the helpless question, 'Then who can be saved?'

TWENTY-NINTH SUNDAY OF THE YEAR

First Reading   Is 53:10-11

This reading is a short excerpt from the fourth Servant Song (52:13-53:12). Already, the Servant has been described as one 'struck down by God, and afflicted' (53:4). But his sufferings are vicarious: 'crushed by our iniquities' (v. 5), with 'the iniquity of us all' laid upon him (v. 6). Our reading stresses, again, that it was 'the will of the Lord to crush him' (v. 10) – and then draws an unexpected and startling conclusion from his death. Offered as a sacrifice of atonement for the sins of others, it is a veritable triumph of failure. The Servant carries out his mission for humankind in and through his sufferings and death. And death marks the beginning of glorification for him. For others it will be the source of many blessings; it will be their 'justification' (v. 11). By reflection on this and similar passages, the early Christians came to an understanding of the saving achievement of the suffering and death of Jesus. (See Good Friday, p. 87.)

Second Reading   Heb 4:14-16

Jesus the high priest who has entered the heavenly sanctuary (6:20; 7:26; 8:1; 9:11) offers solid motivation indeed for holding fast to the faith we profess. Our high priest has already passed through all the heavens to penetrate into the highest of them where God dwells. The high priest is named: Jesus, the true Son of God. The religion which has such a priest, the very Son of God, in such a sanctuary, is a religion to which we must cling despite all difficulties. But may not this surprising greatness of the high priest imply an aloofness towards human misery? Not so: our high priest can sympathize with us in all our trials and sufferings. Jesus had suffered trials as we do, and throughout his life. 'Without sin' indeed – but this fact does not make him less our brother.

Having such a high priest, Christians can advance with full confidence to present themselves before God. The 'throne of grace' is the throne of God's mercy. It is precisely because it is accessible to sinners that it is throne of grace; access is through the priesthood of Christ, the link between God and humankind. Christians who approach the throne encounter the loving mercy of God who bestows on them his favour (*charis*). The sympathy of Jesus is 'seasonable', 'opportune' ('grace to help in time of need'); it is expressed in practical aid to those who are tempted, accommodated to their situation and suitable above all because timely. Our high priest has entered heaven but he is united to us still by his understanding of our trials and difficulties. The distance between us, abolished by the incarnation, has not been broadened again by the ascension; he is always ready and able to help us because he is always our compassionate high priest.

Gospel   Mk 10:35-45

In 10:33-34 we have the third and most detailed prediction of the passion in this gospel. Sadly, the stark words fall on ears deafened by selfish ambition. Jesus asks of one who would follow him a readiness to face and share his sufferings. The power of the risen Lord will in due course break through the present self-seeking of James and John and give backbone to their facile enthusiasm; they will indeed courageously walk in the way of their Master.

The episode of the two brothers (vv. 35-40) originally had no connection with the prophecy of the passion; it finds its place as an illustration of the Marcan incomprehension motif. Matthew spares the two disciples by attributing this ambitious request to their mother (Mt 20:20-21), while Luke omits the story altogether. The brothers approach the Messiah (8:29) and quite firmly put their request, but in general terms. Jesus receives them graciously and asks what they have in mind. They demand nothing less than the first places in Jesus' triumph. 'In your glory' – 'glory' (*doxa*) as at 8:38 and 13:26 is the eschatological glory of Jesus at the parousia; so, at least, Mark understands it. The original setting of the verse is uncertain and the brothers are motivated more by selfish ambition than by any clear idea of what they want. They were disciples of One whom they had acknowledged as Messiah; they were on to a 'good thing' and they were determined to make the most of their good fortune. The episode admirably suits Mark's purpose of emphasising the chronic incomprehension of the disciples and, with its sequel (vv. 41-45), carries a barbed message for his readers.

The other ten are not less incomprehending than John and James; they are indignant at being circumvented by the shrewd pair (v. 41). This is an appropriate occasion for another telling lesson in discipleship (vv. 42-45). Jesus solemnly asserts that, in the community of his disciples, there is no place for ambition. His Church is a human society: there is need for authority, there must be leaders. But those who lead will serve their brothers and sisters, and the spirit of authority is *diakonia*. Surely, Jesus has intended the paradox and asks for it to be taken seriously. There is the shining light of his own example: he served God's purpose, the salvation of humankind, by laying down his life in the service of men and women. There really can be no justification at all for styles and trappings and exercise of authority inspired by the powers and princes of this world. Centuries of tradition cannot weigh against the stark words of the Lord: 'It shall not be so among you': we have no right to urge the burden of history against a demand as stark as that. Sooner or later we must find courage to admit, not only in word but in deed, that we have not hearkened to this word of the Lord.

The ground of the paradoxical behaviour required of disciples is to be found in the example of the Son of Man (v. 45). The saying specifies in what sense Jesus is to 'serve' people: he will give his life as a ransom for them. *Lytron* ('ransom') was originally a commercial term: the ransom is the price that must be paid to redeem a pledge, to recover a pawned object, or to free a slave. In the Septuagint the term is predicated metaphorically of God who is frequently said to have bought, acquired, purchased, ransomed his people (e.g. Ps 49:8; Is 63:4).

In its Marcan form the saying is related to Isaiah 53:10-11 and 'ransom' is to be understood in the sense of the Hebrew word *asham* of Isaiah 53:10, 'an offering for sin,' an atonement offering. By laying down his life for a humankind enslaved to sin, Jesus fulfils the saying about the Servant in Isaiah 53:10-11. Jesus has paid the universal debt: he has given his life to redeem all others. But this is metaphor, not crude commerce. The death of Jesus, in the Father's purpose and in the Son's acceptance, is a gesture of sheer love. Any suggestion that the death of the Son is, in any sense at all, the literal payment of a debt, the placating of an offended God, is blasphemy. God is ever motivated by love, not 'justice'.

THIRTIETH SUNDAY OF THE YEAR

First Reading   Jer 31:7-9

It was Jeremiah's conviction that faithless Jerusalem would fall, a conviction voiced (as elsewhere) in his letter to those exiled to Babylon in 598 B.C. (29:16-20). Yet, in the same context, he can frame a promise: 'For I surely know the plans I have for you, says the Lord, plans for welfare and not for harm, to give you a future with hope' (29:11). This hope is held out not to those left behind in Jerusalem but to he exiles – a point more forcefully expressed in the vision of two baskets of figs (24:5-7).

There is, then, the remarkable feature that the same Jeremiah who so pitilessly demolished false hope yet put before his people a positive hope for the future. His efforts to bring his people to their senses had failed, but it is the greatness of the man and the grandeur of his faith, that precisely during the most tragic moment of his life he spoke his optimistic oracles, notably those of chapters 30-33, 'The Book of Consolation.'

This collection includes earlier oracles of Jeremiah originally addressed to northern Israel (which had been devastated by the Assyrians in 721). Our passage (31:7-9) appears to be an adaptation of such an earlier oracle of Jeremiah to the situation of the exiles in Babylon. It is certainly reminiscent of Second Isaiah and may have been influenced by the Isaiah tradition. At any rate, it carries a message of hopeful joy. It first presents God as a good shepherd gathering together his scattered flock; and ends with Yahweh as 'a father to Israel' who will not allow his 'first-born' to be totally destroyed. The 'remnant', purified by frustration and suffering, will constitute the new people of God; and all this by God's gracious mercy and not through any merit of their own. Even the most helpless of the people, the blind, the lame, the woman with child, will share in the joyful event of salvation. Such a great redemption will be a matter for the world to know about (v. 7).

Second Reading   Heb 5:1-6

In the passage 5:1-10 the author of Hebrews set out to show that Christ has perfectly met the requirements of priesthood – he argues in terms of the levitical high priesthood. In v. 1 he states that a high priest is one chosen from among humankind (*ex anthropón*) instituted as a mediator between God and humankind, who defends the cause of humans before God, and offers human gifts to God, especially sacrifice for sin.

Then, in v. 2 he demands that the priest must be compassionate. Such a requirement is nowhere demanded of priests in general: the author is thinking of Christ. Hence he can specify that the priest be indulgent toward the ignorant and erring who sin because they are human; all the more because he, too, is human, he, too, is 'beset with weakness.' The reference in v. 3 is to the obligation of the high priest on the Day of Atonement to offer sacrifices for his own sins, for those of the priests, and only then for the sins of the people (Lev 16:16-17).

A presupposition of priesthood is divine vocation (v. 4). That a high priest must have this call is proved by the history of Aaron and his sons who were chosen and designated by Yahweh (Ex 28:1; 29:5,10-15).

Therefore, a true high priest must both show great benevolence and indulgence to sinners and be chosen and called by God.

In proving that Christ possesses these qualities the author proceeds in inverse order, dealing first with his vocation (vv. 5-6) and then with his fellowship in human suffering (vv. 7-10). For the author, Psalm 2:7 gives the ground of the priesthood of Christ and Psalm 110:4 the explicit and solemn declaration of his priesthood (vv. 5-6).

The priesthood of Christ flows not from his passion alone but from his passion crowned by his exaltation. (Curiously, our reading stops at v. 6 – the reader should certainly go on to v. 10). Our Saviour, confronted with imminent suffering and death, prayed to his Father 'who was able to save him from death', but according to John 12:27-28,32; 17:5; Acts 2:25-31, this deliverance from death went beyond deliverance from tasting death to deliverance from the grip of death, through resurrection and glorification.

'Being made perfect' recalls the cry of Jesus: 'It is fulfilled' (Jn 19:30): by his passion and death Jesus was perfected in his priestly office. So perfected, he has become to all who believe in him the author or cause of salvation (v. 9). Christ, then, has the qualities of high priest. The most decisive proof is the declaration of his Father. He has designated his Son as high priest according to the order of Melchizedek – that is, an eternal high priest (v. 10). (See Fifth Sunday of Lent, p. 64.)

Gospel   Mk 10:46-52

This narrative focuses on the blind man, who is thereby presented as a model of faith in Jesus in spite of discouragement and as the one who eagerly answers the call of the Master and follows him in the way of discipleship.

For Mark the story sounds a new departure in the self-manifestation of Jesus. He finds himself acclaimed, repeatedly, as 'Son of David', a messianic title. Far from imposing silence, as hitherto, he calls the man to his presence and openly restores his sight. The way is being prepared for the manifestation of the humble Messiah (11:1-10). The days are near for him to be delivered up and he set his face to go to Jerusalem (10:32). God's purpose is already working itself out. Very soon the true nature of his messiahship will be clearly seen.

In v. 51 Jesus challenges the man to make his request. His question is the same as that of James and John (v. 36) [See previous Sunday]. The simple and humble request of Bartimaeus is so different from their selfish demands; he understands so much better than they the authority of Jesus who does not dominate but has come to serve (vv. 42-45).

Unlike them (v. 39) he is aware of his need and of his helplessness and finds his only hope in Jesus' nearness.

And Jesus responds to his need: 'your faith has made you well.' 'Faith' is confident trust in God and in the healing power of Jesus (see 5:34). 'Made you well,' literally 'saved you' has the same overtones of salvation as in 5:28,34.

'Followed him on the way' could mean that the man joined the crowd on the way to Jerusalem. There can be no doubt that Mark means: he followed Jesus on the way of Christian discipleship. The phrase 'on the way' and the following of Jesus form an inclusion with v. 32. Only a person of faith, enlightened by Jesus, can walk his way without consternation and without fear.

THIRTY-FIRST SUNDAY OF THE YEAR

First Reading   Deut 6:2-6

The section 6:1-19 of Deuteronomy is a commentary on 5:1-10 (the first part of the decalogue); it reaffirms the obligation to reject all other gods. There is, however, a shift of emphasis: the love of God has become the first great imperative. The decalogue is no longer merely a law. It becomes the living words of Moses – 'today' (v. 6). This blend of old and new law claims an obedience (vv. 20-25) which is founded on one basic premise: 'we were Pharaoh's slaves ... ' (v. 21). A land 'flowing with milk and honey' (v. 3) is a Canaanite phrase. Coming from the desert, the Hebrews must have been dumbfounded by the relative fertility of the land of Canaan. This fact created a problem for them as is clear from a Northern prophet like Hosea. And, spiritually, Deuteronomy is heir of Hosea.

'Hear' (v. 4) is *shema*; the word gave its name to the *Shema*, the 'creed' which every Israelite man (women and children were dispensed!) recited morning and evening; it opens with this passage from Deuteronomy. V. 4 asserts that Yahweh is (the) 'one Yahweh'. Israel owes undivided loyalty, with its whole being, to this unique God. In Deuteronomy this is the meaning of 'love of God.' The context is always one of total adherence to God, walking in his ways, keeping or doing his commandments, heeding his voice, and serving him – covenantal love.

Second Reading   Heb 7:23-28

In this chapter the author of Hebrews intends to prove the superiority of Christ over the levitical priests. He begins by showing the excellence of the type of the priesthood of Christ, that of Melchizedek (7:1-10), and passes to direct contrast between Christ and the levitical priests.

Our reading (vv. 23-28) is the conclusion of this argument. In v. 23 the uniqueness and permanence of Christ's priesthood is set against the multiplicity and impermanence of priests whom death prevented from maintaining office. V. 25 forms a transition: it concludes the argument of 7:20-24 and introduces the peroration of 26-28; it is an excellent definition of the priestly office of Christ. The salvation brought by him is not transitory but permanent (and therefore marked with perfection): he is a perfect Saviour and everlasting Advocate (see Jn 12:34; 1 Jn 2:1-2).

Christ is holy, without falsehood or malice, without moral imperfection: the language suggests a contrast between the deep ethical purity of Jesus and the ritual purity of the levitical priests (v. 26). V. 27 is a reference to *yom kippur*. On that Day of Atonement emphasis was on sacrifice of expiation, and the high priest had to sacrifice for his own sins before sacrificing for the people – in fact he stands in need of daily sacrifice even for himself. What a contrast with the perfection of Christ who has offered his sacrifice once for all, and not for himself but for the people only. The concluding verse (28) sounds a note of triumph: the Law sets up as priests men subject to sin and mortality, but the solemn word bolstered by a divine oath (Ps 110:4), proclaimed through the mouth of David long after the Law, sets up one who is Son and whose perfection is consummated in priestly achievement and glory.

Gospel
Mk 12:28-34

In this pronouncement story, Jesus gives the answer to the question, 'Which commandment is the first of all?' It was a question the rabbis sought to answer. They looked for the commandment that outweighed all others, the one that might be regarded as a basic principle on which the whole Law was grounded. Because this scribe's question is an honest question by one well-disposed (vv. 32-34) Jesus answers directly. He begins by quoting the opening formula (Deut 6:4) of the *Shema*, and joins it to Leviticus 19:18 on the love of the neighbour. He had been asked to name the first commandment; he responds by naming two commandments. That is because, for him, the one follows directly and necessarily from the other. Love for neighbour arises out of love for God. He had taken and welded the two precepts into one.

In the synoptic gospels only here and in Lk 11:42 is there word of human love for God, and it appears sparingly in the rest of the New Testament. Usually, the emphasis is on God's love for humankind. And this is as it should be. It is because God has first loved us that we love God (Rom 5:5,8; 1 Jn 4:11). Indeed, love for one another is the test of our reality of the love of God (1 Jn 4:20-21). Jesus himself showed in his life and death the quality of this twofold love. His love of God motivated his total dedication to his mission: his love of humankind marked him as one who had come to serve the saving purpose of God, one who had laid down his life as a ransom for humankind (10:45).

The scribe's reply (vv. 32-33) is proper to Mark. He agrees fully with Jesus' answer and further specifies that the true love of God and the loving service of others is more important than elaborate cult. His insistence on love with the whole heart is a recognition that love cannot be measured. Love is incompatible with a legalism that sets limits, that specifies what one must do and must avoid. Jesus' assurance that this scribe is not far from the kingdom of God is, in truth, an invitation. And we sense that this time the invitation will not be in vain (see 10:17-23). Nowhere else in the gospels does a scribe emerge in such a favourable light.

THIRTY-SECOND SUNDAY OF THE YEAR

First Reading   1 Kgs 17:10-16

A story from the Elijah cycle (1 Kgs 17-2 Kgs 2); its setting is the great drought (1 Kgs 17-18) that devastated the land of Israel and beyond. A widow of Zarephath in Phoenicia (modern Lebanon) was down to her last ration of food: a handful of meal and a drop of olive oil. After that she and her child must starve. Yet, at the word of the prophet, she made a cake for him out of her meagre provisions. She took the prophet at his word, and the abundance promised her, the never-ending supply of flour and oil, became hers. She stands out as one of the poor of the Lord, one of those who place all their trust in him, despite poverty and oppression. In its liturgical use the incident becomes a fitting commentary on today's gospel reading.

Second Reading   Heb 9:24-28

The Christian High Priest does not officiate in an earthly sanctuary; his rightful place is in heaven itself. There he appears, now and forever, before God on our behalf. Blood-sprinkling by the high priest in the holy of holies was the actual rite of expiation in the old ritual (Lev 16:14-16). By analogy the consummation of Christ's saving work has taken place in the heavenly Holy of Holies.

Hebrews uses three images to express the work of Christ in the heavenly sanctuary: (1) ritual of the Day of Atonement, which reconciles God and the people (v. 23); (2) appearance in the presence of God (vv. 25-26); and (3) 'intercession' (v. 25). All three images are combined in v. 24.

The theological reality behind these images is that of the presence of the glorified humanity (once a suffering humanity) of Christ with God. Vv. 25-26 offer a recapitulation of ideas expressed in 7:23-24; 9:12,24. Christ does not offer himself again and again to effect a periodical expiation, like the annual expiation of *yom kippur* – otherwise he would have suffered many times over since the beginning of the world – a *reductio ad absurdum*. But now once, and once only, at the consummation of the ages (messianic age), he has appeared for the destruction, through the sacrifice of himself, of sin and the power of hell. V. 27 notes the moments of human destiny: death and judgment. And v. 28 notes Christ's single sacrifice of atonement for the sins of all and his return for the final moment of destiny at the end of time.

Gospel   Mk 12:38-44

Censure of the scribes (vv. 38-44). The scribes prided themselves on their theological learning and – most of them being Pharisees – on their meticulous religious observance.

On both scores they invited and received deference; to that end they affected distinctive dress. It should surely be of more than academic interest that the authentic Jesus-tradition is critical of distinctive 'churchly' garb. The 'best seats' in the synagogue: directly in front of the ark containing the sacred scrolls and facing the people. The charge in v. 40 is more serious. Not only do they make an ostentatious display of long-winded prayer, they are shown to be greedy and exploiters of the helpless. Judaism has some scathing condemnation of unscrupulous scribes. However, the sweeping character of the charges here reflects the animosity between the Church and official Judaism, an animosity more trenchantly expressed in Matthew 23.

This portrait of the scribes stands, and is meant to stand, in sharp contrast to the attitude and conduct of Christian religious leaders (9:33-37; 10:42-45). But what has been, and continues to be, the reality in the Church? Distinctive dress, signs of deference, places of honour at religious and civic functions! It is not easy to see wherein a difference lies between this and the conduct of the scribes outlined and censured here in vv. 38-39.

The Widow's Mite (vv. 41-44). This vignette may have found its setting here partly because of the catchword 'widow' (vv. 40,42). More importantly it is in place because, as an example of true Jewish piety, it contrasts with the counterfeit piety of the scribes. The poor widow who receives Jesus' approbation represents the common people. The 'copper coin' (lep<u>ton</u>) was the smallest in circulation. Mention of two coins is important: the woman could have kept one for herself. Wealthy people had been generous (v. 41); yet this poor widow's mite is an immeasurably greater gift than theirs for she has given of her all – her 'whole living' (v. 44). She had let go of every shred of security and had committed herself wholly to God.

Such is the traditional interpretation of the passage. But we may, and most likely should, view it in a different light. Would Jesus really have approved of a poor widow giving 'out of her poverty … all she had to live on'? Hardly. His immediately preceding castigation of the scribes as those who 'devour widows' houses' is surely in mind. This poor widow is a victim of religious establishment. She had been convinced that it was a 'holy' thing to give her all to the Temple. She is a tragic example of the opposite of what Jesus urged: 'Religion is for men and women, not men and women for religion.'

THIRTY-THIRD SUNDAY OF THE YEAR

First Reading   Dan 12:1-3

The second part of the book of Daniel (chapters 7-12) is apocalyptic, and consists of four visions. The fourth is the great vision: (a) the Time of Anger (chapters 10-11); (b) the Time of the End (chapter 12). Chapter 11 is a veiled presentation of the history of the Ptolemies and Seleucids, culminating in the profanation of the Temple by Antiochus IV. This sparked-off the Maccabean revolt which is the background of Daniel.

The last vision (chapter 12) leaves the sphere of politics and moves to a higher plane. The goal of history is God's kingdom, which will come solely by God's own power and in his good time. Despite the tribulations of the eschatological crisis the elect of God, whose 'names shall be found written in the book' of life will be saved. This 'book of life' is mentioned in Exodus 32:32-33; it expresses the idea that the

Lord has a list of the elect (see Ps 69:29; Rev 20:12-15). Our passage is remarkable as being the earliest clear statement of belief in the resurrection of the dead and the first mention in the Bible of 'everlasting life,' And it firmly introduces the notion of retribution after death (12:2-3). It is a theologically significant text.

Second Reading   Heb 10:11-14.18

The section 10:1-18 of Hebrews is a recapitulation; the author again insists on the superiority of the sacrifice of Christ over the Mosaic sacrifices. In 10:1-14 he treats of the replacement of the standing priests by the priest enthroned. As before, the multiplicity of futile actions is contrasted with the single, permanently effective, action of Christ. While the heavenly high priest is already present with God (v. 12) the universe is still incompletely subjected to his dominion before his future coming (v. 13). But now that Christ is 'perfected' as priest (5:9), the 'sanctifier' has 'perfected' those 'who are sanctified'. Their consciences will be cleansed so that they may properly worship the living God (9:14). In this way Jesus has given his own access to the Father.

The new covenant suffices from now on without need of further sacrifice (vv. 15-18). The sacrifice of Christ has been once for all, and the forgiveness it achieved has been once for all. There is no more sacrifice to be made for sins – because God will remember sin no more. There remains only to appropriate the sacrifice of Christ through the Eucharist – 'proclaiming the Lord's death until he comes' (1 Cor 11:26).

Gospel   Mk 13:24-32

In Mark, Jesus' farewell discourse (chapter 13), after the introduction (13:1-4), falls into three parts: The Signs of the Parousia (5-23); the Parousia of the Son of Man (24-27); the Nearness of the Parousia (28-37). Our reading includes the second part and most of the third part.

Mark certainly believes in a parousia (advent) of a Son of Man and is convinced that it is imminent; in this he shows the common expectation of early Christians. The passage vv 24-27 is a collage of prophetic texts. The cosmic signs which accompany the parousia (24-25) are part and parcel of Jewish apocalyptic descriptions of the Day of the Lord. The parousia marks the definitive manifestation of the Son of Man. Then he will be seen: in fullness instead of being dimly perceived. This is the real message of hope for Christians. This promise and this hope they cling to while the Lord is absent (2:20;

13:34). It is this that enables them, no matter what their present situation, to endure to the end (13:9-13). Already 8:38 had warned that only those who, here and now, in this vale of tears, are not 'ashamed' of a suffering Son of Man will rejoice in his glorious coming. That is why Mark will go on, insistently, to urge watching and readiness for the coming (33-37). And, for the faithful ones, the coming will be joy indeed. The Son of Man will not come to execute judgment. The one purpose of his appearing will be to gather his elect. After his comforting presentation of the parousia, Mark develops that encouragement by stressing its nearness. But he insists that the intervening time must be spent in watchfulness (28-32). There can never be room for complaceny in the life of the Christian.

There can be no doubt that Mark expected an imminent parousia (9:1; 13:30). Was he, then, mistaken? In one sense, obviously, yes; the parousia of the Son of Man did not happen in his generation, nor has it occurred nineteen centuries later. Yet, we can find a basic truth in Mark's conviction. The death and rising of Christ did usher in the last age. Besides, 'parousia' is an apocalyptic symbol which gives dramatic expression to the belief that God's saving plan is perfectly rounded. While we cannot share Mark's view that the End is very near, nor look for a coming of the Son of Man in clouds, we do share his faith in God's victory in Christ. And, for each of us, the 'parousia' will be our meeting with the Son of Man when we pass out of this life into the life of God. It should be our Christian hope that we stand among the elect to be fondly welcomed by him.

THIRTY-FOURTH SUNDAY OF THE YEAR
SOLEMNITY OF CHRIST THE KING

First Reading   Dan 7:13-14

In the first of the apocalyptic visions of the book of Daniel (chapter 7), the seer saw four beasts rising out of the sea (the abode of things evil); an angel explained that these beasts were four successive empires (Babylonian, Median, Persian and Greek [Seleucid]).

Then, in contrast to the beasts, appears one 'like a son of man' (that is, a human figure); again, in contrast to the beasts' origin in the depths of the sea, he appears 'with the clouds of heaven' (v. 13). The 'son of man' is presented to the 'Ancient One' (God) and receives universal and everlasting dominion (v. 14). In keeping with the technique of apocalyptic, the vision is explained to the seer by a heavenly messenger (vv. 26-27) and now it emerges that the 'son of man' of the vision symbolized 'the holy ones of the Most High' – the faithful people of the kingdom. In a later period the Danielic 'son of man' was understood in individualistic terms and, in apocalyptic literature, became a title for the future redeemer. While it is not clear that Jesus referred to himself as 'Son of Man' in this apocalyptic sense, it is certain that the early Church, in its christological endeavour, did give him the title, so understood (see Mk 13:26; 14:62).

Second Reading   Rev 1:5-8

Revelation is presented as a letter to seven Churches – a symbolic number, meaning the Christian communities in general – in the province of Asia. The blessing of grace and peace issues from God, a God not remote but active in our world – the 'seven spirts' – a God especially active and present in Jesus Christ. In this Christian apocalyptic letter the focus is on him. He is Jesus Christ, the Messiah. His titles speak to the situation of John's readers: fidelity unto death, victor over death, God's answer to Caesar's arrogance. He is the example and source of hope for Christians about to face the great persecution. They truly have reason for patient endurance.

Jesus' help is not only for the future; it is, more intimately, in the past and in the present. We were sinners: he liberated us from the evil actions and deeds of our past by dying on our behalf. Do we need further proof that he loves us? His generosity does not stop there. He not only liberated us from bondage, he has raised us to royalty: a royal house of priests, inheriting the privilege of the chosen people. Christians share the authority of the King of kings and stand as priestly mediators in the world of humankind. The 'us' ('made us') is, obviously, inclusive; Christian women share the royal and priestly role as fully as their brothers. This generous Jesus is, indeed, worthy of honour and glory.

From the redemption wrought by Christ in time, John looks to his coming at the end. He will come, from the presence of the Father; none can hide from his presence. He will be manifest to all, even to those whose hostility numbers them with those who had brought about his death. If he appears as Judge, it will not be to condemn. The gracious mercy of this Judge touches hearts: the tribes of the earth will lament in remorse. To underline the seriousness of the promise, God himself speaks; he will speak again only at the close of this book (21:5-8). If he is the Almighty, the eternal, sovereign, Lord, his might is present in the Lamb (5:5-6). He is ever the foolish God who displays his power in the cross of Jesus (see 1 Cor 1:23-25).

John's address is full of comfort. We are assured that our God is the everlasting, the Almighty. But we Christians meet this awesome God in the one who laid down his life for us. John puts, in his manner, what Paul had already declared: 'God proved his love for us in that while we were still sinners Christ died for us' (Rom 5:8). Once slaves of sin, we have been set free, with radical freedom: 'If the Son makes you free, you will be free indeed' (Jn 8:36). Christian privilege brings its challenging obligation: priestly concern for the whole of humankind. But nothing less should inspire those who serve the God who is God of all.

Gospel   Jn 18:33-37

The Johannine scenario of the trial before Pilate (18:28-19:16) is involved and dramatic. John has two stage settings. The outer court of the *praetorium* where the Jews vociferously put pressure on Pilate to find Jesus guilty. Within the *praetorium* where Jesus is held prisoner, in an atmosphere of calm reason, the innocence of Jesus becomes clearer to Pilate. In seven carefully balanced episodes Pilate passes back and forth from one setting to the other, his movement giving expression to the struggle within himself.

And Pilate's struggle between his conviction of Jesus' innocence and political pressure to declare him guilty is evident. On the inner stage, where Jesus and Pilate dialogue, is where the real drama unfolds. From the first the roles have been reversed: it is Pilate, not Jesus, who is on trial. Pilate, like any other, must take a stand for or against the Light. After he had assured Pilate that he does not constitute a political danger because his kingship 'is not of this world' (v. 36). Jesus challenges him to recognize and face up to the truth (v. 37): 'Everyone who belongs to the truth hears my voice.' Because Pilate will not meet the challenge of deciding for the truth in Jesus and against the Jews, he thinks he can persuade the Jews to accept a solution that will make it unnecessary for him to decide for Jesus. This is the Johannine view of the episode of Barabbas, the scourging, and the handing over of Jesus as 'your King'. For John, the trial scene is our own tragic history of temporizing and indecision. Pilate, the would-be neutral man, is frustrated by outside pressure. He, and all who would act like him, end up enslaved to the 'world.' We should face up, honestly, to the Pilate in us. (See Good Friday, p. 92.)

Holy Days

ST PATRICK
17 MARCH

First Reading   Jer 1:4-9

Jeremiah, of all the prophets, is best known to us as an individual. His book contains many passages of personal confession and autobiography, as well as lengthy section of biography. He stands out as a lonely, tragic figure whose mission seemed to have failed. Yet, that 'failure' was his triumph as later ages were to acknowledge.

Jeremiah came from Anathoth, a village four miles north-east of Jerusalem. His father, Hilkiah, was a priest (Jer 1:1). His prophetic call came in 626 (1:2) while he was still quite a young man, and his mission reached from Josiah (640-609) to Zedekiah (697-587) and outlasted the reign of the latter. That is to say, he lived through the days, full of promise, of the young reformer king, Josiah, and through the aftermath, the tragic years that led to the destruction of the nation. It seems that Jeremiah was initially in sympathy with the aims of the reform but was disappointed at its eventual outcome. There is no doubt that he thought highly of the high-minded young king (22:15-156), but he quickly realised that 'you cannot make people good by act of parliament.'

Jeremiah has particular relevance for our day. His predecessors, as far as we know, accepted their prophetic mission with submissiveness – Isaiah indeed with eagerness (Is 6:9). But Jeremiah had to question; there is in him a trace of rebellion. He was not at all satisfied to accept, uncritically, traditional theological positions. He struggled, as the author of Job was to do centuries later, with the problem of retribution (112:1) and asserted the principle of individual (as against collective) responsibility (31:29-30).

But, mostly, it was his own prophetic office that was his burden, and it was indeed a burden far heavier and more painful than that of any other prophet. He needed, all the more, the support of his God. His obedience was so much the greater because of his questioning, because he felt its yoke, because it led to a feeling of being abandoned.

The call of Jeremiah is itself modelled on that of Moses (Ex 4:10-16) and has in turn influenced the account of later calls such as that of the Servant of the Lord (Is 49:1).

Patrick, like Jeremiah, was called from his earliest years, and never ceased to protest his unworthiness. Yet he was conscious that God had given him the Word to spread among the Irish people. It was this sense of vocation that was to keep him faithful to the end.

Second Reading   Acts 13:46-49

Chapter 13 of Acts begins (13:1-3) with the decision of the Christian community at Antioch (in Syria) to launch a mission to the Gentiles. This was a daring new departure because, up to then, the Christian movement was almost wholly Jewish. Barnabas and Saul (Paul), the designated missionaries, moved on to Cyprus and then on to Asia Minor (modern Turkey). At Antioch in Pisidia they preached, on the sabbath, in the synagogue – it was their policy to preach first to Jews. They had quite a favourable reception. A week later, however, the opposition had rallied. In reaction, Paul and Barnabas declared: 'We are now turning to the Gentiles.'

The conclusion of our short reading – 'When the Gentiles heard this they were glad ... Thus the word of the Lord spread throughout the region' – suits, admirably, the welcome of the Irish to the message of Patrick.

Gospel   Lk 10:1-12, 17-20

The passage 10:1-16 is parallel to 9:1-6 (the mission of the Twelve) It does not seem that this sending of the seventy foreshadows the universal mission of Jesus' disciples (as has been suggested); in 24:47 the Gentile mission is entrusted to the Twelve. Two, obviously distinct, sayings (vv. 2-3) reflect the experience of the first missionaries: their own zeal and the opposition they encountered. The warning (v. 4) not to waste time on civilities (elaborate, in the oriental manner) underlines the urgency of the mission. 'Peace' (*shalom*) is the Jewish greeting. One who 'shares in peace' is, literally, a 'son of peace'. 'Son of peace', a Hebraism, means one worthy of peace. Clearly, the greeting is meaningful, a blessing. Food and shelter (v. 7) are not alms but wages (see 1 Cor 9:14).

The mission is not a private sally but a public proclamation of the kingdom. The kingdom is near, so they are not to waste time on those who will not receive them; the message must be brought to others (vv. 10-11). The unreceptive town (v. 12) will not go unpunished; 'on that day' means on the day of judgemnt. Jesus, sent by the Father, has sent the disciples; rejection of them is rejection of God (v. 16).

The ability to cast out demons had, understandably, made a deep impression on the disciples (v. 17). The power had come to them from Jesus (v. 19) and it is by their faith in him that they have been successful. The real cause for rejoicing is that the kingdom has come; for Satan it is the beginning of the end – his fall will be lightning fast (see Jn 12:31). The disciples have received power over the enemy of humankind in all fields (v 19); serpents and scorpions (though these may have a metaphorical sense, see Ps 91:13) exemplify evils in nature, the work of Satan (see Acts 28:3-6).

The assurance of being numbered among the elect is the ultimate reason for rejoicing (v 20). The image of the 'book of life' is a common Old Testament one; see also Rev 3:5; 13:8; 17:8; 20:12,15.

THE ASSUMPTION OF MARY
15 AUGUST

First Reading   Rev 11:19; 12:1-6, 10

In a prophetic vision, John sees the holy of holies of the heavenly temple thrown open and the ark of the covenant visible to all (11:19). The fulfilment will come in the New Jerusalem when God will dwell with humankind (21:3). Here, as assurance to the faithful, the open temple finds a remarkably apposite parallel in Hebrews 10:19 – 'Therefore, brothers and sisters, we have confidence to enter the sanctuary by the blood of Jesus.' Christians have full confidence to 'draw near to the throne of grace' (Heb 4:16). That assurance in Hebrews, no less than in Revelation, is founded on 'the Lamb who was slain.'

Revelation 12 is based on two sources: a narrative describing the conflict between a pregnant woman and a dragon (vv. 1-6, 13-17) and a narrative depicting a battle in heaven (vv 7-12). This sandwich technique, reminiscent of Mark, indicates that the narratives must be understood in conjunction. The woman symbolizes the people of God bringing forth the Messiah; the dragon is the 'ancient serpent' of Genesis 3 – a later reinterpretation of the talking snake of the Genesis text.

By the 'birth' of the Messiah (12:5) John does not mean the nativity but the cross – the enthronement of Jesus. The woman's child was snatched from the destructive intent of the dragon to the throne of God: precisely by dying, Jesus defeated the dragon and was exalted to God's right hand. The expulsion of Satan from heaven in the result of the victory of Christ on earth; this is clearly brought out in the heavenly chorus of 12:10-11.

Second Reading   1 Cor 15:20-26

Some in the Corinthian community, in their Greek view that the human person was made up of two distinct and separable parts (soul and body) with the soul, in practice, being what mattered, despised the body. Logically, they denied resurrection from the dead (15:12). In 15:1-19 Paul not only unwaveringly affirms faith in the resurrection but vehemently defends an understanding of the human person as a psychosomatic unity. Moreover, by stressing the importance of the body, he vindicates the incarnational character of Christianity. His argument is in terms of the resurrection of Christ.

Then, in our passage (15:20-28) he describes the consequences of Christ's resurrection. In fact, not only has Christ risen – he is 'the first fruits of those who have died' (v. 20); his resurrection has implications for all. Paul illustrates the impact of Christ's resurrection on human-kind with a contrast developed more fully in Rom 5:12-21: he sets Adam over against Christ. Adam brought death to humankind and this was a sign of deeper separation from God. Jesus Christ brought resurrection from the dead, and this is an efficacious sign of the saving nature of his death. The resurrection of Christ destroyed the definitive character of physical death; those who are in Christ will live forever (vv. 21-22).

Paul looks to the future, to the moment when all those in Christ will be raised, the moment of the Parousia, of the End (vv. 23-24). Why is there an interval between the resurrection of Christ and of those who belong to him through faith and baptism? It is because the mission of Christ was not complete at his death: 'He must reign until he has put all his enemies under his feet' (v. 25).

Having been exalted to the position of Lord through his resurrec-tion (Rom 1:3-4; 14:9; 1 Cor 15:45), Christ still had to annihilate the hostile powers that yet held the great mass of humanity in subjec-tion to a false value system. At his death the power of forces hostile to authentic human development had been broken, but they had not been definitively crushed. The evil influences operative in the 'world' act on those who are physically alive, and so these must be destroyed first (v. 24), but Death is the master of those who have died, and so its turn necessarily comes next (v. 26). When this definitive victory has been won, when the words of Ps 8:7 (referring to humankind before the fall) and Ps 110 (referring to the Messiah) have been fulfilled, then Christ will present his kingdom to God (v. 24), and he will remit into God's hands the authority given him for his mission (v. 38) The subordination of Christ, precisely as 'Son', to God could not be expressed with greater clarity, and is in total accord with the stress on his humanity in v. 21. (J. Murphy-O'Connor, *1 Corinthians* 143).

Gospel   Lk 1:39-56

In the structure of the Lucan infancy narrative this passage, 'The Visitation', is a complementary episode, a pendant to the diptych of annunciations (1:1-38). Elizabeth is granted the perception not only that Mary is with child but that her child is the Messiah. Her canticle in praise of Mary (1:42-45) echoes Old Testament motifs and anticipates motifs that will be found in the gospel (11:27-28). This narrative serves as a hinge between the two birth stories, of John and of Jesus. And this meeting of women illustrates their respective situations. Elizabeth's pregnancy was not only a sign for Mary; it was also an invitation. The 'haste' of Mary was inspired by friendship and charity.

At Mary's greeting Elizabeth felt the infant stir within her – John, while still in the womb, is precursor (1:17) of the Lord. Enlightened by the prophetic Spirit she concluded that Mary is to be mother of 'the Lord.' That is why Mary is 'blessed among women' - the most blessed of women. Elizabeth went on to praise Mary's unhesitating acquiescence in God's plan for her – her great faith: 'And blessed is she who believed ... '

Mary's reply is her *Magnificat* (1:46-55). This hymn is the conclusion of, and the interpretation of, Luke's Visitation scene. In form a thanksgiving psalm, the Magnificat is a chain of Old Testament reminiscences and leans especially on the canticle of Hannah (1 Sam 2:1-10). There is no clear reference to the messianic birth – and this is surprising in view of the angel's message and the words of Elizabeth. Like the *Benedictus*, this psalm came to Luke from the circles of Jewish-Christian *anawim*. The hymn originally referred to a general salvation through Jesus Christ. It will readily be seen that, without v. 48, the *Magnificat* would fit smoothly into that Anawim setting. But we have the song in Luke's infancy gospel. There it stands between the Old Testament and the New and, like the rest of Luke's infancy narrative, captures the atmosphere of that unique moment. Luke presents the *Magnificat* as a canticle of Mary and we may, and should, read it as such.

Elizabeth had blessed Mary as mother of the Messiah; Mary gives the glory, in joyful thanksgiving, to the God who had blessed her, and through her, Israel: 'My soul magnifies the Lord.' The rest of the opening cry of joy (Lk 1:47) echoes the words of Habbakuk 'I will

rejoice in the Lord, I will exult in the God of my salvation' (Hab 3:18).
God had looked with favour upon his hand-maid, upon her who is the
most perfect of the 'poor of Yahweh.' Here total acceptance of God's
will has won for her, the Favoured One, everlasting glory. At once she
turns the attention away from herself to the Almighty, the holy and
merciful God, who has done great things for her. The Mighty One
shows his power most of all in caring for the needy. In truth, the
'steadfast love of the Lord is from everlasting to everlasting on those
who fear him' (Ps 103:17). All humankind will find hope in what God
has achieved in Mary: loneliness turned into fruitfulness.

The interest then (vv 51-53) switches to Israel and to the manifestation of God's power, holiness and goodness in favour of his people.
These verses are not concerned with the past, or not with the past only,
but represent God's action at all times: what he has done in Mary and
what he, through her as mother of the Messiah, has done for Israel,
shows forth his manner of acting. He does mighty deeds with his arm,
symbol of his power, when he reverses human situations – the proud,
the mighty and the rich he has humbled and left empty, while he has
lifted up and blessed with good things the poor of this world (the
anawim).

This is nothing other than the message of the Beatitudes (Lk 6:20-
21). For, if that message of Jesus were to bring about the desired
change of heart, the poor, the marginalized, would come into their
own. It is God's 'preferential option for the poor' – the option of a God
who scrupulously respects human freedom. He awaits the response
that will achieve the great transformation – but he looks for that
response. The Magnificat anticipates Luke's concern throughout his
gospel, for the poor. It is echoed in Jesus' programmatic statement: '
... the poor have the good news preached to them' (4:18).

The closing verses (54-55) in the mouth of Mary, point to the final
intervention of God. His sending of the Messiah is the decisive act of
his gracious treatment of Israel, the people which, through his covenant with Abraham (Gen 17:7), had become his 'Servant' (Is 41:8-9).
Mindful of his great mercy, he has fulfilled the promise made to the
patriarchs: a promise made to a man is accomplished in a woman.

Elizabeth had singled out Mary's faith for special attention and she
had done so rightly. Still, there remains the more mundane, but
refreshingly human factor that Mary had travelled from Nazareth to
Judea to share the joy of her aged cousin and to lend a helping hand.
One may refer to the Cana episode (Jn 2:1-15). True, it a passage heavy
with Johannine theology – and this is not the place to get involved in

that aspect of the text. What matters here is that John has cast Mary as a charitable and practical woman who could be depended on to supervise, quietly but efficiently, a rural wedding. Each in his way, Luke and John have presented her as the woman for others. Not a surprise casting of her who is mother of 'the man for others.'

ALL SAINTS
1 NOVEMBER

First Reading   Rev 7:2-4, 9-14

The breaking of the seven scroll-seals by the Lamb (Rev 6:1-8:5) unleashed a series of plagues which follows the pattern of events in the Synoptic apocalypse (Mk 13; Mt 24: Lk 21). Before the breaking of the last seal the servants of God were sealed with the seal of the living God, 144,000 of them. The opening of the last seal will unleash the plagues of trumpets (8:6-11:19), which are modelled on the plagues of Egypt. The sealing of the elect recalls the immunity of the Israelites to the plagues that struck the Egyptians. John's unexpected twist is that his servants will be sealed for protection through the great tribulation. They achieve their victory, yes, but in the only Christian manner: 'for they did not cling to life even in the face of death' (12:11).

The 'great multitude' of 7:9-17 is not a group distinct from the 144,000 (itself a 'great multitude'): it is the same group now viewed beyond the great tribulation. In keeping with John's consistent outlook, these are presented as happy here and now; they stand before God and Lamb, celebrating a heavenly feast of Tabernacles (the most joyous of Jewish feasts). As martyrs – the ideal representatives of God's people – they have come triumphantly through the tribulation: the vision is prophetic, anticipatory. A 'great tribulation' was expected to precede the End; for John, the tribulation through which these martyrs come triumphantly is imminent persecution (see 3:10; 13:7-10). These are the victors of the prophetic messages of chapters 2 and 3. The striking paradox (made white in the *blood* of the Lamb) has a haunting beauty; and, as beauty, it speaks truth. It expresses God's and the Lamb's definition of victory: they have won by suffering death, not by inflicting hurt.

Second Reading   1 Jn 3:1-3

We can speak of a person being *named* to an office or a job. In a Semitic context, to be named ('called') is a more forceful expression. Our text says we are named God's children and, in case there should by any doubt, John adds: 'and that is what we are.' We know, that is, experience, our filial relationship to God. We have been born to a new life and share, mysteriously but really, in the life of God (1:29).

The fact of being a Christian, of being born of God, is permanent assurance that one is loved by the Father; each carries in his or her person the attestation of this love. (John will, of course, insist that the Christian live as child of God, 3:4-23). The unbelieving world is incapable of recognizing the true status of Christians because it has not come to know God. For John this means that it had failed to recognize Jesus. As for ourselves, we have to await the coming of the Lord, to see him 'as he is,' before we can arrive at full appreciation of our own Christian reality. Only then shall we see clearly that our future state will be like the glorified state of Jesus. But the process of becoming like Christ has already begun – a familiar stress in John.

Gospel   Mt 5:1-12

Our gospels have two, notably different, versions of the beatitudes: Mt 5:3-12 and Lk 6:20-23. Matthew has nine beatitudes. Luke has four only – but with four corresponding 'woes' (6:24-26). Both versions have grown from an original core going back to Jesus, the additions and adaptations being due to the evangelists. The beatitudes of Jesus are three:

> Blessed are the poor, for the Kingdom of heaven is theirs.
> Blessed are those who hunger, for they will be filled.
> Blessed are the afflicted, for they will be comforted.

These beatitudes do not refer to three separate categories but to three aspects of the same distressful situation. One may ask: what merit is there in being poor, hungry, afflicted? There is none. The 'blessedness' of the poor is in their very need, their distress. God is their champion – as he showed himself to be in Jesus.

Luke has these three beatitudes, plus a fourth: the blessedness of those who suffer persecution for the sake of Christ; and he, like Jesus, looks to the really poor and afflicted. Matthew's longer version contains only three quite new beatitudes: the merciful, the pure in heart, the peace-makers. We get a total of nine only because those of the poor/meek and last two (the persecuted) are duplicates. But there distinctive features in Matthew's beatitudes as a whole. The expression 'poor in spirit' points to a transformation of idea of 'the poor.' In current usage, the designation 'poor in spirit' applies to one who is detached from worldly goods, who is interiorly free in regard to money. In fact, it is frequently related to the possession of wealth: it is possible for an economically rich person to be 'poor in spirit.' That is because we take 'poor' in a specific sense, an economic sense, which may not be the biblical meaning. And that meaning, we now know from the Jewish texts of Qumran is 'humility'; the poor in the spirit are the humble. The parallel beatitude of 'the meek' confirms this meaning. These beatitudes, in Matthew, are no longer addressed to those who lack the necessities of life (Luke/Jesus) but to those characterized by their meekness, their patience, their humility. They are the *anawim* with Jesus himself as the ultimate 'poor man' (11:29). It is evident that 'blessed are those who hunger and thirst for righteousness' is very different from Luke's blessedness of the 'poor' and the 'hungry.' For Matthew, Christianity has broadened and deepened the meaning of the term righteousness (5:20).

Among the really new beatitudes we first look at 'Blessed are the pure in heart for they shall see God' (5:8). The qualification 'in heart' like 'in spirit' points to an interior disposition. What is in question is what we would call 'purity of intention,' demanding perfect correspondence between intention and action. The beatitudes of the merciful and the peacemakers are concerned with action: the conduct of a Christian towards a neighbour who stands in need. The best illustration of 'merciful' is Matthew's description of the last judgment: 'I was hungry and you gave me food ' (25:35-40). As for the 'peacemakers': these evoke a good work highly prized in Judaism. It was observed that, among those who need help, the most needy are often an estranged husband and wife, or friends who have fallen out. To seek to reconcile them, to restore them to peace, is one of the kindest services one can render to the neighbour.

Where Luke applied the beatitudes to Christians as a suffering minority, Matthew has introduced a distinction: he reserves the blessedness promised in the beatitudes to Christians who truly live the gospel ideal. He had re-read the beatitudes in the light of his pastoral preoccupation and he had filled them out. He takes care to remind Christians that the promises of salvation are conditional (5:20). We will not be admitted to the Kingdom unless, after the example of the Master, we have shown ourselves to be meek and humble; unless we have given proof of righteousness and loyalty; unless we have carried out what God has asked of us in particular, unless we have served our brothers and sisters in their need.

The Beatitudes are thoroughly Jewish in form and content. They

challenged those who made up 'Israel' in Matthew's time by
delineating the kinds of persons and actions that will receive their
full reward when God's kingdom comes. They remind Christians
today of the Jewish roots of their piety and challenge each generation to reflect on what persons and actions they consider to be
important or 'blessed.' (Daniel J. Harrington, S.J., *Matthew*, 84)

THE IMMACULATE CONCEPTION OF MARY
8 DECEMBER

The feast of the Immaculate Conception can fit easily into the time of
preparation for Christmas. It celebrates the way in which God prepared
a dwelling for his Son in the midst of the human race, when he chose
Mary and preserved her from sin. The doctrinal aspect is neatly
summed up in the Collect which makes it clear that Mary, though
without sin, is redeemed through the merits of Jesus Christ.

But on this day the Immaculate Conception should not be ap-
proached in too abstract a manner. It is better to let it be a joyful
celebration of Mary in Advent, a feast which, in praising Mary's
fullness of grace, rejoices in God's gracious decision to pour out an
abundance of blessing on a people in need of God's mercy.

The chosen readings give plenty of reasons for celebration. It may
be remarked how, in the Gospel narrative, 'things happen'. We meet,
not a precise definition, but an angel exclaiming, 'Greetings, favoured
one!' This phrase from the Gospel, which, in its more traditional form,
'Hail, full of grace', also provides the Alleluia verse, is the one on
which attention is focused today. (On March 25 the same Gospel is
read but with the emphasis on the Son whom Mary is to conceive.). The
reading from Genesis carries the assurance that in spite of sin the
human race is not to be written off, while Ephesians dwells on how it
is by God's gracious choice that men and women are saved. The use
of these texts for this feast implies, of course, that Mary's place in the
history of salvation is part of God's own plan.

First Reading   Gen 3:9-15, 20

The sad aftermath of the 'fall': the perceptive Yahwist has sketched an
unforgettable picture of the tragedy of sin. The man and woman had
hitherto looked eagerly to their daily encounter with their God (the
clear implication of v. 8). He comes as before, strolling in the garden,
eminently accessible – but they are changed; now, in their guilt, they

flee his face. Humankind cannot remain hidden from God. The man's reply to the second question of Yahweh (v. 11) is his desperate attempt to place responsibility for the results of his actions anywhere but at his own door. First he blames the woman: 'the woman ... gave me'; ultimately he seeks to pin the blame on God – she is the woman 'whom you gave to be with me.' The attempt to involve God is pathetic (but it is still the way of humankind). More tragic is the breakdown of relations between humans – here the man betrays the woman. Solidarity in sin, complicity in crime, are utterly divisive.

We must seek the true meaning of this passage but we should not seek to draw from it what it does not contain. In v. 15 'woman' and 'serpent' are the characters of the story: the 'mother of all living' and the 'cunning' snake. The function of the *nahash*, a talking snake – a stage prop – is to focus attention on the command ('of the tree of the knowledge of good and evil you shall not eat' , 2:17) and to spell out that disobedience is, in effect, a vain attempt 'to be like God.' It will remain the perennial human temptation. Between woman, snake and their progeny there will be perpetual antipathy. The masculine pronoun *autos*, 'he', in the Greek version is simply an awareness that human 'seed' is in question. The Latin *ipsa*, 'she', of the Vulgate does not seem to have come from Jerome himself but reflects a later tradition. If one will use Genesis 3:15 in a messsianic and mariological context (the obvious implication of the choice of the reading on this feast) one must be aware that this is accommodation – and, as such, quite proper. But one cannot maintain that such is the meaning or intent of the Genesis text. A note of hope is sounded in v. 20: 'the mother of all living'. There is hope for the human race because God will have the last word.

Second Reading   Eph 1:3-6.11-12

Ephesians has as its central theme the wonder of grace. From the first, God had devised a merciful plan for uniting humankind with himself, through sending his Son as Saviour. Having enunciated his theme in v. 3 with a three-fold mention of 'blessing', the author proceeds in the following verses to give a description of God's blessing. It consists of God's choice that we should be holy (v. 4), our adoption as God's children (v. 5), our redemption from sin – the forgiveness of our trespasses (v. 7), the revelation of the 'mystery' or divine plan itself (vv 9-10). Mary, the singularly graced (see Lk 1:28), is surely the perfect child of God who inherits and, in her measure, mediates God's blessing.

Gospel   Lk 1:26-38

The infancy gospel of Luke, like that of Matthew, is firmly christological. Here, in 1:32-33, Jesus is described as the Davidic Messiah in terms taken from 2 Sam 7:9-16. The only specifically Christian feature is that Jesus has been identified as that promised Messiah. Luke then moves quite beyond the Old Testament level and uses the technique of Mary's question and Gabriel's answer to point to the true identity of the Messiah (1:34-35). The Messiah is God's Son and his conception is not through marital intercourse (Mary) but through the Holy Spirit (Gabriel). It is Luke's dramatic version of an early christological formula, such as that of Rom 1:3-4. The child is wholly God's work – a new creation.

If the primary emphasis is christological, a secondary aim in our passage is to affirm the status God has granted to Mary. The full stream of divine favour is centred in her. The coming of the Holy Spirit and his overshadowing of Mary highlights both the divine initiative and the beginning of the final process of salvation. Luke, writing in the light of his resurrection-faith, had discerned Mary's stature. She was mother, specially chosen, of Jesus – the Spirit-begotten. She was mother of a unique son, the one who would save his people from their sins. She was, truly, the most blessed of womankind (see 1:42).

Bibliography

Thomas L. Brodie, O.P., *The Gospel according to John*, New York, Oxford University Press, 1993.

Raymond E. Brown, S.S., *The Birth of the Messiah*, updated edition, New York, Doubleday, 1993.

Raymond E. Brown, S.S., *The Death of the Messiah*, two volumes, Anchor Bible Reference Library, New York / London, Doubleday / Geoffrey Chapman, 1994.

Raymond E. Brown, *The Gospel accroding to John*, New York, 1966.

C.H. Dodd, *The Interpretation of the Fourth Gospel*, Cambridge, Cambridge University Press, 1955.

Daniel J. Harrington, S.J., *The Gospel of Matthew*, Sacra Pagina 1, Collegeville MN / Dublin, The Liturgical Press / Columba Press, 1991.

Luke Timothy Johnson, *Luke*, Sacra Pagina, Collegeville MN / Dublin, The Liturgical Press / Columba Press 1993.

J.P. Meier, *Matthew*, New Testament Message 3, Wilmington DE / Dublin: M. Glazier / Veritas, 1980.

J.P. Meier, *A Marginal Jew*, New York / London, Doubleday / Chapman, 1994.

Jerome Murphy-O'Connor, O.P., *1 Corinthians*, New Testament Message, Wilmington DE / Dublin: M. Glazier / Veritas, 1980.

Donald Senior, C.P., *1 and 2 Peter*, New Testament Message, Wilmington DE / Dublin: M. Glazier / Veritas, 1980.

Lionel Swain, *Ephesians*, New Testament Message 13, Wilmington DE / Dublin: M. Glazier / Veritas, 1980.

Index to Scripture Commentary

Old Testament

New Testament

The Gracious Word, Year A

To come to a full understanding of the depths of the lectionary for Sundays and Holy Days, one needs an array of tools. And that's exactly what Wilfrid Harrington and Philip Gleeson provide.

This volume in the series builds on the special character of Year A. There is a special introduction to the Gospel according to Matthew, the Gospel read throughout Year A, and the commentary, Sunday by Sunday, helps to bring out how the problems and needs expereinced in the community for which the Gospel was written are problems and needs still being expereinced among Christian people.

The work is enhanced by etchings from the distinguished Irish artist Patrick Pye – painter, stained glass artist and etcher who is widely recognised as the countriey's foremost religious artist.

216 pages   Paperback

ISBN 1-871552-51-6

The author has worked in parish ministry, in school chaplaincy and as a religion teacher in secondary schools.

Windows on the Gospel
STORIES AND REFLECTIONS
Flor McCarthy, SDB

Fifty-four stories from the author of *Sunday and Holy Day Liturgies* offer glimpses into the heart of the Gospel, following the broad outline of the story. Practically all the parables are touched on, and most of the familiar characters appear.

These stories are offered to everyone searching for a spirituality based on the Gospels.

A scriptural index and a table of references to the lectionary help to meet the needs of preachers and teachers.

173 pages   Paperback

ISBN 1-871552-24-9

All are based on lived experience of the needs of parish congregations in Ireland and the United States

Sunday and Holyday Liturgies, Year A

' ... not only a solid line of thought which might be taken up in the homily, but also a down-to-earth contemporary idiom in which it might be expressed.' Patrick Rogers, CP, *Irish Theological Quarterly.*

248 pages   Paperback

ISBN 0-907271-74-X

Sunday and Holyday Liturgies, Year B

' ... Fr McCarthy has once again put us in his debt.' Tom Lane, CM, *The Universe.*

248 pages   Paperback

ISBN 0-907271-37-5

Sunday and Holyday Liturgies, Year C

' ... brief, useful introductions, headings for readings, homily pointers, prayers of the faithful and communion reflections for all Sundays and Holydays.' P.J. Brophy, P.P., in *Doctrine and Life*

248 pages   Paperback

ISBN 0-907271-72-6

Go Down to the Potter's House
A JOURNEY INTO MEDITATION
Donagh O'Shea OP

This is a new, revised edition of a work which won great acclaim on its first appearance in 1984.

' ... clear, clean and deep, free of the clutter of wordiness and the fog of technical jargon or pious inflation.... In both form and substance Donagh O'Shea is a reliable guide.' *Spirituality Today*

' ... a balanced and inspirational presentation, well worth reading for anyone interested in growth in the spiritual life.' *Sisters Today*

120 pages   Paperback

ISBN 1-871552-26-5

Take Nothing for the Journey
MEDITATIONS ON TIME AND PLACE
Donagh O'Shea, O.P.

' ... a profound mind, deeply enriched by meditation and reading in many languages, subtly aware of the depth, density and labyrinthine nature of human consciousness and exquisitely sensitive to the ultimate mystery of the Godhead.' *Doctrine and Life*

' ... a totally new vision and energy expressed in the most lyrical, incisive and poetical prose ... has restored my hope.' *New Day Magazine*

129 pages   Paperback

ISBN 1-871552-00-1

ALSO BY DONAGH O'SHEA

*The author lectures in spirituality at the Regina Mundi Institute
and at the Beda, both in Rome. In addition, he has conducted
retreats and seminars in Ireland, Britain, Switzerland, the U.S.A.,
Albania and the Philippines.*

In a Fitful Light
CONVERSATIONS ON CHRISTIAN LIVING

This book offers illumination, often from unexpected sources, on
themes prominent in discussions of spirituality today.

' ... delving into great issues ... his thought often startles with
its originality, provoking recognition and association....

'Enthusiasms which in our day are passed off as spirituality are
questioned rather directly and the insidious values bred by consum-
erism exposed. And yet the charm is that seeds of truth are found
even here.' Jim Sweeney, CP in *Religious Life Review*

171 pages   Paperback

ISBN 1-871552-43-5